Chance, Merit, and Economic Inequality

Joseph de la Torre Dwyer

Chance, Merit, and Economic Inequality

Rethinking Distributive Justice and the Principle of Desert

palgrave
macmillan

Joseph de la Torre Dwyer
Independent Scholar
Brooklyn, NY, USA

ISBN 978-3-030-21125-7 ISBN 978-3-030-21126-4 (eBook)
https://doi.org/10.1007/978-3-030-21126-4

This Palgrave Macmillan imprint is published by the registered company Springer Nature Switzerland AG.
The registered company address is: Gewerbestrasse 11, 6330 Cham, Switzerland

For the Unlucky

Preface

Sections of this book that begin with "****" may be skipped but will be of interest to specialists.

Acknowledgements

This book has greatly benefited from the efforts of many individuals. I would like to thank the participants in the 85th Southern Economics Association Annual Meeting who responded helpfully to early versions of Chaps. 2 and 13, the Book Club that allowed me to foist upon them an early version of Chap. 1 and still provided valuable suggestions and encouragement, the Interlibrary Loan staff at the Brooklyn Public Library who aided me in obtaining many important source materials, Sam Smit's assistance in a time of need, the anonymous referees who seriously engaged with my work to help me better see the project's strengths and weaknesses and radically improve its substance, Ben Pauli and Albert Castle for providing careful reading and illuminating feedback, Papa for reading the entire draft and offering some sharp questions, and My Love for generously supporting me through this entire process, reading numerous versions of every fledgling and final chapter, and helping me to ever better refine the text in terms of clarity and content.

Colophon

The data analyses (and the book itself) rely upon R version 3.5.3 (2019-03-11). Major R packages used in the data analyses (and the book) include R-base, bookdown, rmarkdown, knitr, packrat, ProjectTemplate, devtools, lodown, psidR, data.table, psych, car, mice, AER, splitstackshape, fitdistrplus, caret, mgcv, Hmisc, tseries, IC2, ineq, reldist, ggdag, plyr, and MASS.[1] The complete source is available at justdeserts.org.

> Finally, I owe a word of explanation and apology to specialists on any part of my enormous subject. It is obviously impossible to know as much about every [subject] as can be known ... by [those] whose field is less wide. ... On such grounds I ask the indulgence of those readers who find my knowledge of this or that portion of my subject less adequate than it would have been if there had been no need to remember 'time's winged chariot.'—Bertrand Russell, The History of Western Philosophy, Preface

---

[1] R Core Team (2019); Xie (2018a,b); Allaire et al. (2018); Ushey et al. (2018); White (2018); Wickham et al. (2018); Damico (2019); Oswald (2018); Dowle and Srinivasan (2018); Revelle (2018); Fox et al. (2018); van Buuren and Groothuis-Oudshoorn (2018); Kleiber and Zeileis (2017); Mahto (2018); Delignette-Muller et al. (2018); Jed Wing et al. (2018); Wood (2018); Harrell (2018); Trapletti and Hornik (2018); Plat (2012); Zeileis (2014); Handcock (2016); Barrett (2018); Wickham (2016); and Ripley (2018).

Contents

List of Figures

List of Tables

CHAPTER 1

Introduction

> These [individuals] ask for … the same thing: fairness, and fairness only. This, so far as in my power, they, and all others, shall have.—Abraham Lincoln, letter May 30, 1860

How ought we justly allocate economic resources among individuals? That is the central question of this book. I believe that we possess the power to translate one of our most fundamental, shared moral intuitions into a clear account of a unique, determinate answer to our motivating question. That is to say, a philosophically and politically defensible, administratively feasible, and economically efficient distribution of economic resources among individuals.

Contemporary inequality greatly concerns political scientists, sociologists, economists, philosophers, and a growing constituency of voters and policymakers who are uneasy with both the outcomes as well as the key drivers of our economy. Although much of this concern is accentuated by the 2008 financial crisis and consequent Great Recession, inequality of income and wealth further attracts considerable intellectual attention as a sustained phenomenon that has been rising in most wealthy nations, and between nations, since at least 1980.[1]

[1] For example, Katz and Autor (1999).

J. T. Dwyer, *Chance, Merit, and Economic Inequality*,
https://doi.org/10.1007/978-3-030-21126-4_1

Perceptions of this inequality are often coupled with a prevalent feeling that current levels of economic inequality represent a moral wrong that demands both individual action and institutional policy[2] as inequality is too great, poverty is too widespread, and economic mobility is too low. This moral sentiment begs three questions[3]: why should we reduce economic inequality, to what extent, and how can we feasibly do so?[4]

Egalitarians answer the first question by arguing that inequality is a bad in and of itself. Yet, very few confront the second question with a strict principle of equality to the exclusion of all other conflicting principles of justice. Rather, the strategy of most contemporary solutions to inequality has been to seek a stable, delicate balance between conflicting principles of strict equality and strict efficiency, often with the inclusion of a principle of sufficiency or priority that specifically focuses on those below, or furthest below, the poverty line.[5] A growing body of research pursues a second prong, arguing that *too much inequality is itself inefficient* in our real-world, non-ideal market, and thus, both the principles of equality *and* efficiency recommend that we ought to better the economic situation of either the most disadvantaged or the middle class, broadly defined.[6] For example, the International Monetary Fund recently stated, "The evidence of the economic damage from inequality suggests that policymakers should be more open to redistribution than they are."[7]

While this book is seriously concerned with economic inequality among individuals, it takes an atypical view of the relationship between inequality and injustice. Rather than present a similar solution as those described above, I propose to answer our three motivating questions differently and, I hope, more effectively. Fortunately, many individuals are in search of an original solution to economic inequality as recent evidence shows that Americans "object to inequality and increasingly believe government

[2] Tan (2012).

[3] Taking individuals as capable of having a concept of their good and a sense of justice. Rawls (1999 (1971)), 442.

[4] This book takes Wolff's claim seriously, that "the goal of a theorist of distributive justice, it seems to me, is to propose an understanding of distributive justice that might influence policy" Wolff (2003), 226–227.

[5] Atkinson (2015).

[6] "...lower net inequality is robustly correlated with faster and more durable growth, for a given level of redistribution. ...redistribution appears generally benign in terms of its impact on growth..." Ostry et al. (2014), 4; Stiglitz (2013); Pickett and Wilkinson (2011).

[7] Ostry et al. (2016), 4.

should act to redress it, but not via traditional redistributive programs."[8] I thus bring a new normative principle[9] to center stage that is far more widely shared, and much more deeply felt, as a core principle of distributive justice than are equality, efficiency, sufficiency, or priority with respect to the distribution of economic resources.[10]

In selecting a new principle of justice as my foundation, I do not recommend moral monism, that is, that this is the only distributive principle of value. Even at its most ambitious, I will merely want to strengthen the case that this distributive principle is first among equals. More conservatively, however, I suggest that this principle "belongs on the list of genuine intrinsic values"[11] and that a salutary step to balancing multiple principles of distributive justice is to more fully understand and consider each of the relevant, separate principles in isolation at the level of both concept and consequences. Better understanding of concept and consequences may further inform our intuitions, arguments, and policies.

Although it may come as a surprise to those currently concerned with inequality, poverty, and economic immobility as moral wrongs to be undone, the principle of justice that will serve as the foundation of this book is *desert*. Desert is currently a sorely underutilized principle in the anti-inequality, anti-poverty, and pro-economic mobility literature on public policy and in fact is most often used in support of anti-egalitarian arguments, ideologies, as well as policy implementation.[12] This is not surprising as two core intuitions of desert—(1) that some individuals *deserve more* than others and (2) that it is better if individuals receive what they deserve[13]—appear to naturally pull away from equality. So why do I place desert at the center of my proposal?

I will argue that desert via a merit-based view of responsibility is a normative ideal that hinges upon a fundamental moral intuition and is

[8] McCall and Kenworthy (2009).

[9] "[A]ccording to the dominant philosophical defenses of liberalism that are current today, desert has no role whatsoever to play in the fundamental normative principles that apply to the basic social, political, and economic institutions of society." Scheffler (1999), 199; Scheffler (1992).

[10] Mulligan (2018), chap. 3; Miller (1999c); Lamont (1994), 45; Scheffler (1992); Lerner (1980).

[11] Kagan (2012), 629.

[12] King (1999), 219–286.

[13] Notwithstanding Kagan's assertion that "some individuals are more deserving than others," I think the core intuition is in fact that some individuals deserve more than others. Kagan (2012), xiii.

among "the best candidates to fill a theoretical role whose contours are dictated by the normative beliefs that we already hold."[14] I will thus follow Miller and attempt to use political philosophy to offer "a clearer and more systematic statement of the principles that people already hold"[15] and would want to hold upon considered reflection. That political right and left share a common intuition is buttressed by the fact that the most revered Presidents of the United States on left and right, both Presidents Roosevelt (FDR) and Reagan, repeatedly and explicitly stated their support for this fundamental moral intuition[16] and I believe it implicitly guides most major economic policy in the United States.[17] As such, I hope that this makes my solution attractive to the vast majority of individuals without regard to partisan affiliation. Second, I place desert at the center of my proposal because the problem of unequal economic distribution may be usefully divided into at least two logically separate considerations—(1) inequality and (2) *undeserved* inequality—and it is only the latter that we object to[18] because only the latter is unjust.[19] The principle of desert, properly implemented, completely eliminates *undeserved* inequality by ensuring that each individual receives exactly what they deserve, no more and no less. In addition, it does so via *ex post* interventions on rewards—interventions that are simpler, more precise, less intrusive, and thus more just than complementary *ex ante* interventions currently dominant in thinking about economic inequality and opportunity.

To my mind, it is desert—the ancient idea that justice means giving to each what they deserve[20]—rather than equality, efficiency, priority, or

[14] Sher (2014), 87.

[15] Miller (1999c), 51.

[16] Olsen (2017).

[17] "... the American Idea that justice is done when ... rewards are proportionate to merit and effort." Ryan (2011), 6.

[18] "I want to insist on this point: the key issue is the justification of inequalities rather than their magnitude as such." Piketty (2014), 264; Pojman (1999), 285; Kagan (1999).

[19] Those who self-identify as egalitarians are gradually endorsing this position. Cf. Olsaretti (2003b), 11; Temkin (1993).

[20] Vallentyne (2015), 41; Feldman (1955a), 573; Mill (1991), 179; "Justice is a constant and perpetual will to give every man his due." Roman jurist Ulpian in the Digest of the Roman book of law Corpus Juris, ca. 200 BCE. Pojman and McLeod (1999), 4; For more contemporary definitions of justice and, thus, desert, two accounts of justice that I have found attractive are justice as fittingness (of treatment) and justice as equilibrium (of burdens and benefits), Cupit (1996b); Sadurski (1985).

sufficiency that offers a more compelling rationale for redistribution.[21] For those consequentialists who find themselves more attracted to these other principles of distribution, however, I argue in Chaps. 4–6 that allocations of *Just Deserts* realize to a greater extent than that exhibited in our current economy, and may even maximize, the fundamental values of equal opportunity, economic efficiency, and individual liberty.[22] Likewise, I demonstrate in Chap. 12 that allocations of *Just Deserts* within the United States may eliminate at least one-quarter of present income inequality, guarantee a reduction in current poverty levels, while simultaneously realizing maximum economic mobility. That is to say, while many have long thought that the concepts of "personal responsibility" and "hard work" are inherently antithetical to redistribution, I show that they are entirely supportive of broad but just redistribution.

How do I propose to fulfill such ambitious promises? Throughout the course of this book, I will make a few simple claims on behalf of my proposal—what I shall call the *Just Deserts* proposal—that track Cohen's analytic of political philosophy: (1) what are the correct principles of justice?; (2) which social states of affairs ought to be brought about?; and (3) what should the state do?[23] Parts I, II, and III of this work will address these respective questions. Thus I begin with an examination of a powerful normative ideal, a morally monistic concept of justice as desert, from within the bounds of ideal philosophy in Part I. From there, I then strengthen the case that desert is what we want, all things considered, by attaching the consequences of a principle of desert to the motivations and rationales for other principles of distribution in Part II. Finally, I construct a detailed public policy of desert and demonstrate its distributional consequences within the bounds of non-ideal philosophy using economic modeling and analysis of nationally representative survey data in Part III.

To begin, Chap. 2 will identify an overlooked, fundamental source of inequality and a lack of economic mobility in the United States, in fact, all known societies—specifically, *chance*. This same chapter will then clarify and sharpen a deep commitment to a shared, fundamental moral intuition that views this source of inequality as unjust, generating a theory of *moral*

[21] For example, cf. Marshall et al. (1999).

[22] Others have also noted the concordance between equal opportunity and freedom. Fishkin (2014).

[23] Cohen (2011c), 227.

responsibility and the moral agent. This leads us to Chap. 3's argument on behalf of an original theory of desert, specifically a unique, determinate luck-egalitarian theory of the principle of desert. I clarify the distinction between this and other principles of distribution by usefully formalizing the theory of desert in order to explain precisely what justice demands with respect to each individual's allocation. Scholars in the social sciences and humanities may be interested to know that this formalization may also serve as an operationalized theory of the concepts, "privilege" or "systemic inequality," and allow them to measure and discuss these concepts more formally.[24]

In the current literature, other dominant principles of distribution currently make procedural claims with which this principle of desert may at first seem to conflict. The next few chapters will show how distribution according to a luck-egalitarian principle of desert satisfies the underlying consequentialist needs of these principles of distribution, including (Chap. 4) *equal opportunity*'s need for a "level playing field," (Chap. 5) *efficiency*'s need to maintain aggregate economic output, productivity, and welfare, and (Chap. 6) liberalism's and libertarianism's need for individual *liberty*. By clarifying a "level playing field," we see that the *Just Deserts* proposal provides equality of opportunity to all individuals via an agnostic, *ex post* intervention. By synthesizing luck egalitarianism with optimal tax theory, I demonstrate that the *Just Deserts* proposal may be implemented under certain conditions as economists' first-best endowment tax, being thus able to guarantee maximum aggregate productivity and output with no deadweight loss. Last but not least, by better understanding an endowment tax, properly identifying the "individual," and examining the Lockean and Nozickean provisos underpinning contemporary libertarianism, we see that the *Just Deserts* proposal enables maximum individual economic liberty and the capacity of each individual to pursue their own happiness.[25]

Having demonstrated that no procedural requirement of these other principles of justice is in conflict with the principle of desert, Chaps. 7–10 will draw upon the desert-based distributive justice and intergenerational economic transmission literatures to specify the remaining necessary com-

[24] For an argument with great affinity to my own, "that only morally deserved inequalities justify unequal lots," cf. Spiegelberg (1944).

[25] Cf. Fishkin (2014).

ponents of a theory of desert with respect to a public policy governing the allocation of economic resources. That is, (1) what is the proper *quality* according to which one individual deserves more economic rewards than another, (2) what specifically constitutes the economic rewards to be allocated according to desert under our current discussion, (3) who or what deserves such rewards, and lastly, (4) how may we simply and precisely measure desert for such rewards? These chapters will outline the principles underlying an original empirical method necessary in order to take a precise measurement of desert and its corresponding rewards. Economists might be particularly interested in the original methods used to measure income distribution and inequality of opportunity beginning at Chap. 7.

Chapter 11 will argue that the *Just Deserts* proposal is not merely ethically, philosophically, and methodologically viable, but leads to an explicit policy prescription. Those readers who simply wish to understand the mechanics of implementing the *Just Deserts* proposal as public policy may begin with this chapter in which I formalize four variations on this policy prescription. Chapter 12 then analyzes the new economic distributions based upon the implementation of the principle of desert among the population of the United States. Here I show that *Just Deserts* as public policy is fully feasible today and satisfies important remaining normative principles of justice set aside during Chaps. 4–6: *equality* by eliminating at least one-quarter of economic inequality, *priority* and *sufficiency* by wiping away a guaranteed quantity of poverty, and *economic mobility* by reaching the maximum theoretically observable limit thereof. Lastly, I argue that even if this *Just Deserts* policy is imperfect under non-ideal circumstances, it is still guaranteed to be more just than our current economy.

Finally, Chap. 13 speculatively sketches the contours of the *Just Deserts* economy after policy implementation and finds three important implications. First, the *Just Deserts* economy would usher in a new era of philanthropy as many of the disadvantaged populations of today would no longer be disadvantaged. Second, the *Just Deserts* economy would drastically ameliorate the economic position of women despite the sexes' empirically distinct relationship to economic labor. Third, the *Just Deserts* economy would sharply change the way we think about disability, both adding a rigorous formalization to disability theory and clearly demonstrating a focus on different abilities rather than disabilities.

As the *Just Deserts* proposal covers a lot of ground across literatures in political science, economics, and philosophy, taking a widely shared, fundamental moral intuition and arguing that its logical consequence is a luck-egalitarian theory of desert, an underutilized principle of distribution that actually possesses very strong claims to represent distributive justice, all things considered, Chap. 14 will conclude with a summation of our initial motivations and subsequent arguments toward a viable public policy of distribution. The only price we must pay upon implementation thereof is that each of us receives precisely what we deserve, no more and no less. In the end, I hope this book persuades many of its readers that a principle of desert is the most just, most ecumenical,[26] and most efficacious way to solve the felt moral problems of inequality, poverty, and economic immobility.[27]

In sum:

- The *Just Deserts* proposal identifies chance as a uniquely important element of unmerited economic inequality.
- The *Just Deserts* proposal establishes itself upon a shared, fundamental moral intuition as a just means of distribution.
- The *Just Deserts* proposal is the most efficacious means to address the problems of inequality, poverty, and economic mobility because it is likely to receive broad support across the entire political spectrum due to its foundation upon a fundamental moral intuition and its ability to satisfy a host of other dominant principles of economic distribution.
- The *Just Deserts* proposal, according to mainstream economics, is perfectly efficient in at least some of its policy variations.
- The *Just Deserts* proposal's policy prescription is already completely feasible given current technology and knowledge.
- The *Just Deserts* proposal, most importantly, is more just than our current economic system because each individual will receive precisely what they deserve.

[26] On the need for a supportive ethos, or constellation of social norms, in order to realize successful public policies, cf. Carens (2015).

[27] Some might feel that distributive justice gives us a *prima facie* reason to act, "Justice is a practical virtue, it is concerned with how we should act." Cupit (1996b), 4; others may not. While I mount no substantial defense of desert as a "prescription for right action," I feel I can always fall back on Feldman's rather simple axiology: "behave in such a way as to make the world as good as you can." If *Just Deserts* is a plausible formulation of distributive justice and the world would be better with *Just Deserts* than without, that is at least a *prima facie* recommendation that we ought to implement *Just Deserts*. Feldman (1955a), 584.

PART I

Just Principles

CHAPTER 2

The Die Is Cast: Chance, Merit, and Inequality

I believe that every right implies a responsibility; every opportunity, an obligation; every possession, a duty.—John D. Rockefeller, Jr.

In the United States today, morally arbitrary chance dominates the distribution of economic resources. This is neither new nor particular to this nation—as the old saying goes, "An ounce of luck is worth a pound of gold." Although chance is morally arbitrary, neither just nor unjust, the ways in which our institutions deal with chance is a matter for distributive justice.[1] This book aims to demonstrate and defend a distribution of economic resources that is more just than that which flows from our current distributional institutions because the new distribution would flow from the concepts of responsibility and desert. I will argue that the principle of desert demands that rewards be uniquely sensitive to responsibility rather than chance and I will formalize precisely how we may accomplish this through a proposal I call *Just Deserts*. Having argued that we ought to remove chance from one of the most important realms of our lives—the distribution of economic resources—I will share and defend a detailed policy prescription as well as model its implementation upon the distribution of economic resources within the US population in order that we may better understand what it would mean to reward each individual

[1] Rawls (1999 (1971)), 87; Sadurski (1985), 122–131.

J. T. Dwyer, *Chance, Merit, and Economic Inequality*,
https://doi.org/10.1007/978-3-030-21126-4_2

with their *Just Deserts*, nothing more and nothing less. Given the centrality of desert to our notions about justice,[2] I argue that not only will this distribution be both "fair and feasible,"[3] but perhaps the "most fair, fully feasible" distribution we can realize.

2.1 Out of Control

Inescapably, we are at different times both the undeserving beneficiaries, and unwilling victims, of chance. The question that I would like to answer in this chapter is the following: how ought we morally assess an individual who is morally responsible for an outcome when that outcome is, to some extent, governed by pure chance? Thus, Chap. 2 begins by offering a theory of moral responsibility, a necessary precondition to a theory of desert.[4] While trodding familiar ground for moral philosophers, I newly assemble the literature in service to my ends—always aiming at the *Just Deserts* proposal.

2.1.1 Clarify Terms and Uses

To answer this question clearly, I must first clarify terms. I will use the word "individual" through this book as synonymous with philosophers' term of art, moral agent.[5] By outcome, I mean that one simply selects some observed fact about the actual world—the reading of a thermometer at point *p* and time *t*; the average speed of individual, *i*, over the course of such and such a race; the mass of the planet Jupiter right now.

2.1.1.1 Empirically Descriptive, Not Prescriptive Responsibility

Next, the terms *responsible* and *responsibility*. In contemporary vernacular language, we use these terms with multiple meanings. The statements, "You are ***responsible*** for cooking dinner tomorrow night" and "Each of us has a ***responsibility*** to respect others" are ***normatively prescriptive*** statements

[2] "Desert is central to our pre-reflective thought." Sher (1987), ix; Many people have a "pre-theoretical certainty that at least some people deserve something..." Zaitchik (1977), 373.

[3] Wolff (2003), 222.

[4] "People must, in a robust sense be responsible for [X] to be morally deserving of [Y]." Temkin (2011), 55; Cf. Pojman (1997); Cupit (1996a); Feldman (1996); Smilansky (1996).

[5] Parthemore and Whitby (2013).

that assert that which a moral agent *ought to do*, whether past, present, or future. As I have very little to say regarding what a moral agent ought to do, at no point in this book will I use the term "responsible" in a normatively prescriptive statement.

On the other hand, the statements, "You are *responsible* for the injuries my friend suffered yesterday" and "Sam shares *responsibility* for the bank robbery last week" are not only ***normatively but also empirically descriptive*** statements that always ***retrospectively measure*** past outcomes and what a moral agent *did do*.[6] Lastly, "This bad weather is *responsible* for my cold" and "These birds are *responsible* for the destruction of the garden" are empirically descriptive statements without normative content that always retrospectively measure past outcomes and what an *object* did do.[7]

2.1.1.2 Merit-Based and Accountability-Implying Responsibility

As I will present what is known as a "merit-based" view of moral responsibility as a normative ideal and will further argue that *Just Deserts* are the proper reward to individuals, this chapter provides a theory by which one may precisely measure *agent responsibility* for a particular outcome—or what one might call "thoroughgoing, blame-licensing, accountability-implying moral responsibility."[8] By "accountability-implying moral responsibility," I mean that the statement "Sam shares responsibility for the bank robbery last week" (whether reflecting a judgement,[9] attitude,[10]

[6] For the lack of importance between ascriptive and descriptive statements, cf. Feinberg (1970a), 137ff., Cf. Feinberg (1970e), 25, 26n1; for a further division into causal agency and simple agency, not germane to my purposes, cf. Feinberg (1970a), 132–136.

[7] We might refer to these latter two types of statements as *moral responsibility* and *object responsibility* statements and, together, they constitute the class of *empirical responsibility statements*. Note that Fischer and Ravizza use *causal responsibility* instead of *object responsibility*. They also usefully point out that moral responsibility is not to be confused with legal responsibility, corporate responsibility, role responsibility, and so on. Fischer and Ravizza (1998), 1–2.

[8] Hurley (2003), 92; From a more juridical perspective, Hart speaks of "liability responsibility." Hart (1968), 215–227; As an aside, I must note that I do not use accountability in Bok's sense, that is, to hold accountable is not to "take some action to reflect [an individual's] will, attribute it to [the individual], and ask what it reveals about [the individual's] will and character, and about the ways [that will and character] might be improved." Bok (1998), 152.

[9] This is the "ledger view" of moral responsibility. Fischer and Ravizza (1998), 8–10n12.

[10] Strawson (1962).

or something else) may legitimately serve as a basis for a backward-looking intervention upon the individual, Sam. By the end of the chapter, I will have introduced a multidisciplinary vocabulary, as well as a formalized theory, with which one may discuss such agent responsibility.

2.1.1.3 From Normative Ideal to Regulatory Ideal

While I will begin by excavating a shared, fundamental moral intuition from the perspective of ideal philosophy, we will need to later relax these conditions and consider a policy translation of our normative ideal of agent responsibility into the perspective of non-ideal philosophy and viable public policy. That is to say, the normative ideal will also function as a "regulatory ideal—a standard for designing, assessing, and reforming institutions, laws, and social practices."[11] In recognition of this end goal, I want to make it explicit that the value of the normative ideals of desert and responsibility does not require that we know that any person has ever exhibited greater than zero agent responsibility—for example, the normative ideal does not rest on the truth of some form of libertarian[12] free will or the falsity of determinism.

Many philosophers, in fact, have forcefully argued that such a notion of free will is "metaphysical nonsense,"[13] implies a moral illusion,[14] or is a mistaken byproduct of either pride[15] or evolutionary adaptation[16]—positions to which I am somewhat sympathetic.[17] Due in part to this skepticism, philosophers have been hostile to the empirical possibility of deep agent responsibility and thus staged a "revolt against desert"[18] in the last century. Nonetheless, these arguments are not conclusive.[19] Furthermore, and as alluded to above, the premise that no human has ever exhibited this agent responsibility fails to undermine the weaker

[11] Arneson (2003), 236.

[12] This libertarianism should not be confused with the political philosophy of self-ownership to be discussed later in the book.

[13] Smart (1973), 54.

[14] Smilansky (2000).

[15] Taylor (2003).

[16] Ruse (2003).

[17] Pereboom (2003).

[18] Barry (1965), 112.

[19] Unfortunately, both the claim that determinism is true and its opposite are unfalsifiable. Strawson (1994), 20.

claim that this is a "very plausible and appealing"[20] way, after reasonable consideration and/or "wide reflective equilibrium,"[21] to conceptualize moral responsibility. Philosophical arguments against agent responsibility may possess even less force against the distinct Rawlsian *political* claim that the normative ideals will offer us the most attractive account of "the concept [of distributive justice that our present political culture] regards—*here and now*—as fair and supported by the best reasons."[22]

Nonetheless, I believe that my argument has no need of these fallback positions. My account of distributive justice flows through a version of agent responsibility and a principle of desert that attempts to appeal to multiple interested factions (including proponents of merit-based and consequentialist responsibility, incompatibilist and compatibilist views of moral responsibility, and even scientific determinists) via an agnostic and empirical method willing to let the chips fall where they may.

2.1.2 Return to Original Question

To return to the original question, to what extent is an individual agent responsible for an outcome when that outcome is, to some extent, governed by pure chance? To begin with a twist on a classic tale from Williams,[23] imagine that you are chosen to serve on a jury tasked with determining agent responsibility—the accountability-implying moral responsibility of a particular individual for a particular outcome that would legitimate a corresponding, backward-looking intervention (punishment or reward):

> Cautious Chris was driving a car on a rainy day at a speed well below the posted speed limit when a child unexpectedly, and purely by chance, stepped out from between two parked cars only a fraction of a second before Chris' car reached the same location. Luckily, the child's only injury was a broken arm. On the basis of compelling evidence, you believe that Chris was taking great precautions, more than the typical driver under the conditions, and that no other driver traveling at Chris' speed would have avoided this outcome. To what extent was Chris responsible for the child's broken arm, if at all?

[20] Fischer and Ravizza (1998), 11.
[21] Daniels (1996).
[22] Rawls (1985), 238.
[23] Williams (1981).

> Let us now change the facts a bit. What if the car struck the child's arm identically to the first case and produced an identical injury, but this time, there was enough time to stop the car if Reckless Ryan had not been driving just under the posted speed limit? In fact, compelling evidence leads you to believe that all other drivers traveling in this rain were driving significantly more slowly than Ryan and would have avoided this outcome. Do you have different reactions to the two scenarios despite their identical outcomes? Are your judgements, sentiments, or other reactions with respect to agent responsibility[24] and blameworthiness for the child's broken arm different for the two drivers?

I believe most readers would agree with the following statement, "In both cases, a child unexpectedly, and purely by chance, stepped out from between two parked cars. Yet, it certainly does appear that there is some moral difference between the two cases such that we place more blame on Ryan than on Chris. That difference, moreover, seems to find its basis in Chris' caution and Ryan's recklessness."

2.1.2.1 Maybe Only Outcomes Matter?

Perhaps one might argue to the contrary that there is zero moral difference between the two cases because the only thing that matters, with respect to moral responsibility, is outcomes and consequences—in this case, an identically broken arm. Consider then an extreme case inspired by Nozick:[25]

> Imagine that Strong Sam, unprovoked and without precedent, picks up Light Logan and throws Logan down a well. At the bottom of the well Logan lands unexpectedly, and purely by chance, on a child. Luckily, the child's only injury is a broken arm. To what extent was Logan responsible for the child's broken arm?

[24] I am not asking you to examine your beliefs with respect to legal liability. While "strict liability" or "absolute liability" might treat Chris and Ryan identically, morality comes before the law, and I want you to consider the empirically descriptive, backward-looking, moral responsibility of our drivers, not their legal liabilities.

[25] Nozick (2013).

2.1.2.2 No, Control Matters!

I would imagine that most readers would respond along these lines, "Logan was not at all responsible for the child's broken arm. Logan was thrown, unprovoked, down the well by another party." Although it was in fact Light Logan's body that broke the child's arm, we only hold individuals morally responsible and thus accountable for those outcomes that are, at least to some extent, *within their control.* As Nagel writes, "people cannot be morally assessed for what is not their fault, or for what is due to factors beyond their control."[26] Or more positively stated, "If an agent is morally responsible for [X], then the production of [X] must be something over which the agent has control."[27] Philosophers call this widely shared, fundamental moral intuition,[28] *the control principle.*[29] As we shall see, this intuition ineluctably leads us, or so I shall argue, to the controversial conclusion that luck has a precise mathematical place within an account of *Just Deserts.* To prematurely state my reply to the chapter's opening question:

[26] Nagel (1979), 24.

[27] Pereboom (2003), 29.

[28] "[M]ost substantive moral theories hold agents morally accountable only for that for which they are agent-responsible [attributively responsible]..." Vallentyne (2008); "Morals constitute a kind of internal law, governing those inner thoughts and volitions which are completely subject to the agent's control... where the agent rules supreme and luck has no place." Feinberg (1970e), 33, "If we charge [individuals] with the consequences of fortuitous events [i.e., chance], the ["moral"] records will lose their accuracy and fail, accordingly, to achieve their purpose." Feinberg (1970a), 125; For a rare exception, cf. Scanlon (2000), chap. 6.

[29] Arneson (2004); Nelkin (2013); Also, this is a non-egalitarian reformulation of Cohen's point, "...egalitarian redress is indicated to the *extent* that a disadvantage does not reflect genuine choice." Cohen (2011d); Due to its strong support by egalitarians when individuals are disadvantaged due to factors beyond their control, Lake names minor variations on this principle the "egalitarian intuition" or the "responsibility principle." Lake (2001), 12–13; "An action is free in the sense required for moral responsibility only if it is not produced by a deterministic process that traces back to causal factors beyond the agent's control." Pereboom (2003), 3; also cf. 126; Note that this definition of control is of *categorical* control (what Hurley names *regressive* control) Hurley (2003), 111 that is thicker than Hurley's account in which "[Simple] Control ... involves maintenance of a variable at a target value in the face of exogenous disturbance, *where the variable is caused to take values jointly by factors endogenous and factors exogenous to a control system* [Dwyer's italics]." Hurley (2003), 95. Instead, control means caused to take values exclusively by endogenous factors.

- *Our moral assessments of an individual who is agent responsible (morally responsible and thus accountable in a way that may justify backward-looking intervention upon the agent) for any* Outcome Y *is directly related to the extent that* Outcome Y *depends upon factors categorically within the individual's control.*

2.2 Responsibility by Degrees

There is a lot packed into the control principle and, as I plan to "revise ordinary common-sense norms of responsibility and deservingness to bring them into conformity with [the control principle],"[30] it would be helpful to specify what I mean by the phrase "*depends upon factors categorically within the individual's control.*"

2.2.1 Non Compos Mentis *Quick Mike*

For that reason, I want to spend the next few pages enriching our understanding of the control principle. To begin, I turn to a thought experiment derived from the opening scene of the film, *Unforgiven.*[31]

> In a saloon in the American West of the late 1800s, a young prostitute, Delilah Fitzgerald, laughs at a man known as Quick Mike. In an apparently *uncontrollable* rage, he attacks her with a knife, throwing his partner and Delilah's co-workers to the side. At this point, the owner of the saloon places a gun at the back of Quick Mike's head and his uncontrollable rage suddenly vanishes. The question is: given Quick Mike's uncontrollable rage and the control principle, how do we morally assess Quick Mike as morally responsible for his actions and the resulting harm to Delilah?

I assume that most readers' intuitions will incline toward the statement that Quick Mike was, to some extent, morally responsible for Delilah's harm. If, on the other hand, Quick Mike had suffered a *literally uncontrollable* rage, the control principle would offer no moral grounds to hold him responsible and blameworthy for harming Delilah at all. Although

[30] Arneson (2007), 269.
[31] Eastwood (1992).

we might still *prudentially* apply certain preventive or protective forward-looking interventions upon Quick Mike in order to limit *future harm*—such as one would do in response to a rabid dog—we would exempt Quick Mike from punishment (or any other backward-looking intervention) for *past harm*. Our common law system agrees with this intuition that we lack the relevant grounds for moral responsibility statements when assessing defendants who are *non compos mentis*, which literally means "not having *control over*[32] one's mind." Thus, in these types of cases, we cannot hold Quick Mike morally responsible in the specific way necessary to conclude that he is blameworthy and accountable as "incapacity... is incompatible with responsibility."[33] Yet, what if we follow our intuitions with respect to the story and stipulate that Quick Mike was in fact *compos mentis*, how do we then reach a moral assessment?

2.2.2 Circumstances Accommodate Competing Theories of Moral Responsibility

The important element I would like to draw attention to is that Quick Mike was clearly able to control his rage but did not do so *until his circumstances changed*—namely, sensing a loaded firearm at the back of his head. As I will elaborate, circumstances are the key to understanding both our everyday, and more sophisticated, moral assessments of an individual who is morally responsible for a particular outcome. Furthermore, I believe that competing accounts of moral responsibility can find a good deal of common ground in this statement. To elaborate, whether one's account of moral responsibility is (1) Strawsonian,[34] that moral responsibility "requires that the agent be an apt candidate for [the] application [of a participant-reactive *attitude*]"[35]; (2) "reason-responsive," that moral responsibility requires that the agent's behavior is *responsive to reasons* and that alternative outcomes belonging to the agent are logical possibilities (the agent has "guidance control")[36]; or (3) "merit-based," that moral

[32] Lewis and Short (1879), s.v. com-pŏs (conp-), pŏtis, potis, def 1.
[33] Feinberg (1970g), 274.
[34] Strawson (1962).
[35] Fischer and Ravizza (1998), 8.
[36] Fischer and Ravizza (1998), 28–41.

responsibility requires that the agent have *categorical control over the object of responsibility*, I will argue that circumstances as I define them will constitute precisely the type of empirical "discoveries" to which our moral assessments—whether "attitudes and responses" or considered beliefs—would be "sensitive," and thus "change."[37]

2.2.3 Assessing Extenuating Circumstances

Nearly every day, we assert that the most important facts underlying our moral assessments with respect to moral responsibility are the circumstances that in fact actually obtained relevant to the particular observed outcome of interest. As a first bit of evidence, consider our extraordinary ability to identify extenuating circumstances and mitigating factors that leave fixed the outcome in question (as well as the moral valence or weight thereof), but do change our *moral assessment*. As you reflect upon your own life as a moral agent, you may notice that every few months you fail to speak kindly to your spouse *because* of an issue at work, you lie to your parent *because* you do not want to disappoint them, you skip a religious service *because* a promotion is on the line, or you miss an appointment with a friend *because* of romance. In general, we all sometimes fail to do what we ought to do "*because*" of some external circumstance.

Yet, did an issue at work really *cause you* to speak harshly to your spouse, absolutely powerless to do otherwise, in the way Strong Sam really caused Light Logan to travel down the well? For most non-philosophers, clearly not. Acting under the belief or sensation that we are categorically able to do otherwise, we do in fact hold ourselves agent responsible for each and every one of these minor moral failings. Just as true, however, we use these circumstances to adjust our moral assessments of ourselves. As I will soon argue, we use circumstances not merely to adjust our moral assessments of self and others, but they are a principal basis of such moral assessments. As such, any moral assessment of an individual who is morally responsible for an outcome must take account of these extenuating circumstances that reduce, but do not seem to extinguish, agent responsibility.

[37] Fischer and Ravizza (1998), 4.

- Outcome Y *necessarily depends to some extent upon factors beyond the individual's control. Moral assessments of agents based upon moral responsibility likewise depend upon the circumstances that in fact obtained.*

2.2.3.1 The Flavors of Chance

If our moral assessment of an individual who is agent responsible for any *Outcome Y* is contingent upon circumstances beyond that individual's control—what I will hereafter refer to as *circumstances of chance*—how do we identify such relevant circumstances? As we are apt to narrow what counts as a relevant circumstance, it may be useful to highlight what I believe are superficially different kinds of circumstances of chance and that we are more apt to notice some kinds of circumstances over others, even though all such circumstances are theoretically identical. Borrowing from Nagel, I will focus on three such kinds that we might call material, internal, and social circumstances.[38]

Let us adapt a case from Singer[39] in order to more clearly examine the way circumstances of chance may alter our moral assessment of the individual for *Outcome Y*.

> One day, you are walking on a path alongside a small pond when you notice a child drowning in the pond. For whatever reasons, you decide that you are going to jump into the pond, swim to the child, and bring them safely to shore. Now try to imagine that just as you leave the path you realize that you must first overcome [[a river rapids]] to save the child and that only a few humans have ever overcome [[rapids]] such as these in less than five minutes. Let us stipulate, however, that *it is categorically within your power and control to succeed (or not succeed)*. Seeing absolutely no alternatives, you fight the [[rapids]] with tremendous effort and just as you are about to take your first step into the pond you realize that you failed to save the child. Compelling evidence leads us to believe, however, that you absolutely would have rescued the child were it not for the [[rapids]]. What is your moral assessment of your failure to save the child? Note that in this case, material circumstances

[38] Note that Nagel refers to resultant, circumstantial, causal, and constitutive luck. I have chosen terms that both comprehend Nagel's framework and more clearly distinguish themselves to non-philosophers.

[39] Singer (1972).

of chance made it more difficult, *but by stipulation not impossible*, for you to save the child in time.

As an example of internal circumstances of chance, one might imagine that the circumstantial obstacle was not a river rapids but a terrible phobia[40] of ponds that only you possess. Lastly, as an example of social circumstances of chance, one might imagine that the circumstantial obstacle was instead a religious belief of your particular (sub)culture that for an adult to enter this pond is to become defiled for eternity.

At first, one may feel that I have presented three scenarios (rapids, phobias, religious belief) whose dispositive facts differ. I would suggest that this stems from the fact that it is easiest to appreciate the power of material circumstances because they affect all human moral agents while internal circumstances affect only one individual and social circumstances affect only one (sub)culture of individuals, and thus may not apply to you in particular. Given this tendency of human psychology, I should stress to the reader that we may stipulate that each of the three cases presented you with circumstantial obstacles of *identical difficulty* whose exclusive provenance was chance—that is, you had absolutely zero control over the placement of the rapids, the type of phobia, or the particular religious belief held by your culture. If you do not feel these circumstantial obstacles to be of identical difficulty, please simply adjust the size of the river, the severity of the phobia, and the sacred nature of the pond until they are of identical difficulty in your mind with respect to rescuing the drowning child. As such convergence is possible, this serves as a hint that circumstances of analytically different types may all be measured, with a single as yet undefined metric with respect to moral responsibility and attendant moral assessments.

To continue, what is your moral assessment of your failure to save the child? Although our cognitive biases may resist this conclusion from the trio of identical cases, given our stipulations that it was categorically within your power and control to succeed (or not succeed), you must hold yourself agent responsible *to some extent* for this outcome. Have no fear, though,

[40] Cf. "a paralysing and insurmountable fear of heights..." Olsaretti (2003a), 202; "a person who resolutely masters his fear in order to rescue someone,..." Sher (1987), 135; "Certain sorts of mental disorders—extreme phobias, for instance—may also issue in behavior that the agent does not control in the relevant sense." Fischer and Ravizza (1998), 35.

a verdict of guilty (*morally responsible* for a bad outcome) still leaves wide latitude for the sentence (or in this case, our moral assessment). Given the severity of the extenuating circumstances, the right moral assessment is the smallest possible negative assessment. Of course, were none of these extenuating circumstances present—allowing you to easily rescue the child—and you still failed to do so, our theory states that our moral assessment of you (judgement, feelings, etc.) would be much harsher.

2.2.3.2 In Good Times and In Bad

Up to this point, we have been proceeding in a somewhat legalistic manner insofar as the justice system often looks to extenuating circumstances or mitigating factors that might decrease the strength of a negative moral assessment for a bad and/or unlawful outcome for which one is, to some extent, morally responsible. Some have even argued that moral responsibility must necessarily reference blame (for a bad outcome).[41] Do we, however, have a similar, or identical, intuition that circumstances of chance change our moral assessments for good outcomes as well as bad?

> Imagine that there is an individual, Two-Face,[42] who has been cursed to determine their moral conduct solely upon the flipping of an unbiased coin. Heads, Two-Face is literally compelled by supernatural forces to aid the elderly, tails, to do them harm. Two-Face goes through life flipping an unbiased coin, and, against all odds, it always lands heads up. Instead of robbing elderly ladies at the corner, Two-Face helps them to carry their groceries home. Although we may be thankful for this improbable string of coin tosses, how do we morally assess Two-Face for these good outcomes?
>
> Now imagine that Two-Face has an identical twin, True-Face, so named because they always choose to do the right thing no matter how difficult that may be. Although they accurately confide to us that they are plagued by selfish feelings, odd desires to harm strangers, and temptations to cheat and betray friends, their behavior reflects a worthy moral compass and is in fact *identical* to Two-Face's good deeds. How do we morally assess True-Face for these good outcomes?

[41] Wallace (1998), 12.
[42] This is a variation on a villain in the Batman mythology. Kane and Finger (1942).

As stated, Two-Face's actions were entirely due to the chance outcomes of a series of coin tosses beyond their control—this is a particular and local version of hard determinism in which, additionally, Two-Face is neither "reason responsive" nor an apt candidate for a participant-reactive attitude.[43] Thus, Two-Face holds zero agent responsibility for the improbable string of good deeds as it is the curse that is in fact *object responsible* for the entirety of the outcome.[44] We therefore withhold any moral assessment of Two-Face for these outcomes. On the other hand, although we do not yet know how to precisely measure our moral assessments, True-Face's behavior seems to exhibit that not only are they morally responsible for these outcomes—they were in some sense within her control—but we might offer True-Face an extraordinarily strong positive moral assessment as if they had somehow found a way, against severe countervailing odds, to cross the river rapids in time and rescue the drowning child.

Thus, it seems to me that a corollary of the control principle is that we can indeed morally assess individuals for that which is within their control, whether or not its valence is good or bad. In fact, our normative ideal of agent responsibility and the moral assessments that flow therefrom is concerned not only with morally good and bad outcomes, but any and all outcomes irrespective of their moral status, whether morally tinted outcomes (e.g., saving a child's life) or not (e.g., winning a game or raising one's hand).[45] Further, our moral assessments are sensitive to relevant circumstances of chance, whether they promote or inhibit *Outcome Y*. This chapter thus claims to formalize a method by which to precisely identify the right moral assessment of any individual exhibiting moral responsibility for any observed outcome.[46]

[43] Lake (2001), 23.

[44] While it may raise a number of unnecessary new issues, some readers might find an analogy between Two-Face as cursed human and Two-Face as deterministic computer program revealing. Cf. Noorman (2012).

[45] "Merit spans both the moral and the nonmoral realms." Sher (1987), 109; "Indeed, our Strawsonian view of moral responsibility allows for moral responsibility for 'morally neutral' behavior. For instance, one can be morally responsible for simply raising one's hand (where this is not a signal or in any way morally significant)." Fischer and Ravizza (1998), 5n5, 8n11.

[46] Note that this leaves two options for Arneson, either "character" or "disposition" is autonomous effort or it is a vector of outcomes toward which one exhibits autonomous effort. Arneson (2007).

- *Agent responsibility and the attendant moral assessments apply to good, bad, and amoral outcomes and is sensitive to all circumstances of chance (material, social, internal, and otherwise) that either promote or inhibit the outcome in question.*

2.2.4 Measure for Measure

Let us begin to think more explicitly about how we might precisely measure one's responsibility for a particular outcome and, thus, render a precise moral assessment of the individual. That the extent to which we hold ourselves responsible *for an identical outcome* may change according to changes in the relevant circumstances of chance reveals something of the true nature of agent responsibility. One useful analogy is that of "willpower." It is not a binary question of whether one wills to speak kindly to one's spouse or not that determines the outcome, but a question of the strength or power of our will within a specific circumstantial context—"voluntariness [] in this sense is a matter of degree."[47] Under certain circumstances, such as a saloon owner's gun to one's head, we know that even a weak will to nonviolence, like Quick Mike's, may cease the attack. Under other circumstances such as a river rapids, however, we expect that only a very powerful will to save a drowning child has any chance of success. This is because the will does not have unmediated access to realize outcomes—as if the will to speak kindly to one's spouse, or to save a drowning child, robotically or magically led to such outcomes irrespective of relevant circumstances of chance. Rather, willpower exists as an exertion of force upon the ever-changing tide of circumstance. It is this exertion of force upon circumstances—what I will hereafter refer to as autonomous effort[48]—not the outcome, that I will argue below is the true basis of all legitimate moral assessments of agent responsibility.[49]

[47] Feinberg (1970a), 149.

[48] I find this a more felicitous phrase than "autonomous action." Sher (1987), 37.

[49] Miller makes a similar claim vis a vis desert when considering the case of "a cowardly man [who] performs a courageous deed," stating, "Indeed, [] we may even regard the merit of the action as increased by its atypical character..." with respect to circumstances of chance. Miller (1999a), 139n1.

- *The conceptual primitives of this account of moral responsibility are (1) the individual, (2) the observed outcome, (3) circumstances of chance, and (4) autonomous effort.*

2.2.4.1 Autonomous Effort Cannot Be Measured
While I have suggested "willpower" as one useful analogy to help us consider the problem of precisely measuring agent responsibility, I must now reveal a detail of my argument: it is impossible to directly measure an individual's agent responsibility for any *Outcome Y*.[50] There exists neither a true universal unit nor instrument of measure up to the task—agent responsibility and autonomous effort are theoretical concepts, not empirical phenomena. At first this appears to be a fatal blow to any attempt to realize *Just Deserts*—if we can't measure agent responsibility or autonomous effort, how can we possibly render a moral assessment, let alone reward individuals according to desert?

To begin to solve this dilemma, let us examine our typical informal solution that we use to render everyday moral assessments. Note that when one wishes to informally determine an individual's agent responsibility and autonomous effort for *Outcome Y*—what I will hereafter refer to as an *observed outcome of interest*—one reflects upon their knowledge of other individuals who are, or have been, similarly situated to the individual in question. True across many, but certainly not all, competing accounts of moral responsibility, one uses the best knowledge available about human nature, cultural scripts, moral and religious beliefs, social roles, and any other circumstantial factors—in sum, the entirety of circumstances of chance (material, social, internal, and otherwise)—that may make this observed outcome of interest more or less difficult to realize in order to account for extenuating circumstances.

- *We may measure the extent to which* Outcome Y *depends upon factors beyond the individual's control through the best knowledge of, and appropriate comparison with, other individuals similarly situated.*

[50] This is a key, and often confused, point. At this stage, I will leave it as a puzzling metaphysical statement but note simply that it does nothing to change our non-ideal policy prescription. Cf. Roemer (1998), 8–12.

2.2.4.2 Comparison as a Means to Measure Circumstances

As this may sound strange at first, allow me to clarify what I mean by *appropriate comparison* and why I claim that this is a quotidian, routine, and informal measurement grounded in our shared, fundamental moral intuition.[51] The first comparison one is apt to make, in attempting to measure the agent responsibility of another individual for an observed outcome of interest, is with oneself: One asks, what would I feel in that situation, how easy or difficult would it be for me to overcome my lifelong religious beliefs to save a child, and so forth? This is akin to what psychologists of empathy refer to as "imaginative transposition." Yet, as John Locke noted, "it is unreasonable for [individuals] to be judges in their own cases, that selflove will make [individuals] partial to themselves and their friends; and on the other side, that ill nature, passion and revenge will carry them too far in punishing others."[52] In other words, self-interest inclines each individual to correctly highlight chance *inhibitors* of good outcomes as *external* to their own agent responsibility while incorrectly conflating chance *promoters* of good outcomes as *internal* to their own agent responsibility, and vice versa when appraising the agent responsibility of others with whom the agent does not self-identify.[53]

Recognizing that a comparison with only oneself (knowing that "we congratulate ourselves on our blessings, which we call our achievements [and] blame the world for our blunders, which we call our misfortunes")[54] is apt to lead to biased judgement, one widens the circle of comparison. One thus takes a second step. In the case of our two drivers, we compared Cautious Chris and Reckless Ryan not simply with ourselves, but with other moral agents, in particular, *with other drivers*—a *prima facie* relevant class of moral agents. Thus we noted that Chris took more precautions than most drivers while Ryan took fewer. These facts became part of our respective moral assessments in which we place greater blame on Ryan than on Chris for an identical outcome—the child's broken arm. But have we widened our circle of comparison too far by making an *undifferentiated* comparison with all other drivers?

[51] Cappelen et al. (2010).

[52] Locke (1997 (1689)), sec. 13.

[53] And vice versa again for the above four statements when considering bad outcomes.

[54] Taylor (2003), 15–16.

> Imagine that Cautious Chris was 65 years old and Reckless Ryan was 16 when they had their respective "accidents." Further evidence compels us to believe that Chris, although taking more precautions than most drivers, was actually less cautious than most 65 year-olds. And Ryan, although taking fewer precautions than most drivers, was actually more cautious than most 16 year-olds. Does this, and should this, change your judgement, sentiments, or other reaction with respect to Chris and Ryan's agent responsibility for the child's broken arm?

Surely one's age is a factor beyond one's control. It is a matter of chance pure and simple, yet in the actual universe we inhabit, cautious driving seems to ***depend upon*** the circumstance of age. That is to say, cautious driving is a significantly easier outcome to realize for 65 year-olds than for 16 year-olds—it requires significantly different autonomous effort for Ryan to achieve the identical outcome of cautious driving as Chris. Now, if I am correct that any plausible, competing account of moral responsibility must adjust its moral assessments of Chris and Ryan upon learning that cautious driving seems to depend upon the circumstance of age, there is thus common ground for the statement that age is a factor that alters, but does not extinguish, Chris and Ryan's moral responsibility for the identical outcome of their driving choices and behaviors.[55]

To extend this concept, if the outcome, rescuing a drowning child, depends to some extent upon the circumstances of age and sex (both being beyond one's control), it would be better if we could take account of the circumstances of age and sex at the same time. In this way, we would be sure to compare each individual with other individuals ***most similarly situated***, separating the ways their observed outcomes depended upon chance factors of age and sex from the ways such outcomes depended upon their autonomous effort.[56] While the outcome likely does not depend upon all circumstances of chance, the general rule for our informal assessments is that accounting for more circumstances of chance is apt to generate a better

[55] For a brief review of the public policy discussions of adolescent brain development, cf. Steinberg (2013).

[56] Technically, "most similarly situated" does not mean that the only individuals who could offer relevant information to our assessment of a 55-year-old female are other 55-year-old females. This is a weakness of Roemer's proposal that leads to undesirable and unnecessary mathematical and theoretical complications as I will discuss in great detail below. Roemer (1998).

measure of agent responsibility. The ideal measure of agent responsibility, however, will account for all circumstances of chance upon which the outcome, to some extent, depends.

- *The best knowledge of, and appropriate comparison with, other individuals similarly situated is improved by accounting for all circumstances of chance upon which the outcome depends.*

2.2.4.3 Mathematical Identity of Moral Responsibility

In the field of agent responsibility, it is thus against the background of similarly situated individuals that we are able to separate circumstances of chance from factors within the individual's control in order to isolate and precisely measure the agent responsibility and autonomous effort of the individual for the observed outcome of interest. But what of my claim that we cannot directly measure individual responsibility? Arneson states:

> the factors that influence choice that are entirely beyond the agent's power to control and for which she cannot reasonably assume responsibility and the residual factors that are reasonably imputable to the agent are inextricably tangled. We do not in principle know how to separate them, but even if we did, in practical terms the extent to which I am genuinely responsible for a given choice I make or inadvertent failure to attend is impossible to measure.[57]

This statement, echoing earlier ones by Sidgwick, Slote, Miller,[58] and others,[59] goes too far. In my view, although we humans cannot *directly* observe or measure agent responsibility or autonomous effort, it does

[57] Arneson (2007), 265.

[58] "For in any case it does not seem possible to separate in practice that part of a man's achievement which is due strictly to his free choice from that part which is due to the original gift of nature and to favouring circumstances..." Sidgwick (1999), 53; "Indeed, in arguing that one very basic question about deserts for work seems unresolvable, I have made it plain that I can offer no practical scheme for justly distributing goods in society." Slote (1999), 217, Slote (1973), "Certainly, it would be extremely difficult to separate the voluntary from the non-voluntary... and so to tell which of a man's qualities were proper grounds for desert. Perhaps the revised principle for ascribing good desert would be impossible to use in practice." Miller (1999a), 137, Miller (1976).

[59] For example, Fishkin (2014), sec. II.B.3.

not follow that we cannot measure them at all. There are exactly two contributing factors—***mutually exclusive, exhaustive, and independent***— to which we might assign retrospective, empirical responsibility for an observed outcome of interest: (1) factors beyond the individual's control, that is, circumstances of chance and (2) factors NOT beyond the individual's control, that is, autonomous effort. Thus, moral responsibility of the sort I am discussing consists of a mathematical identity that we may exploit to our advantage that allows for *Outcome Y* (any observed outcome of interest) to depend upon a generalized functional relationship:

$$Outcome\ Y = f(\text{Circumstances of Chance, Autonomous Effort}) \tag{2.1}$$

This mathematical identity guarantees that if we can measure both *Outcome Y* and relevant circumstances of chance and we know the function holding all the pieces together, then we can logically deduce autonomous effort—that is, Arneson's *residual*.[60] These facts of mutual exclusion, exhaustion, and independence help to explain the machinery of our shared, fundamental moral intuition. Circumstances help us to estimate autonomous effort, or how responsible an individual is for the observed outcome of interest, and thus help us to arrive at our moral assessment.

2.2.4.4 *Triple Claim: Mutually Exclusive, Exhaustive, and Independent*

Allow me to take a brief moment to defend this triple claim with respect to our normative ideal—that circumstances of chance and autonomous effort are mutually exclusive, exhaustive, and independent. Mutual exclusion and exhaustion are somewhat tautological truths as there are innumerable ways one might cut the universe into *A* and ¬*A*—we have simply selected agent control as the disambiguating element such that *A* contains factors that are beyond this moral agent's control and ¬*A* contains factors that are NOT beyond this moral agent's control.[61] Now one might ask, challenging the mutual exhaustion claim, but are there not factors *partially* within our control and *partially* beyond our control? No, such things are by

[60] In this way, *Outcome Y* is not a "fallible marker for [responsibility, but its] necessary condition." Wolff (2003), 221.

[61] Circumstances of chance are thus synonymous with Hurley's "thin luck." Hurley (2003), 107ff.

definition observed outcomes of interest—a different level of abstraction from factors, the indivisible atoms of outcomes.

2.2.4.5 *Independence*

Next, what do I mean when I say that circumstances of chance and autonomous effort are independent? I mean that perfect knowledge of all circumstances of chance provides absolutely zero information as to an individual's autonomous effort.[62] This independence is necessary in order to ensure that we do not hold individuals morally responsible and thus accountable for those factors beyond their control—including their genes, culture and laws, the context of conditional benefits and burdens, even their brain's operations of perception, calculation, judgement, and so on.

2.2.4.6 *Agent Responsibility for an Outcome Means Nothing for Moral Assessment of Such Responsibility*

We can better see with this mathematical identity that observed outcomes of interest necessarily depend to some extent upon circumstances of chance. This means that agent responsibility for the outcome itself is always contrastive and partial.[63] Rather than undermining our assessments of moral responsibility, it is the partial extent to which an individual is agent responsible for an outcome that precisely determines the appropriate moral assessment. This partial extent is autonomous effort—those factors in the universe over which the individual has independent and categorical control.[64] We pay rigorous attention to circumstances of chance, however, because empirical circumstances of chance (combined with information about the outcome) are the only means we have of revealing what really

[62] Formally, we could write, $P(AE = \alpha\epsilon_i | CC = CC_i) = P(AE = \alpha\epsilon_i)$ for discrete random variables or $f_{AE}(\alpha\epsilon_i | CC = CC_i) = f_{AE}(\alpha\epsilon_i)$ for continuous random variables.

[63] This is important as Vallentyne considered partial responsibility underdeveloped in moral philosophy. "In particular, the issue of partial responsibility for an outcome (rather than it being all or nothing) needs further development." Vallentyne (2008); for a comprehensive and detailed account of partial freedom, cf. Boeninger (2011).

[64] I think this seriously threatens Hurley's argument that a "regressive account of responsibility" is not coherently compatible with causal (e.g., choice or control) conceptions of responsibility. Hurley (2003), 24–28.

matters in these moral assessments—the "effort" condition of moral responsibility.[65]

Observed outcomes on their own provide insufficient information to determine the appropriate moral assessment because (1) identical outcomes are possible via highly different exhibitions of autonomous effort and (2) radically diverse outcomes are possible via identical exhibitions of autonomous effort (including the negation of the apparent outcome of interest). Thus, it is necessarily via the consideration of circumstances of chance that extenuate, but do not extinguish moral responsibility, that we may confidently express stronger or weaker sentiments or judgements of admiration, provide rewards, and vice versa.[66]

- *The definition of control necessary for moral responsibility requires that factors within A's control are mathematically independent of everything except the moral agent.*

2.3 *** Implications, Objections, and Rebuttals

At this juncture, allow me to defend against objections that this theory of moral responsibility is too thin or otherwise defective.[67] I shall briefly discuss (1) Aristotle's exculpatory ignorance and force, (2) moral luck, (3) outcome-tokens and outcome-types, (4) the principle of alternate possibilities, (5) the place of "character," (6) random autonomous effort, and (7) irrational behavior.

2.3.1 Ignorance and Force

Aristotle supposed that agent responsibility requires (a) a moral agent with the capacity to deliberate and decide and (b) that the outcome must

[65] Given this exclusive, exhaustive, independence, I think that Sher's argument loses its critical force. Sher (2003).

[66] This may be viewed as an extension or corollary of the control principle. Arneson (2004), 3.

[67] While some have argued that such a thin theory of the moral agent may fail to secure the "dignity and autonomy" associated with contemporary liberalism, I do not see the loss of dignity or autonomy–nor do I explicitly seek to attract liberals until Chap. 6. Sandel (1999), 185.

be voluntary (i.e., chosen, or within their control) and, respectively, that ignorance and force are two responsibility-extenuating conditions.[68] Do ignorance and force play the same role in the account of agent responsibility I have presented?

In all real-world cases, the account I develop also concludes that ignorance and force constitute extenuating circumstances. Yet, I believe that the precise content of our intuitions does not allow ignorance to *necessarily* extenuate responsibility. As I describe it, agent responsibility for an observed outcome of interest is extenuated to some extent when (1) the observed outcome of interest to some extent depends upon the degree of ignorance or force and (2) the particular circumstances that obtained were high ignorance or high force. Yet, we can generate any number of thought experiments in which condition (2) obtains but condition (1) does not—for example, Sam would have shot Pat *with or without* ignorance that Sam was hallucinating an appropriate object of Sam's gunfire. Here, I find that Sam's ignorance is absolutely not exculpatory.[69]

2.3.2 "Moral Luck"

What are the implications of our account if Sam deliberately and knowingly shoots at Pat and a duck, by pure luck, intercepts the effects of Sam's firearm? Our account roundly rejects "moral luck"—the idea that we may morally assess individuals for factors beyond their control. While some philosophers have shown sympathy to such an idea—for example, asserting that *attempted* murder might receive lesser *retrospective punishment* than *realized* murder even if chance is the *one and only difference*—this "moral luck" premise is undercut. Assigning different punishments to attempted murder and murder makes sense under real-world epistemic conditions of ignorance[70] where, specifically, we do not in fact know that chance is the only difference between the different outcomes.[71] Here, the law uses

[68] Indeed, most philosophers have started with the intuition that a moral agent who is agent responsible must exhibit these two conditions. Aristotle (1999), sec. III.1–5.

[69] Young (2016), 967–68.

[70] Cf. Latus (2000).

[71] "There is an irreducible margin of vagueness in the legal concept of responsibility which often leads courts to mechanically apply admittedly arbitrary rules... to cases in which *[the true extent of agent] responsibility is essentially uncertain* but which require that 'a line be drawn somewhere' [Dwyer's italics]." Feinberg (1970e), 26.

the observed outcome of interest (along with circumstances of chance) to empirically estimate autonomous effort and finds that estimate to differ between failed and successful murder outcomes. Yet, if we had knowledge not available in the real world and we somehow knew Sam's autonomous effort, it would be implausible to treat Sam (with a duck) and Sam (absent a duck) differently—the duck is irrelevant to a moral assessment of Sam. It is Sam, not Sam-and-a-possible-duck, who is the object of our moral assessment.

2.3.3 Outcome-Tokens and Outcome-Types

To underline our intuition that guides our account, "moral responsibility... must be something one can neither escape by good luck nor tumble into through bad luck."[72] While the observed outcome of interest (e.g., Pat's injury from Sam's bullet, a child's broken arm) *motivates* the search for responsible agents, individuals are agent responsible for their autonomous effort and that is the focus of our moral assessments. For example, the moral assessment of two individuals deliberately and knowingly driving in a reckless manner ought to be identical, no matter that by pure luck only one of the drivers in fact injured a child. By focusing on autonomy and following it away from observed outcomes to its singular location in autonomous effort, this theory correctly grasps "the kind of absolute moral responsibility that... has for a long time been central to the Western religious, moral, and cultural tradition, even if it is now slightly on the wane [and that may be] a natural part of the human moral-conceptual repertoire."[73]

Furthermore, analyzing observed outcomes into outcome-types and outcome-tokens[74] helps to dissolve some of the confusion over binary[75] and partial responsibility, that is, that agents are either responsible or not while simultaneously "our ordinary ascriptions of responsibility do not seem to be "all-or-nothing" judgements with no allowance for degrees

[72] The fact that Feinberg does not believe such deep responsibility is possible does nothing to diminish the excellence of the definition thereof. Feinberg (1970e), 32.

[73] Strawson (1994), 8–9.

[74] Wetzel (2014).

[75] I think Feinberg's analyses superb, yet they often allow the legal perspective to override the pre-institutional perspective. For example, see the search for "the cause" of some event. Feinberg (1970a), 142–144.

of responsibility."[76] Both binary and partial responsibility are intuitive and true in that it is true of *all* outcomes that one is or is not agent responsible—the velocity of Mercury at the time of Caesar's death or whether one says "Please" and "Thank you." At the same time, among outcomes for which one is to some extent agent responsible, there are outcome-types that seem to more highly depend upon one's autonomous effort—whether one says "Please" and "Thank you" as compared to the electoral winner in your local race for congressional representative. Stated briefly with new terms of art, as circumstances of chance play a greater role in an outcome-type (reckless driving) the more we *attenuate* our moral assessments of all individuals with respect to reckless driving; as circumstances of chance play a more improbable role in an outcome-token (a particular child's particular injury) the more we *extenuate* our moral assessments of the particular individual in the particular case at hand.

2.3.4 *The Principle of Alternate Possibilities*

As a further puzzle, how does the present theory deal with the "principle of alternate possibilities"—"that a person[, Sam,] is morally responsible for what [Sam] has done only if [Sam] could have done otherwise."[77] Frankfurt launched an important argument against this principle such that, under certain conditions, we rightly feel that an individual bears responsibility for an outcome even if the thought experiment stipulates that it was not compossible with the laws and state of the universe that this outcome failed to obtain. For example, under conditions of *counterfactual* overdetermination or *simultaneous* overdetermination, Sam shot Pat irrespective of Sam's autonomous effort.[78]

Rather than weakening our attachment to free will libertarianism, concession of the principle of alternate possibilities might strengthen our attachment to the premise that individuals are responsible—exactly as our fundamental shared moral intuition suggested—not for observed outcomes, but only for that which is within their categorical control, their autonomous effort. While some have scoffed at resting as weighty

[76] Fischer and Ravizza (1998), 80.

[77] Frankfurt (1969), 829; For various formulations, cf. van Inwagen (1986), 154, 156, 157, 161.

[78] Cf. "Erosion" and "Erosion*," respectively. Fischer and Ravizza (1998), 157–169.

a concept as moral responsibility upon such a "flicker of freedom," there is nothing absurd about suggesting that while outcomes also depend upon circumstances of chance, moral assessments depend exclusively upon the flicker of freedom that is autonomous effort. More audaciously, even if outcomes in the universe we inhabit are ***independent*** of autonomous effort—that is, we live in a deterministic universe—while backward-looking moral assessments could be nothing better than random for humans, individuals could still be agent responsible for any ***autonomous effort***.

2.3.5 Character

Another set of objections to this theory might wonder how things like character fit into this account. Perhaps an individual, Sam, has spent years building a certain sort of character such that certain actions are now completely rote, perfunctory, and habitual (perhaps even ***determined*** by their character)—lacking in the deliberation Aristotle thought necessary. Can Sam exhibit agent responsibility for such acts? There is only one question we need to ask in order to morally assess Sam with respect to the outcome-type, *Outcome Y*: (1) what was Sam's relevant autonomous effort? It does not matter whether that autonomous effort were exhibited two seconds ago or two decades ago, as long as our moral assessment refers to the same individual who exhibited the autonomous effort.

2.3.6 Random Autonomy

What can we say to the objection that the need for autonomous effort's independence from circumstances of chance could be met simply by allowing autonomous effort to be purely random? Moral responsibility surely doesn't rest on a metaphysical roll of the dice. While it is true that the independence criterion may be met by indeterministic dice, there is no reason to suppose autonomous effort is random in this way. First, and most superficially, the word random does not mean unintelligible, irrational, or other such notions that seem divorced from moral responsibility. To be random with respect to circumstances of chance is simply a synonym of mathematical independence. To the individual, however, there is nothing unintelligible, irrational, or chancy about this precise quantity of autonomous effort—the "factors within the individual's control" that are exclusively subject to the individual's own law—factors neither "alien-deterministic," "truly random," nor "partially random."[79] This autonomous effort with respect to this outcome-type is absolutely rational and sensible within the autonomous world of the individual's volitional economy.

2.3.7 *Defective Classical Rationality*

Rather than urging that autonomous effort could be random, what if autonomous effort is occasionally random as suggested by recent work in economics, psychology, and philosophy that seems to show definitive evidence of cognitive biases and irrational observed outcomes of interest, undermining a classical view of a rational actor? It is important to note that such observations are not proof of the moral agent's characteristics, but rather of the material constraints within which the moral agent is forced to exhibit moral agency.[80] While brains may be irrational, predictable,[81] and even predictably irrational, the agents linked to brains may not—or so the argument might go.[82]

- *Moral responsibility is exclusively determined by autonomous effort, which is perfectly independent with respect to circumstances of chance, even the circumstances of our human perceptions, cognitive biases, limitations of knowledge, and possible manipulation by other actors.*

[79] Pereboom (2003), 54.

[80] Just as dark glasses might impair one's capacity to see a doorway in a dark room without the dark glasses doing harm to one's eyes' and brain's capacity to process visual stimuli, human cognitive biases might impair one's capacity to exhibit rational observed outcomes of interest without harming the moral agent's capacity to ratiocinate. Hurley (2011).

[81] I think Campbell overstates the strength of the predictability argument and thus their tactic to avoid it. Campbell (2003), 58–59.

[82] In this way, Fischer and Ravizza's three-part analysis of strong reasons-responsiveness collapses to one single element: there are never failures in the connection between what reasons there are and what reasons the agent recognizes, nor between the agent's reasons and their choice. There are only failures in the connection between choice and action. Fischer and Ravizza (1998), 41–46.

2.4 The Mysterious Seat of Moral Responsibility

Although I have made the rather undefended claim that we may not directly measure autonomous effort—the factors within one's control for which one may legitimately be held agent responsible—it would seemingly be so much easier if we could do so, and some readers and researchers will be tempted to try. It is important to recognize that this is not only completely otiose, but risks allowing a highly detrimental bias to creep into our measurements of autonomous effort. Let us turn to an adaptation of a very provocative story from Barry to help counter those ill-fated temptations.[83]

> Across the nation, a population of *identical* students took a rigorously unbiased math test. Before taking the test, however, students were *randomly* placed into three groups, "Industrious," "Average," and "Lazy." Each group of students was given access to a study room during the course of one week which contained the study materials for the test. The study room for "Industrious" students was painted a cream color, contained soft classical music, a subtle scent of lemon, and an ergonomic chair. "Average" students' study room had bold graffiti on the walls, current pop singles as music, a neutral scent, and a hard, simple chair. "Lazy" students' study room had multiple televisions on each wall, punctuated the cacophony of televisions with startling noises, smelled like gasoline and trash, and had no chair. Although the students were *identical in all ways before this week*, "Industrious," "Average," and "Lazy" students spent 12, 6, and 3 hours studying for this test, respectively. Unsurprisingly, after taking the test under identical conditions, the students' average scores differed by group assignment, 150, 100, and 50, respectively. While the "Industrious" students are inarguably stronger in the mathematics covered in the test (robustly demonstrated by the higher average score), to what extent are the "Industrious" students agent responsible for the *difference* between their scores and those of the other students?

2.4.1 *Agent Responsibility and Economy*

Barry says that the "Industrious" students are agent responsible for their "extra hours spent studying," or as he says, their hard work. On what

[83] Roemer (1998), 21.

grounds should we reject this? First, note that *hard work* is a normative statement of agent responsibility, unhelpfully prejudging the question. We have not directly observed agent responsibility nor even the difficulty of the hard work, however, only the extra hours studying. Barry suggests that these extra hours, however, represent a greater cost incurred for "Industrious" students and that this constitutes greater agent responsibility.

From the crucial perspective of the moral agent themselves, however, given their respective circumstances of chance, it was in fact identically difficult for the "Industrious" students to study 12 hours as it was for the "Average" students to study 6 hours. No cost or benefit is an island. While there may indeed be more disutility to extra hours studying, this must be balanced against the disutility of working in a hard chair or remaining in a room that smells of gasoline. It is not that it was easier for "Industrious" students to study 12 hours than 6 hours, it is that the balance of utilities and disutilities for the "Industrious" group of students to study 12 hours was precisely identical to the balance of utilities and disutilities for the "Average" group of students to study 6 hours and the "Lazy" group of students to study 3 hours.[84]

Although this story utilizes material circumstances of chance to make its point, the same scenario could be obtained by social or internal circumstances of chance as well. In all cases, the difference in hours studying between the groups in this story were in fact completely dependent upon the circumstances of chance and not the autonomous efforts of the students themselves. In identical fashion, the difference in test scores between the groups in this story were in fact also completely dependent upon the circumstances of chance. As such, just as Two-Face was not agent responsible for outcomes completely dependent upon a morally arbitrary circumstance of chance, neither are the "Industrious" students (or any other group) agent responsible for the difference between their scores and those of the other groups of students, as the difference in scores was exclusively dependent upon the difference in random assignment to study rooms.

[84] Pace Sher, while it may seem to be "a piece of bad luck" that some must "exert more of what *looks a lot like effort* to [exert] the same amount of effort," we shall not be fooled into believing that what looks like effort (observed outcomes of interest) is indeed effort (autonomous effort). Sher (2003), 210.

2.4.2 *Agent Responsibility is Never* A Priori

Perhaps Barry would counter that it is not a question of disutility, it is simply that the number of hours spent studying was a free choice of each student, absolutely within their control, and the "Industrious" students *chose* to study more hours and perform better on the test. Yet, this is an *a priori* assumption, and although it may reflect the way we feel about some of our own observed "good" behaviors (and the "bad" behaviors of some others), it is nonetheless subject to empirical examination. Agent responsibility does not allow us to *a priori* decide that we are 1% responsible for river crossings, 80% responsible for automobile accidents, and 100% responsible for hours studying for math exams and the resulting test scores, irrespective of circumstances of chance. For humans, the extent of one's agent responsibility for an observed outcome of interest necessarily requires empirical measurement of circumstances of chance and as such always requires empirical data.

If Barry were to disagree here, stating that no possible evidence could change the fact that the moral agent within each student has absolute agent responsibility for the number of hours studying for the test, irrespective of circumstances, then we are no longer discussing agent responsibility the way most of us understand it via the normative ideal. Such a theory of *ascriptive responsibility*, however, is immediately open to a *reductio ad absurdum* argument as it suggests that even if we filled the study room for the "Industrious" group of students with bees, spiders, atomized hallucinogens, and a thin layer of hot lava, they would still be 100% agent responsible for the difference in the amount of time spent studying for the exam as well as their test score in comparison to the other previously identical students. As this is an absurd position contrary to our fundamental moral intuition, we may confidently state that agent responsibility requires empirical knowledge of circumstances of chance as autonomous effort shows itself in no other way than in context with circumstances of chance.

- *Autonomous effort may never be directly measured but is always knowable as the empirically derived residual in the mathematical identity that links outcomes, circumstances of chance, and autonomous effort.*

2.4.3 Agent Responsibility and Independence

It is possible that Barry or others might counter that "hours spent studying" was the wrong measure of autonomous effort—the factor within the individual's control for which they are legitimately agent responsible—and we should instead measure something more fundamental if we want to measure the students' *true choice* of hours studying, for example, a certain neurochemical.[85] Unfortunately, while some researchers may enjoy the search for The Fountain of Personal Responsibility, this quest is unnecessary and superfluous. We already know where to look: one's individual, autonomous effort toward any observed outcome of interest is, by definition, *something upon which the observed outcome of interest may depend yet has no meaningful relationship to circumstances of chance*—that is, autonomous effort is Arneson's residual.[86]

It is perhaps surprising that, from the perspective of ideal philosophy, it is not possible for the state of study rooms, parental pressure, employers' exhortations, disease, torture, drugs, or even lava to affect autonomous effort in any way as it is absolutely and strictly independent of circumstances of chance.[87] While it is a truism that observed outcomes may depend upon circumstances of chance such as hot lava, we must recognize that it is observed outcomes alone that depend upon circumstances of chance, not the moral agent's autonomous effort itself.

I have taken pains to belabor this point because it is absolutely crucial to a theory of responsibility, and thus *Just Deserts*. Furthermore, it directly contradicts potential interpretations of some luminary scholars, including Rawls, Miller, Olsaretti, Cohen, and Temkin who have occasionally equivocated, confusing vernacular meanings of "Effort" (i.e., observed proxies for autonomous effort) with that mutually exclusive, exhaustive, and independent concept at issue, autonomous effort. Rawls writes, "Even the willingness to make an effort, to try, and so to be deserving in the ordinary

[85] It is immaterial whether the neurochemical is assumed to be an actual representation of autonomous effort or merely a correlate, and therefore proxy or surrogate measure.

[86] As an individual's autonomous effort is independent of all circumstances of chance, this completely dismisses Persson's problem mentioned by Arneson. Arneson (2007), 285.

[87] This normative ideal of the moral agent seems thus to be the "ghost in the machine." Ryle (1949); nonetheless, compatibilists may rather easily support my argument. Cf. Knight (2009), chap. 5.

sense is itself dependent upon happy family and social circumstances"[88] as well as "it seems clear that the effort a person is willing to make is influenced by [their] natural abilities and skills and the alternatives open to [them][89] ... and there seems to be no way to discount for their greater good fortune."[90] Miller similarly writes, "Efforts and choices, too, are affected by circumstances over which the individual making them has no control."[91] Olsaretti argues, "Since the efforts people make depend on, and are inextricably bound up with, factors that are beyond individuals' control, such as their abilities and lucky circumstances, an effort-based or choice-based desert principle, while seemingly attractive, may seem impracticable."[92] Cohen states, "The practical difficulty of telling how much of [effort] merits reward hardly justifies rewarding it at a rate of 0 percent, as opposed to at a rate somewhere between 0 percent and 100 percent..."[93] Temkin claims, "One can't simply assume that Mary deserves to be better off than John, based on the extent to which they differed in maximizing their potential. Perhaps if John had been given Mary's initial starting point, he would have acted as Mary did..."[94]

Each of these statements treats "Effort" as dependent upon something outside the moral agent's control, yet the autonomous effort we wish to isolate in the normative ideal of agent responsibility is that which remains after we have stripped all circumstances of chance away. Thus, we must be clear that, by definition, autonomous effort is an ultimate and original source of control that is absolutely independent of every circumstance of chance in the entire history of the universe. As a corollary, we have guaranteed that there is one, single mathematical distribution of autonomous effort in which all moral agents participate.[95] Thus, Rawls' claim that "the effort a person is willing to make is influenced by [their]

[88] Rawls (1999 (1971)), 64.

[89] For an argument against at least Rawls' "uncritical assumption that people differ in effort-making abilities," cf. Sher (1987), 28–30.

[90] Rawls (1999 (1971)), 274.

[91] Miller (1999c), 276n20.

[92] Olsaretti (2003b), 13–14.

[93] Cohen (2011d), 12.

[94] Temkin (2011), 75.

[95] To be explicit, I am arguing that there is only one distribution of autonomous effort for all moral agents throughout all time and space. This is an important point that extricates us from the mathematical difficulties of different autonomous effort distributions across types. As Roemer states it, "...if we could somehow disembody individuals from their circumstances,

natural abilities and skills and the alternatives open to [them]" is not about autonomous effort but about some observed outcome of interest. Likewise, Hart and Honoré claim too much when they state, "whatever the metaphysics of the matter may be, a [free and deliberate] human action is never regarded as itself caused."[96] It is not the *action* that is never caused as Feinberg argues with respect to the "coldly jealous husband,"[97] but the autonomous effort behind the action. Of course, speaking from the perspective of ideal philosophy, we have not made any such claim that autonomous effort actually exists anywhere in the universe. For all we know, hard determinism may in fact be true and the number of actions believed to be within our control will eventually shrink to zero.[98] For all we know, attributions of agent responsibility are merely "reactive attitudes" that do not objectively describe reality.[99] Nonetheless, any plausible account of responsibility must adjust its reactions upon learning that the outcome depends upon circumstances of chance.

To sum up our conclusion, as all outcomes are dependent upon a mutually exclusive, exhaustive, and independent pair—circumstances of chance and autonomous effort—and there is no way to directly measure autonomous effort, the truest measure of agent responsibility is the remainder or residual after accounting for the dependence of the observed outcome of interest upon all circumstances of chance. This of course shares a strong affinity with what some have called the autonomous spark and "morally essential core"[100] of each outcome for which only the individual is agent responsible.

- *Individual, autonomous agent responsibility—autonomous effort toward* Outcome Y—*is independent of all circumstances, depending upon absolutely nothing else but the moral agent. It is the one sacred, unobservable element within each individual that circumstances can*

then the distribution of the propensity to exert effort would be the same in every type." Roemer (1998), 15.

[96] Hart and Honoré (1959).

[97] Feinberg (1970b), 157.

[98] Nagel (1979), 35.

[99] Strawson (1962).

[100] Nagel (1979), 30; Perhaps this is also what Campbell has in mind when they state, "Moral freedom, then, pertains to inner acts." Campbell (2003), 50.

never touch and is measured only against the background of such circumstances.[101]

2.5 In Sum, This Chapter Has Argued

- *Our moral assessments of an individual who is agent responsible (morally responsible and thus accountable in a way that may justify backward-looking intervention upon the agent) for any* Outcome Y *is directly related to the extent that* Outcome Y *depends upon factors categorically within the individual's control.*
- Outcome Y *necessarily depends to some extent upon factors beyond the individual's control. Moral assessments of agents based upon moral responsibility likewise depend upon the circumstances that in fact obtained.*
- *Agent responsibility and the attendant moral assessments apply to good, bad, and amoral outcomes and is sensitive to all circumstances of chance (material, social, internal, and otherwise) that either promote or inhibit the outcome in question.*
- *The conceptual primitives of this account of moral responsibility are (1) the individual, (2) the observed outcome, (3) circumstances of chance, and (4) autonomous effort.*
- *We may measure the extent to which* Outcome Y *depends upon factors beyond the individual's control through the best knowledge of, and appropriate comparison with, other individuals similarly situated.*
- *The best knowledge of, and appropriate comparison with, other individuals similarly situated is improved by accounting for all circumstances of chance upon which the outcome depends.*

[101] "A good will is not good because of what it effects or accomplishes, because of its fitness to attain some proposed end, but only because of its volition, that is, it is good in itself… Even if, by a special disfavor of fortune or by the niggardly provision of a stepmotherly nature [circumstances of chance], this will should wholly lack the capacity to carry out its purpose—if with its greatest efforts it should yet achieve nothing and only the good will were left (not, of course, as a mere wish but as the summoning of all means insofar as they are in our control)—then, like a jewel, it would still shine by itself, as something that has its full worth in itself. Usefulness or fruitlessness can neither add anything to this worth nor take anything away from it." Kant (1993 (1784)), 4.

- *The definition of control necessary for moral responsibility requires that factors within A's control are mathematically independent of everything except the moral agent.*
- *Moral responsibility is exclusively determined by autonomous effort, which is perfectly independent with respect to circumstances of chance, even the circumstances of our human perceptions, cognitive biases, limitations of knowledge, and possible manipulation by other actors.*
- *Autonomous effort may never be directly measured but is always knowable as the empirically derived residual in the mathematical identity that links outcomes, circumstances of chance, and autonomous effort.*
- *Individual, autonomous agent responsibility—autonomous effort toward* Outcome Y*—is independent of all circumstances, depending upon absolutely nothing else but the moral agent. It is the one sacred, unobservable element within each individual that circumstances can never touch and is measured only against the background of such circumstances.*

CHAPTER 3

Autonomy and Desert

Ah, but a man's reach should exceed his grasp. Or what's a heaven for?—
Robert Browning, "Andrea del Sarto," 1855

Having established a theory of moral responsibility—that the sole and exclusive basis for the type of thoroughgoing moral responsibility that justifies a backward-looking intervention upon the individual is autonomous effort and never circumstances of chance—the *Just Deserts* proposal needs to integrate this within a theory of desert. At this point, while some may feel that such integration is nearly trivial,[1] others may challenge that it is

[1] "A necessary condition for actively deserving anything is that one is responsible for some act for which some treatment is fitting." Pojman (1999), 286; "When we are pronouncing judgments of desert, we are inevitably making judgments about persons whom we hold responsible for their actions." Sadurski (1985), 117; "How do basally deserving acts differ from basally responsible acts? The answer is, I think, that there is no difference." Knight (2011), 162; "..which suggests that responsibility matters not non-instrumentally, but as a reliable indicator of something else, e.g., moral deservingness." Lippert-Rasmussen (2011); "The concept of desert serves to signify the ways of treating people that are appropriate responses to them, given that they are responsible for those actions or states of affairs." "Treating people as they deserve is one way of treating them as autonomous beings, responsible for their own conduct." Rachels (1978), 157, 159; Also, cf. Feinberg's "theory of responsibility" that deals with "the complex situation in which persons... are therefore said to deserve..." Feinberg (1970c), vii; "...for an agent to be morally responsible for an action is for this action to belong to the agent in such a way that she would deserve blame if the

J. T. Dwyer, *Chance, Merit, and Economic Inequality*,
https://doi.org/10.1007/978-3-030-21126-4_3

imperative to defend an intrinsic connection between agent responsibility for an outcome and desert.

3.1 Narrowly Define Desert

Before attempting any such defense, I should delimit the scope of what I mean by desert as this is a contentious topic in current philosophical literature. By desert I mean "distributive desert"[2] in which there is a strictly defined, fully transferable,[3] already existing reward[4] to be exhaustively and simultaneously divided among all relevant individuals and that must be represented by a positive rational number of some unit in which 0 means "absolute zero," for example, 12.9 apples or 1 pie. I do not mean *rank-desert* by which some deserving object might "deserve" a silver medal or first prize. I do not mean *customary-classification-desert* by which some deserving object might "deserve" a grade of B+ or a two-star review—it being plausible that all relevant objects "deserve" a B+ or "deserve" only four-star and two-star reviews (but not three-stars).[5] I also do not mean *moral desert* by which "morally virtuous [individuals] deserve pleasure and the morally vicious deserve to suffer."[6] Nor do I mean *retributive desert* by which some individual might "deserve" some form and quantity of (legal) punishment on account of some (criminal or civil) offence.[7]

action were morally wrong, and she would deserve credit or perhaps praise if it were morally exemplary." Pereboom (2003), xx; "It would seem that there are some things like rewards and punishments which, to be deserved, presuppose the responsibility of the person concerned." Kleinig (1973), 57–58; and, a bit more obliquely, "a person's having been able to have done otherwise is a *necessary condition* of ascribing desert."[Barry's emphasis] Barry (1965), 108.

[2] In Part III, more narrowly, "economic desert." Cf. "Where I talk of theories of economic desert, I have in mind theories which specify distributions of income and wealth in accordance with desert." Wolff (2003), 220.

[3] While perfectly transferable means there is no portion of the reward that is non-transferable, fully transferable shall mean that there is no individual, i, whose deserved reward, R_d, is less than their current portion of non-transferable reward, R_{nt}. For interesting analyses of non-transferable rewards, cf. Olsaretti (2003b), 19; Scheffler (2003), 83–87; Kagan (2003), 98.

[4] "Now some modes of treatment–reward and punishment in particular–presuppose a responsibility on the part of the recipient." Cupit (1996b), 167ff.

[5] Cf. Miller (2003), 29–32.

[6] Hurka (2003), 45.

[7] Hurka (2003), 52.

Furthermore, I shall exclude any consideration of cases in which there is only one individual[8] and shall ignore any desert claims of past or future individuals who do not currently exist (as well as any non-individuals, e.g., buildings, cultures, ecosystems)[9] on the reward. Lastly, I should note that I am trying to generate an account of *pre-institutional* distributive desert.[10] All of this is important to note because my argument is thus immune from discussions of whether an individual deserves a binary reward (e.g., a pension *or not*), rank-order reward (e.g., medical treatment *before or after* another individual), and so on. These examples, which seem to have heavily influenced the literature, are not about distribution in the important ways that I have defined above. In this way, these caveats allow me to say that while I am sympathetic to claims that "justice is simply the getting of what is deserved,"[11] I only wish to demonstrate the attractive theory and consequences that flow from adhering to the claim that "distributive justice is simply the getting of what is distributively deserved."

3.2 Desert Is One Principle Among Many

What does it mean, then, to deserve and how is this connected to responsibility? Many philosophers have understood desert as a three-part relation of the form:

$$i \text{ deserves } R \text{ because of } q \qquad (3.1)$$

where i is the moral agent, R is the reward, and q is the "desert-basis" quality possessed by i.[12] This theory, although containing the necessary elements of scope, metric,[13] and grounds,[14] is unfortunately far too general and does not explicitly, or even implicitly, make reference to agent

[8] Some have claimed that all justice requires plurality. "Justice is a concept which … makes no sense if applied to somebody considered completely in isolation from everybody else." Ewin (1981), 72.

[9] Allegedly, " 'Personal desert' is no pleonasm." Feinberg (1970d), 55.

[10] Cf. McLeod (1999a); Olsaretti (2004), 15.

[11] McLeod (2003), 126.

[12] Olsaretti (2003b), 4; Lamont (1994), 45–46; Feinberg (1963); Feldman and Skow, however, argue both that there are no strong arguments for a three-part relation nor is the adicity of desert particularly important. Feldman and Skow (2015).

[13] Or stakes (Olsaretti (2015), 263ff.).

[14] Wollner (2015).

responsibility—a necessary component to a theory of desert as I have just asserted. As the formalization stands now, one might colloquially "deserve" a reward because of any possible "desert-basis" at all, including scores on a math test, blue eyes, or having a maternal grandmother whose birth year coincided with the most recent visit of Halley's comet. Instead, I will argue that one's distributive deserts are strictly sensitive to one's autonomous effort toward the observed outcome of interest.

3.2.1 Bring in Agent Responsibility

If agent responsibility[15] is necessary to generate a true desert-based principle, the entitlement principle of desert must in fact be a four-part relation of the following form:

$$\text{Principle of Desert:} \quad i \text{ ought to receive } R_{iY} \text{ because of } \alpha\epsilon_i \rightarrow Y \tag{3.2}$$

where $\alpha\epsilon_i \rightarrow Y$ is the autonomous effort of moral agent, *i*, toward observed outcome of interest, *Y*, and R_{iY} is the precise quantity of the corresponding individual reward. First, according to this formulation, note that individuals exhibit agent responsibility for their autonomous effort toward observed outcomes of interest but they do not exhibit agent responsibility for rewards themselves,[16] nor for realizing rewards—individuals ought to receive rewards, but whether they do or do not in fact receive those rewards has no bearing on agent responsibility or desert.[17] Second, desert is backward-looking as $\alpha\epsilon_i \rightarrow Y$ may only be observed in the past[18]—one cannot assess future agent responsibility.[19] Third, R_{iY}

[15] It should be noted that this is completely separate from "ultimate responsibility" which of course does not exist for any individual with respect to any of their observed outcomes of interest such as hours studying or their score on a test. Persson (2007), 91ff.

[16] There is comfortable agreement with the statement that "giving people what the deserve on account of their efforts is not the same as giving them what they are responsible for." Hurley (2003), 9.

[17] Pace Sher (2014), 36.

[18] "Desert is a 'backward-looking' concept, if we regard the present as the limit of the past..." Miller (1999b), 98; "When talking about desert, we are evaluating certain actions which have already happened." Sadurski (1985), 117; "Desert is never simply forward-looking." Kleinig (1999), 86.

[19] For a rare counterargument, cf. Feldman's attempt to attack the temporality requirement of desert. Cf. Feldman (1995b).

corresponds to, but is conceptually distinct from, Y_i as well as all other relevant observed outcomes. For example, if one runs a race in which one might deserve olive branches, one does not necessarily deserve every consequence of one's autonomous effort toward running the race—that is, an elevated heart rate and blisters on one's feet. More pithily, just as Temkin has correctly stated that "full [agent] responsibility for one's choices doesn't entail full [agent] responsibility for one's predicament,"[20] we should add, "nor that one deserves one's predicament." Fourth, this is a self-contained and non-cyclical formula—one does not deserve one's desert-basis.[21]

3.2.2 *Competing Alternatives*

Now, how can I defend my formalization above? Consider that Barry's math students compete for scholarship money of $5000 cash, R_Y, to be distributed in some just way to each student, i, in accord with each individual student's score on the test, Y_i. Philosophers have previously argued over the meaning of "desert," for example, many saying that one of the students, i_1, "deserves" the largest reward because they (q_1) realized the highest score; others saying that i_2 "deserves" the largest reward because they (q_2) exhibited the most autonomous effort toward receiving the highest score; still others saying that i_3 "deserves" the largest reward because they (q_3) have the most economic need for the reward; while others might say that only i_4, "deserves" the largest reward because they (q_4) are the only student who satisfies the stipulation that the scholarship money must go to the child of an immigrant; and, lastly, some saying that there is no "desert" here at all because one may only deserve a reward based upon one's virtue or moral character.[22] No camp has convinced the others as to which desert-basis is the correct, legitimate, or only defensible[23] definition of "desert," and Lamont has even argued that desert is not a rich or determinate enough concept to internally decide upon which represents a better philosophical understanding of desert.[24] I disagree and argue

[20] Temkin (2011), 65.
[21] Zaitchik (1977).
[22] For this view and links to historical antecedents in Plato, Aristotle, and Kant, cf. Temkin (2011), 54, 67.
[23] Olsaretti (2003a), 194–195.
[24] Lamont (1994).

that only i_2 deserves the largest reward because it is the only formulation that involves autonomous effort—an absolutely necessary component to desert.[25]

3.2.3 *Assessment and Credit*

Given these competing alternatives, how can we defend the claim that desert and moral responsibility are inextricably bound as both rest upon autonomous effort? Below, I sketch various lines of argument that I see as important. First, many philosophers argue that the proper desert-basis must be an object of appraisal (or moral assessment).[26] There are only three relevant things we might assess: circumstances of chance, autonomous effort, and their combination. While some might argue that we do in fact assess their combination (the observed outcome of interest, "Ryan was driving the vehicle that broke the child's arm"), this fails to appreciate the intermediate status of observed outcomes of interest with respect to our moral assessments. As mentioned above, the evidence suggests that we extenuate our moral assessments of ourselves and others as we learn of circumstances of chance upon which that observed outcome depended (Ryan's age). That is, we use observed outcomes in our quest to assess autonomous effort, inasmuch as possible, to the exclusion of all circumstances of chance.

3.2.4 *The "About" Condition*

Second, most who write about desert agree that the desert-basis must be "about" the deserving individual,[27] for example, "the facts which constitute the basis of a subject's desert must be facts about that subject."[28] To my mind, this "about" condition requires that such a fact be relevant to the above moral assessment *of the moral agent* rather than a moral assessment of something other than the moral agent. While many are ecumenical

[25] "One possibility, which seems to me attractive, is that... only a principle of desert that sanctions only and all those departures from equality that result from factors over which the relevant individuals have control satisfies [a principle of desert that is defensible as a principle of distributive justice]." Olsaretti (2003a), 202.

[26] Olsaretti (2003b), 6.

[27] Olsaretti (2003b), 4–7; Feldman and Skow (2015).

[28] Feinberg (1970c), 59.

with respect to desert-bases, strictly speaking, we should see that the only thing that is ever truly a property or fact *about* the individual—that is, the moral agent—is their autonomous effort.[29] Circumstances of chance, on the other hand, are properties *of* individuals. While your eyes and your grandmother are undoubtedly yours, they do not tell us anything *about* the moral agent to whom they belong relevant to a moral assessment of you.

Now one might claim that one's eyes (or one's passion for poetry) are constitutive properties of one's identity, yet such talents, preferences, events, traits, character, acts, properties, and so on[30] (if not synonymous with autonomous effort) merely give us evidence of the moral agent's (a) pure circumstances of chance or (b) a combination of circumstances of chance and autonomous effort. In and of themselves, neither (a) nor (b) tell us anything about the moral agent to whom they belong that is relevant to a moral assessment thereof.

To take this "about" argument one step further, Cupit has claimed that "rewards and punishments become not only less defensible but less intelligible when they are imposed for what people are, not for what people do."[31] That is to say, even if one sought to stretch what is "about" the individual to include circumstances of chance, circumstances of chance are not things that the individual does—in fact, just the opposite, they are things that are done to the individual.

> Desert as a candidate principle of justice, we could say, has to be *active desert*, that is, it is desert on the basis of the choices they make and the activities they undertake, rather than on the basis of the sheer possession of unequally distributed unchosen factors, or on the basis of certain things happening to people not as a result of their choices.[32]

Autonomous effort is the only thing the individual may truly be said to "do." Everything else is "arbitrarily given" and thus not about the moral

[29] Sher connects this "about" requirement to our status as deliberating agents. Sher (1987), chap. 9.

[30] Sher (1987), 152ff.

[31] Cupit (1996b), 139.

[32] Olsaretti (2004), 28 [Olsaretti's italics].

agent in the "undistanced, constitutive sense necessary to provide a desert base."[33]

3.2.5 *Expected Consequences*

Third, many philosophers say that desert involves "expected consequences,"[34] the elimination of "untoward interventions,"[35] or even that which is "fitting."[36] It is clear that what underlies these various formulations is a motivation to place luck on one side of the ledger and non-luck on the other. Luck is, of course, identical to our concept of circumstances of chance. In fact, the "expected consequences" of any autonomous effort is, technically defined, precisely the consequences one would see if luck were neutralized. What is the elimination of "untoward interventions" but the elimination of any interference of unexpected luck with someone's autonomous effort? What could be more "fitting" than for one's autonomous effort to translate in a seemingly direct and unmediated fashion (relative to other individuals) into outcomes, free of the particular (and technically "unexpected") good or bad luck that obtained in contribution to one's outcome?

3.2.6 *Interior Locus of Desert*

Fourth, numerous philosophers have grasped the growing interiorization of the locus of desert—or what I would call a retreat from the ever-widening scope of our understanding of circumstances of chance—as we came to explain more of the exterior world via objective causes. Consider Miller's claim that "we can detect an historical trend" toward the proposition that "desert should depend entirely upon what is within a man's control, that is on his efforts."[37] Or "one of the defining characteristics of desert … is that it does require some minimum degree of voluntariness."[38] Or Scheffler's diagnosis of contemporary political philosophers' avoidance

[33] Sandel (1982), 85.
[34] Sher (1987), 40–52.
[35] Goodin (1985).
[36] Cupit (1996b).
[37] Miller (1999a), 137; Miller (1976).
[38] Lamont (1994), 53; Likewise, "We can only speak of "rewards" and "punishments" where there is voluntary effort involved at some point." Barry (1965), 108.

of desert stemming from skepticism about "individual agency, a form of skepticism which is the contemporary descendant of skepticism about freedom of the will."[39] Of necessity, autonomous effort is the endpoint of Miller's historical trend.

3.2.7 *Seeming Instability and Multiplicity*

Fifth, the inextricable link between desert and autonomous effort is consistent with the notion that there is a core to the concept of desert simultaneous to a seeming instability and multiplicity of desert-bases.[40] With a three-part relation of desert, one may be apt to see almost anything as a desert-base. Unlike the near-empty formalization of the three-part relation of desert (where only the individual holds weight), the correct four-part relation clarifies that while myriad observed outcomes of interest and rewards may be involved in desert statements, autonomous effort is the necessary underlying feature common to all proper desert statements. It is the autonomous effort exhibited toward the score on the test and toward blue eyes, if any, that is a necessary, although not sufficient, condition for desert.

Given the strength of this intuition that the desert-base is connected to moral assessments, "about"[41] the individual, independent of luck, highly interior (e.g., effort, will), and stable yet multivalent, a very natural conclusion[42] is that desert necessarily implies the desert-basis of autonomous effort—*ex hypothesi*, the only thing in the universe that is ultimately and

[39] Scheffler (1992), 309–310; Likewise, "[A]n act of will [] is the primary locus of both moral responsibility and control." Hunt (2000), 201; To reward or punish express "reactive attitudes" that are "essentially reactions to the quality of others' wills." Strawson (1962).

[40] For example, a suggestion that there may be innumerable desert-base types, but with a one-to-one relationship to rewards, along with the suggestion that innumerable desert-base types have a many-to-one correspondence to each and every reward (e.g., an apology, punishment, prize, medical treatment, wage, etc.). McLeod (1996), 277–280.

[41] McLeod (2003), 126n8.

[42] As noted in Chap. 2, I think I can also drop some premises about determinism and alternate possibilities by linking desert to autonomous effort—whether or not observed outcomes of interest ever depend upon autonomous effort or not. Cf. "determinism is incompatible with judgements of desert," Miller (1999b), 99. Miller also marshalls Sidgwick in support of this proposition, "The only tenable Determinist interpretation of Desert is, in my opinion, the Utilitarian...". Also, "a person's having been able to have done otherwise is a necessary condition of ascribing desert." Barry (1965), 108.

originally about the moral agent in the appropriate way.[43] As Lamont rightly suggests, "For a quality to count as a ground for desert, the person concerned must, in some sense, be able 'to take credit for' that ground"[44]—yet, how could one possibly take proper credit for what is due to pure luck, completely beyond one's control? It is for these reasons that no properly specified desert-basis is a circumstance of chance (such as blue eyes) or an observed outcome of interest (such as test scores, virtue, or character).[45]

3.2.8 *Naming Competing Alternatives*

Yet, it is not enough to show that autonomous effort is tightly linked to the concept of distributive desert but we must also exclude other alleged desert-bases if I am to argue that autonomous effort is the one necessary and sufficient desert-basis. If we begin by refusing to "allow casual everyday speech to blind us to the distinctions in question,"[46] we become open to recognizing that "this individual deserves R" is not a synonym for "this individual ought to receive R" or "this individual is entitled to R"[47] or even "the world would be better if this individual received R."[48] Such generic distributive justice statements are axiological in that they require, but do not specify, the underlying value that motivates their principle of just entitlement. If we focus on the underlying values, we can see that desert is merely one species[49] of independent and non-parasitic[50] principles

[43] As Geoffrey Cupit argues (toward a different conclusion than *Just Deserts*), an individual cannot typically deserve on the basis of a fact about one's grandmother because such facts do not typically affect the status of the deserver. Recalling our fundamental moral intuition's rejection of moral luck, it is quite clear that one's moral status may never depend upon circumstances of chance and, thus, must depend entirely upon the agent's autonomous effort. Cupit (1996b), 38.

[44] Lamont (1994).

[45] This of course presumes that virtue (and character) theorists mean something different from autonomous effort toward virtue or moral character.

[46] Miller (1999b), 93.

[47] Miller (2003), 27; Pace Matravers (2011), 141.

[48] McLeod (1999b), 277–280, McLeod (1996).

[49] Pojman (1999), 286.

[50] Olsaretti (2003a), 196ff.; Olsaretti (2004), 15ff.

of just entitlement.[51] Thus, the above q_1, q_2, q_3, and q_4 clarify that we have, for example, ***outcome-based***, ***autonomous effort-based***, ***need-based***, and ***rule-based*** entitlements based upon different ethical principles of justice.[52] Indeed, we should see that every principle of distribution has a particular *entitlement-basis* for the statement, "ought to receive." Pace Lamont, one's value-system determines which entitlement-basis one uses, not the meaning of desert. One ought to distribute scholarship money on the basis of ***observed outcomes*** if one seeks to satisfy a distributive principle of *efficiency*; on the basis of ***autonomous effort***—that for which one is absolutely responsible—if one's principle is *desert*; on the basis of ***need*** if one's principle is *sufficiency*; on the basis of ***rules*** if one's principle is *the rule of law*, and so forth. In sum, goods ought to be distributed to individuals on the basis of some entitlement or obligation,[53] desert being only one such possible entitlement.

3.2.9 Desert's Power Flows from the Control Principle

Although my distributive desert theory may appear controversial to some, *Just Deserts* simply "follow[s] out the full implications of this concept [of personal responsibility resting upon the control principle] in our use of the concept of desert."[54] In addition, this necessary link between desert and autonomous effort explains the powerful normative force of desert claims—they align perfectly with our fundamental moral intuition that "people cannot be morally assessed [nor, *a fortiori*, be the target of a backward-looking intervention] for what is not their fault, or for what is due to factors beyond their control."[55] The power of the principle of desert flows from our moral assessments of moral agents, which are a reflection of agent responsibility.

[51] Admittedly, as McLeod has pointed out, many philosophers of desert want to distinguish between "entitlement" and desert where "entitlement" means "institutional desert." This understanding of "institutional desert" is not what I mean when I say distributive desert. McLeod (1999a), 189.

[52] For the addition of "process-based" rewards, cf. Dick (1975), 251ff.

[53] Economics may also use the term "entitlement rules" rather than "entitlement." Cf. Brandolini (1992).

[54] Miller (1999a), 137; Miller (1976).

[55] Nagel (1979), 24.

3.2.10 Adding More Details to Desert

I argued above for a four-part relation of desert, but we need to add further details before we will have comprehensively explained the principle of desert. While arguments over outcome-based, autonomous effort-based, need-based, and rule-based distribution are arguments over the best entitlement principle of distribution, arguments over the legitimacy of distributing scholarship money based upon autonomous effort toward the test score as opposed to autonomous effort toward mathematical mastery are arguments over what Knight has termed the "appraisal grounds" of the principle of desert.[56] According to Knight, we have clearly identified the "basal grounds" of desert as autonomous effort—the grounds (distinct from the basal grounds of sufficiency, efficiency, and so forth) upon which an individual is *deserving* of some reward—but we have yet to identify the "appraisal grounds" of desert. These appraisal grounds require a crucial defense, based upon prudential and/or moral grounds, of why this particular reward ought to *correspond* to (or be fitting treatment according to)[57] autonomous effort directed toward this particular outcome of interest—a question I will explore further in Chaps. 7–10. But first, appraisal grounds further include a *sensitivity* principle whereby we may precisely identify how each individual's rewards are sensitive to different values of relevant autonomous effort and it is there that I turn next.[58]

3.3 The Desert-Basis Revisited

Although the above has clarified the content of the desert-basis as the autonomous effort toward the observed outcome of interest, this still leaves open the question of how individual allocations of the reward are sensitive to differences among the desert-basis. That is to say, we have determined the horizontal equity of desert but not its vertical equity.

56 This also helps us to keep in mind that arguments against a particular appraisal grounds argument are not good arguments if one wishes to undermine the principle of desert as the best principle of distributive justice.

57 "It is the notion of treating which provides the link between the desert basis and what is deserved." Cupit (1996b), 47.

58 For the analysis of "appraisal grounds" into (1) a correspondence between desert-basis and reward and (2) a sensitivity of reward upon desert-basis, cf. Knight (2011), 155.

Horizontal equity is the equal treatment of equals while vertical equity is the appropriately unequal treatment of unequals.[59] Both concepts require (1) an *entitlement* and (2) an *entitlement-basis*, where entitlement is the equal or unequal treatment and entitlement-basis signifies in what respect equals are equals or unequals are unequals. Vertical equity, however, additionally requires (3) a *principled sensitivity* in order to explain why a unique, determinate distribution of rewards among unequals is appropriate.[60] As such, *Just Deserts* must define and defend (1) a reward, (2) a desert-basis, and (3) a sensitivity of the reward to the desert-basis.

3.3.1 Not Proportional Reward

While it is strictly because of $\alpha\epsilon_{iY}$, where this is equivalent to $\alpha\epsilon_i \rightarrow Y$ (i.e., the individual's autonomous effort toward the observed outcome of interest, Y), that the individual deserves a reward, one cannot simply link the desert-basis to the reward. For example, consider a refashioning of Aristotle's "proportional reward" for desert:

$$R_{iY} \propto \alpha\epsilon_{iY} \tag{3.3}$$

Here, rewards, R_{iY}, ought to be proportional to autonomous effort toward the observed outcome of interest. John Roemer has argued that "proportional reward," as I have called it, "is poorly defined: obviously, proportionality depends upon the units in which [the entitlement-basis] and the relevant [entitlement] are measured."[61] First, as with virtue, one might be hard-pressed to determine the proper units with which to measure autonomous effort. Second, any non-proportional transformation of our reward units, e.g., from olive branches to "natural log of olive branches," fails to offer an identical unique, determinate mapping of reward to desert-basis. Rather than a simple link of the desert-basis to the reward, the means by which the vertical equity specification of desert

[59] Lambert (2001), 138.

[60] Olsaretti also contends that desert requires vertical equity with the "comparative justice requirement." Olsaretti (2004), 24.

[61] Roemer (2012), 179.

may survive this unit-transformation test is a functionally defined formal sensitivity of desert,

$$R_{iY} \propto \hat{Y}_i = f(CC_{LE}, \alpha\epsilon_{iY}) \tag{3.4}$$

3.3.2 *Luck-Egalitarian Desert*

To clarify this formalization, this is a theory of luck-egalitarian desert: that if a reward in need of distribution, R_Y, corresponds to autonomous effort toward a particular outcome of interest, $\alpha\epsilon_{iY}$, then each individual ought to receive an allocation of the defined reward of interest (entitlement), R_{iY}, in proportion to their *counterfactual* outcome of interest, $\hat{Y}_i$ (where the hat indicates its counterfactual status), had they exhibited circumstances of chance functionally identical to mean circumstances of chance among all individuals, "luck-egalitarian circumstances of chance," CC_{LE}, in combination with their original, empirically derived autonomous effort toward the observed outcome of interest. As this is dense, technical language, wrapped in a lengthy sentence, allow me to offer a lighthearted, illustrative example.

> Imagine that you and Mozart are the only two relevant individuals and you both enter a piano competition in which, *ex hypothesi*, the appraisal grounds require that an individual's autonomous effort, $\alpha\epsilon_{iY}$, toward the observed outcome of interest, Y = goodness of piano performance, corresponds to a reward, R_Y = 10 kilograms of chocolate. As is true for all observed outcomes of interest in the universe, one's observed performance depends entirely upon two mutually exclusive, exhaustive, and independent factors:
>
> 1. CC_i, a vector of circumstances of chance that actually obtains for the individual, i
> 2. $\alpha\epsilon_{iY}$, autonomous effort toward the observed outcome of interest, in this case, toward the goodness of the piano performance exhibited by individual, i
>
> Next, although real-world vectors of circumstances of chance contain myriad circumstances, imagine for the sake of illustration that there are only two within the relevant vector of circumstances of chance for this outcome, $CC_i = \{p_i, t_i\}$:
>
> 1. p_i, talent for piano performances
> 2. t_i, talent for piano timing

To again keep things simple, imagine that the goodness of one's piano performance, Y_i, is produced via the function, $Y_i = p_i + t_i + \alpha\epsilon_{iY}$, that is to say: add one's talents for piano performance and timing together with one's autonomous effort toward the goodness of one's performance.

As it so happens, Mozart has amazing circumstantial talent and thus his relevant vector of circumstances of chance (factors absolutely beyond his control—i.e., pure and unadulterated luck) exhibits the measured values, $CC_{Mozart} = \{600, 400\}$ while you have poor circumstantial talent, $CC_{You} = \{6, 4\}$. When it comes to autonomous effort, however, Mozart exhibited a 10 while you exhibited a 15. As is clear, the goodness of Mozart's performance is unquestionably greater, 1010 vs. 25 ($Y_{Mozart} = 1010 = 600 + 400 + 10$; $Y_{You} = 25 = 6 + 4 + 15$). Given our stipulation that 10 kilograms of chocolate is appraised as the corresponding reward, how are your desert-entitlements sensitive to your desert-bases—that is, what do you each deserve?

Surprisingly, you clearly *deserve* a greater reward than Mozart because you exhibited greater autonomous effort toward the piano performance even though Mozart's performance was better. The sensitivity question demands, however, that we can say precisely how much greater a reward you deserve. At first, you may have been tempted to define vertical equity as strict proportionality, and say 50% more chocolate along with Aristotle ($50\% = (15 - 10)/10$). Instead, the correct answer is that you deserve 0.97% more chocolate than Mozart.

To explain this finding, the supporting reasoning states that if you had each counterfactually received "luck-egalitarian circumstances of chance" with respect to this observed outcome of interest, relevant talent valued at 505 ($505 = [(600 + 400) + (6 + 4)]/2$), our functionally defined desert sensitivity states that your reward should be proportional to $520 = 505 + 15$ and Mozart's should be proportional to $515 = 505 + 10$ ($0.97\% = (520 - 515)/515$).

Does Mozart have any grounds to complain about receiving a lesser reward for his performance that was better than yours? Have we been too harsh, dogmatic, or moralistic in our distribution of reward? Based upon a principle of desert, absolutely not. While Mozart may be *entitled* to more based on a number of other distributive (and non-distributive) principles and the words "deserve" and "reward" may even be used in the vernacular in such ways, the principle of desert requires us to assess each pianist solely upon their autonomous effort and to distribute rewards commensurately.

Mozart made a radically genuine choice to exhibit precisely 10 units of autonomous effort and, importantly, there was literally nothing in the universe (except Mozart the moral agent) preventing him from exhibiting 15, or 20, or 2000 units of autonomous effort toward this particular piano performance and receiving a relatively larger reward.

To continue, I hope it is clear that the *Just Deserts* formalization above is not a principle of luck-egalitarianism, but of luck-egalitarian desert.[62] Moral agents do not deserve equal luck, rather the argument is that when there are rewards placed into a desert-relation, moral agents deserve that their rewards are exclusively sensitive to autonomous effort. To elaborate, I do not believe that all members of the population deserve to play piano as well as Mozart (strict outcome egalitarianism),[63] nor do they deserve the same values among all the elements within the vector of circumstances of chance (radical luck-egalitarianism),[64] nor even do they deserve the same functional value of the vector of circumstances of chance (generic luck-egalitarianism, also "expected consequences"). The principle of desert's sole aim is that, ***with respect to rewards***, we may strip away all the chance differences between you and Mozart and allocate rewards sensitive to the only factor genuinely and completely within individual control, autonomous effort.

This generalized formula has the advantages that (1) it always realizes a distribution such that rewards are absolutely insensitive to luck but exclusively sensitive to agent responsibility,[65] (2) it does not fail the unit-transformation test, (3) that sensitivity is always ***in strict accord with expected consequences—that is, the underlying, empirically derived function of the observed outcome of interest itself***,[66] and (4) importantly, rewards do

[62] "Any plausible desert theory, then, will require that the differential effects of brute luck on advantage be neutralized." Vallentyne (2003), 175; Although I believe desert can stand alone, for a relevant sketch of an egalitarian's support for my principle, cf. Christiano (2007), 79–81.

[63] Pace Anderson (2015); For a more sophisticated critique of Anderson's mistaken narrowing of luck egalitarianism, cf. Vallentyne (2015).

[64] Bedau (1967).

[65] By stipulation, we have divided the universe in such a way that Rawls' and Miller's arguments lack force as it is simply not possible for "choices and efforts [, i.e., autonomous effort, to] depend on contingencies that are not under [the individual's] control [i.e ,circumstances of chance]." Miller (1999c), 148.

[66] For example, if doubling autonomous effort leads to a 50% change in outcome-type 1 (e.g., goodness of piano recital) but a 200% change in outcome-type 2 (e.g., average speed

not need to stand in a causal relationship to the rewarded autonomous effort, that is, one might deserve chocolate for a kind act even if kind acts never empirically caused their agents to receive chocolate. Speaking in the language of the "responsibility-sensitive" literature, the luck-egalitarian principle of desert is a "reward principle" that always satisfies Fleurbaey's horizontal equity "compensation principle"[67] for any economy and any conditions.[68] That is, luck-egalitarian desert implies responsibility-sensitive reward in which no one is ever "worse off than others through no fault [or choice] of their own."[69]

- *One principle of entitlement among many, a principle of desert uses autonomous effort toward* Outcome Y *as its entitlement-basis, while offering a luck-egalitarian principle in defense of its version of vertical equity.*

3.4 Chance, Merit, and Inequality

I would now like to move away from abstract theory to practical implementation and explicitly address the distribution of economic resources, or what Wolff calls "economic desert."[70] As a note on terminology, a *distribution* describes the division of the reward among the entire population; an *allocation* describes how much of the reward is received by one individual; and a *mapping* describes the rules that govern each individual's allocation.

> Imagine for a moment that there are two individuals, Sherlock and Irene, *identical in all ways* save morally arbitrary appearances, who have each just received a gift of $1000. Interrupting their private joys, a mad scientist suddenly forces them into a lottery during which they are unable to communicate with each other, and after which their memories of this lottery will

during a 400 m race), doubling autonomous effort will be associated with 50% greater reward in the former case and 200% greater reward in the latter.

[67] As Fleurbaey notes, this tension had been sensed by Dworkin and Barry. Cf. Dworkin's "endowment-insensitivity" and "ambition-sensitivity" as well as Barry's "principle of compensation" and "principle of responsibility." Dworkin (1981b), 311; Barry (1991), 2:142.

[68] This includes homogeneous as well as heterogeneous economies, as discussed in Chap. 5. Fleurbaey (2008); Fleurbaey and Peragine (2013).

[69] Temkin (1993), 13.

[70] Wolff (2003), 220.

> be completely erased. An unbiased coin is repeatedly tossed, the outcomes of which determine a new distribution of their now combined gifts of $2000. According to the lottery, Sherlock receives $1900 while the remaining $100 goes to Irene. To what extent is either individual agent responsible for their allocation? Does either deserve their allocation?

The observed outcomes of this lottery depended solely upon an element of chance that was entirely beyond the control of either party, and so, according to the *control principle*, we should have no doubts about our answer. It is incoherent to hold either party agent responsible for these outcomes. In spite of a clear answer with respect to agent responsibility, however, desert is silent because nothing has yet fulfilled Knight's appraisal grounds and linked some desert-basis to the gifts ($2000).

> Imagine, then, that Irene and Sherlock are the only relevant moral agents and that their autonomous effort toward their score on Barry's math test is the corresponding desert-basis for the $2000. Just before they take the test, however, the mad scientist informs Sherlock and Irene that an anonymous benefactor has provided for a new, larger, and stranger lottery. As a mad experiment, they will now play for a corresponding pot of $1,000,000. Once again, an unbiased coin is repeatedly tossed, the outcomes of which determine not their winnings, nor the state of the study room, but their very selves—Sherlock ends up with extraordinary math talent while Irene is left with little. Although both exhibited identical autonomous effort, Sherlock's score is far better than Irene's. What do they each deserve?

While other principles of distribution might claim Sherlock is entitled to $990,000 of the $1,000,000, according to the principle of desert, unequal allocations cannot be a just distribution of resources given their identical autonomous effort. Sherlock has no reasonable desert claims to a greater share. Similarly, Irene's worse performance on the test did not depend in any way, shape, or form upon a single factor within her control. In sum, they each exhibit an equal entitlement-basis for any deserved rewards.

3.5 The Lottery You Can't Refuse

Let us now rotate our perspective on these thought experiments to sharpen the point as to the often overestimated presence of agent responsibility in the real world.

> Imagine that there is no mad scientist. Instead, Sherlock is simply born into a family of great means and Irene is merely born into poverty. Each has received gifts of fortune, but Sherlock's are extraordinarily valuable ($990,000) while Irene's are not ($10,000). They are *identical in all other ways* save morally arbitrary appearances. To what extent is Sherlock agent responsible for this difference in benefits he stands to receive based merely upon chance? To what extent is Irene agent responsible for less? Do they deserve these differences?

Some philosophers[71] call birth the *natural lottery*[72] for it appears to share all the necessary characteristics with the mad scientist's lottery described above when properly viewed from the perspective of the morally autonomous and agent responsible core of the individual, namely, (a) a lottery[73] based purely upon morally arbitrary chance, (b) with no opportunity to alter the lottery outcomes, and (c) with no market opportunity to purchase an insurance policy against lottery outcomes.[74] Far from inconsequential, the natural lottery, rather than agent responsibility, may be the single strongest controlling factor with respect to the resources at each individual's disposal throughout their lifetime.[75] And yet, our society does little to change this, allowing circumstances of chance to govern Sherlock's life of luxury and Irene's brief life of penury.

Given our acceptance of the control principle and the fact that the size of their gifts did not depend upon a single factor within their control, it is clear that neither Sherlock nor Irene are agent responsible for those gifts. Without relevant autonomous effort, it is chance, and chance alone, that is empirically responsible (via object responsibility) for the size of their

[71] Rawls (1999 (1971)), 64; Knight (1935), 54–57; "It is this fundamental human plight of being born into our initial stations and their inequalities which is sometimes rather vaguely referred to by the phrases 'chance of birth' or 'accident of birth.'" Spiegelberg (1999), 151, Spiegelberg (1944).

[72] Gosepath (2011); Lamont and Favor (2014); Lippert-Rasmussen (2014); Markovits (2008).

[73] While I tend to agree with Hurley's arguments that we should only discuss "constitutive luck" rather than the "natural lottery," I merely need the reader to see the "natural lottery" as circumstances of chance, thin luck. Hurley (2003).

[74] One might infer from Heathcote that precisely the lack of such insurance markets inhibits economic growth. Marrero and Rodríguez (2013); Heathcote et al. (2008).

[75] "For it is chance in a specific and very definite sense which is ultimately responsible for all we initially are and have. … It follows that all initial inequalities in the form of privileges and handicaps are ethically unwarranted." Spiegelberg (1999), 151; Spiegelberg (1944).

gifts upon which their different lifetime economic outcomes are jointly dependent with their respective autonomous efforts.

Whether they deserve the value of their gifts is another question. While we cannot speak definitively at this juncture, we can state the following: If the value of their gifts were (part of) the corresponding reward for some desert-basis (autonomous effort), then Sherlock would only deserve $990,000 if that were the allocation determined by the desert formula above.

- *Our moral assessments that flow from agent responsibility as well as our determination of desert treat the entirety of the natural lottery in identical fashion to all other circumstances of chance as the entirety of the natural lottery is absolutely beyond the individual's control.*

To conclude, the *Just Deserts* proposal suggests, not that the observed outcomes of interest in Sherlock and Irene's story may be unjust, but (a) that encompassing rewards may be unjust because undeserved and (b) that we should transfer some good(s) from Sherlock to Irene as rewards provided Knight's appraisal grounds are satisfied. Yet, our society does not currently implement a public policy that ensures that each receives their *Just Deserts*, no more and no less. In fact, while our society appears to provide Knight's appraisal grounds, our institutions instead reward each individual for their circumstances of chance as if these circumstances were the autonomous effort for which the individual is agent responsible. Moreover, our society allocates a distribution that is "so suffused with arbitrary influences on legitimate possession that it cannot count as fair."[76] Rather than rectifying unjust distributions based upon chance, our society's public policies currently exacerbate them.[77] The *Just Deserts* proposal will address this injustice.

[76] Wolff (2003), 224.

[77] This puzzle as to why our public policies do not match our moral beliefs, why a *Just Deserts* proposal is not already in place, is explained partly by the only recent acquisition of some conceptual and empirical tools as well as the obvious self-interest of those currently enjoying the greatest relative and absolute amounts of unmerited rewards.

3.6 *** Implications, Objections, and Rebuttals

At this juncture, allow me to address objections that this theory of desert might be too thin or otherwise defective. I shall briefly discuss (1) deserved gross inequalities and deprivation, (2) challenges to the intrinsic connection between desert and responsibility, (3) determinism, (4) noncomparative desert, and (5) brute luck and option luck.

3.6.1 Desert Is Too Harsh

While it is commonly accepted that the principle of desert may plausibly lead to gross inequalities[78] or even gross poverty, it is important to note the strong links between desert and freedom. The account of freedom I have in mind is not merely an equal right to negative liberty as freedom from interference by others. Distributive desert implies a robust positive freedom, equal to all, to realize any possible reward.[79] As will become more clear in the chapters that follow, there is thus nothing "harsh" about deserved gross inequalities or deprivation when such are the appropriately corresponding deserved rewards for individuals' genuine choices expressed via their autonomous effort—if Mozart *chooses* to exhibit relatively little autonomous effort (a factor absolutely within Mozart's control), there is nothing harsh in honoring that choice. Desert necessarily holds vertical equity at its core and thus, "inequalities [in reward] are justified only insofar as they reflect differential exercises of responsibility, and equalities [in reward are justified] only insofar as they reflect equivalent such exercises …"[80]

[78] Pace Segall (2013), 150–151.

[79] Technically, this freedom does not include realizing an allocation equal to the entire reward although such an allocation is logically possible.

[80] Knight (2009), 230; also, contrary to most of the luck-egalitarian literature, Sher (2014), 22, those with a lesser allocation of the reward are not the "crucial party" able to make a claim of injustice. Even the individual with the greatest amount of reward may legitimately demand and receive compensation as redress.

3.6.2 Do Responsibility and Desert Fall Apart?

3.6.2.1 No Responsibility, No Desert

Consideration of the relationship between lotteries and desert may illuminate the connection between responsibility and desert. To begin, some have argued that "… the outcomes of lotteries … are inherently, to some greater or lesser extent, undeserved: The losers always deserve more (sometimes much more) than they get; the winners never deserve as much (sometimes not nearly as much) as they receive."[81] I believe this is too strong a claim. Others have suggested that with respect to lotteries, "no one morally deserves anything at all."[82] This is correct but apt to be misinterpreted. Closer to the mark is the statement that when we "[t]hink of a person who wins a large sum in the lottery. … Other things being equal, there is no injustice in her receiving it."[83] Yet, "other things being equal" is left critically unspecified.

The existing confusion around lotteries and desert is possible because Knight's appraisal grounds are typically missing. If there is a lottery for 12 pies and there are no desert-relations in which (any portion of) those 12 pies stand as a reward, then it is absolutely true that no one deserves any of those pies at all. If, however, some or all of those pies were a reward in some desert-relation, a lottery for the 12 pies almost certainly contravenes desert and leaves some with more or less than they deserve (although it may very well be that the loser deserves less). Thus, it is not lottery *outcomes* that we consider unjust, it is the intervention of a lottery outcome upon a desert-relation that is unjust.

3.6.2.2 Autonomous Effort Toward Lottery Outcomes?

Yet, this seems to suggest that one might counterintuitively deserve some rewards by exhibiting autonomous effort toward lottery outcomes. This suggestion underscores the importance of Knight's appraisal grounds for desert. Time and again, desert is misunderstood by generating thought experiments in which the desert-basis and reward are vaguely, or not at all, specified. This suggestion is counterintuitive because there are no good

[81] Goodin (1999), 240, Goodin (1985).
[82] Temkin (2011), 56.
[83] McLeod (1999a), 193.

appraisal grounds to tie rewards to individuals' autonomous effort toward a lottery outcome. As such, this is a clearly invalid desert-relation.

Not only must we clearly define the desert-basis and the reward, it is important to see that in some cases such as the natural lottery, it's possible that (some of) the reward has already been distributed among the relevant moral agents. This previous distribution of good, *G*, for which no moral agent is responsible must not be confused with the distribution of *G*-as-reward. Stated differently, Irene might deserve some of the value, *G*, previously distributed by the natural lottery not because of her autonomous effort toward G itself but because of her autonomous effort toward some *Y* (doing good, climbing mountains, etc.) that we appraised as corresponding to *G*-as-reward.

3.6.2.3 No Apparent Responsibility, No Desert?

There are, however, other challenges to the connection between desert and responsibility—ones in which individuals only ***apparently*** exhibit zero autonomous effort toward the observed outcome of interest. For example, Knight argues for "responsibility-sensitive justice" wherein horizontal equity holds in all cases except where two individuals apparently exhibit zero responsibility ("for example, [one of them is] hit by a meteorite") at which point "responsibility-sensitive justice" states that "there can be no responsibility-based justification for compensation" because "no one is responsible for the victim's bad brute luck non-acts."[84] Pojman presents a similar case where the individual suffers a painful disease, "is not responsible for contracting it,"[85] yet still might deserve compensation.[86] Feldman presents diners of a restaurant who become ill with food poisoning and "deserve several things" even though they "bear no responsibility for the fact that they were poisoned." Likewise, Feldman considers that grieving parents whose child has died "deserve various things" even though "no one bears any responsibility for their misfortune."[87]

While I don't think that these alleged desert-relations are within the scope delimited at the beginning of the chapter, our approach may nonetheless shed new light. It is true that, as in a lottery, these individuals

[84] Knight (2011), 152, 166.

[85] Pojman and McLeod (1999), 63.

[86] For Pojman, this unites "active desert" and "compensatory desert," Pojman (1999), 286–287.

[87] Feldman (1995b), 69.

are not responsible for their bad lottery outcomes. In each of these cases, however, it is precisely because we assume that the victims of bad luck exhibited equal autonomous effort as other non-victims toward some *Y* and we appraise *R* as the corresponding reward that they must be compensated[88] because they bear identical responsibility as others for their, now unjust, quantity of some reward *that has been previously distributed by luck*. Desert continues to necessarily rely on responsibility when rewards correspond to the proper desert-basis—we are not interested in diners' autonomous effort toward food poisoning by negligent chefs but in individuals' autonomous effort toward *Y* (whatever corresponds to the reward that is, or subsumes, good health). Likewise, we are not concerned with the quality of the meteorite victim's "non-acts" because we focus on their autonomous effort toward the appropriate outcome (e.g., the math test), not a particular circumstance of chance that intervenes on the appraised reward. When an individual exhibits identical autonomous effort as others toward Y and a factor by stipulation completely beyond their control (a meteorite, a negligent chef, a fatal illness) intervenes upon the desert-relation, we consider such intervention demands a counter-intervention in order to realize a just distribution of rewards.

3.6.2.4 No Autonomous Effort, No Desert?

What if, among all relevant moral agents, not a single individual exhibits any autonomous effort toward the math test? While my intuition is that no such desert-relation exists, it is important to note that zero autonomous effort does not mean zero responsibility—an individual is always agent responsible for their autonomous effort, whether zero or something else. With respect to desert, whenever all relevant individuals exhibit identical autonomous effort (even if zero autonomous effort), each deserves an identical share of the reward according to our formula above.

3.6.2.5 Identical Responsibility, Different Outcomes, Different Deserts?

Another related objection that some might raise is that this theory of desert is intuitively wrong because it would apply punishments to all reckless drivers even though only some of them were observed to injure children. While I do believe that this is the best form of retributive desert,

[88] For the fact that bad luck reduced their quantity of some good(s) below their deserved quantity of *R*, isometric to the aforementioned good(s).

I have not presented a theory of retributive desert but of distributive desert where we are seeking a just distribution of some existing good. Furthermore, "distributing" punishment is qualitatively different from distributing chocolate. It is not the case that there are 1000 early bedtimes, 19 ostracisms, or 5 million days in jail subject to a just distribution.[89]

Yet, one might raise the same objection about our math test.

> Imagine that two identical individuals employ the same strategy on the math test about questions to which they cannot find the answer: flip an unbiased coin. By luck, one of the individuals receives a higher score on the test even though they exhibited identical autonomous effort and their answers were identical except where the coins were involved. Does one individual deserve more of the reward than the other?

According to our theory, no. Is this counterintuitive? Given that, ideally, deserved rewards are sensitive to factors within the individual's control, *Just Deserts* sets luck to one side and asks that our luck-free moral assessments directly translate to desert.

3.6.2.6 Indeterministic Outcomes, Effort, Desert

Likewise, when multiple individuals place a bet and some appear to put more effort into making the correct bet than others (e.g., through prudent research), some object that we do not then redistribute the pot according to apparent effort. First, our theory ignores *apparent effort* and focuses exclusively upon autonomous effort—factors absolutely within the agent's control. Second, there are many valid types of entitlement and distributive desert is only one species thereof—that distributive desert does not apply in all microscenarios does not suggest that our account is mistaken. Third, stating that the winner of an indeterministic bet "deserves" the pot *because they won the bet* and not because of a well-defined desert-relation is a mistaken attempt to undermine desert by discussing some other entitlement. Fourth, the importance of some other species of entitlement

[89] Nonetheless, if we stipulated that there is a desert-relation between reckless driving and some punishment and I were asked to generate a theory of retributive desert, I would likewise find it perfectly intuitive to allocate an identical backward-looking punishment to all reckless drivers with the same autonomous effort toward safe driving based upon factors within their control, with no difference between the one who hit a child (by pure luck) and the 100 who did not (by pure luck).

in this scenario offers little support for an argument that other principles are more important than (or preferred to) our account of desert. If Sherlock deserves nine pies and Irene deserves three pies for their autonomous effort on the math test, there is nothing unjust about them later entering their rewards into a bet about which the prior desert-relation is silent. Once the principle of desert has been satisfied, Sherlock and Irene may then sell, buy, bet, consume, and even destroy their rewards and the principle of desert is silent. Thus, examples in which we do not intuitively see the principle of desert are rarely the defeaters they are taken to be.

3.6.3 Determinism

Another objection some might suggest is that our theory of desert must be incorrect if determinism is true *and* we do in fact deserve things like chocolate or economic resources. If these two premises were true, we might deserve things where the desert-basis is autonomous effort or something else. If the latter, this theory of desert is incorrect. If the former, this theory is not necessarily incorrect, it merely recommends reward egalitarianism. That is, if Sherlock and Irene live in a deterministic universe and so their performance on the math test is *independent* of their autonomous effort, then the "expected consequences" of any autonomous effort are always the same. If, in addition to the control principle, however, a further intuition is that "for all rewards, some individuals deserve more of that reward," then those entities incapable of directly observing autonomous effort (e.g., humans) cannot realize distributive justice in this case as, *ex hypothesi*, knowledge of circumstances of chance and observed outcomes of interest provides no information about autonomous effort in a deterministic universe. Of course, nothing precludes some suprahuman entity from noting and rewarding their autonomous efforts.[90]

3.6.4 Absolute Desert

Another objection some may raise is that my theory of distributive desert is entirely comparative. Although the freedom via desert discussed above is robust, it is not absolute. As we can see from the vertical equity specification

[90] Of course, such a situation would also require a different kind of vertical equity than I have suggested.

above, the principle of desert realizes responsibility-*sensitive* reward (a strictly comparative or relative principle), not responsibility-*contingent* reward (a strictly noncomparative or absolute principle). Further, this relativity has two dimensions: what each individual deserves is necessarily relative not only to the size of the reward to be distributed but also relative to the autonomous efforts of all other relevant individuals. As a consequence, one cannot know what Sherlock deserves if one is ignorant of what any other individual in the population deserves.[91]

Of course, if we were in possession of an absolute table of correspondence between autonomous effort and reward (enabling a noncomparative principle of desert),[92] one might be able to say that 12 pies or $1,000,000 is far too large or small a reward for Sherlock and Irene. One might further see that rewards ought not be sensitive to autonomous effort in the way I have suggested—in strict accord with the underlying, empirically derived function of the observed outcome of interest itself. Yet, not only do we not have such a table, there is little reason to suppose that the distribution of 12 pies for autonomous effort toward Y (assuming we have found the correct appraisal grounds) could be anything but comparative. Thus, the specification of vertical equity with respect to desert is represented as Eq. (3.4) and Sherlock and Irene each deserve $500,000.[93] As such, sensitivity means that the desert-basis is strictly "about" the moral agent while the desert-entitlement depends upon the desert-basis and some constant, luck-egalitarian circumstances of chance as determined by

[91] "...the justice of your treatment is (partly) constituted by how it compares to how others are treated. The epistemic correlate to this is that the justice of a particular person's treatment cannot be known without knowing how others in the relevant comparison class are treated." McLeod (2003), 126n10; Pace Lake (2001), 91ff.

[92] "The idea that there is some absolute amount of money that a person could deserve solely by virtue of the work that he has done and without regard to how others have performed makes no sense." Miller (2003), 32; "Our beliefs about desert include a concern with patterns as patterns." Hurka (2003), 50; "I wish to claim that justice is also necessarily comparative, that it always involves comparisons between persons or groups." Sadurski (1985), 14ff.

[93] That is, I "hold that what a person is due is based on some essentially comparative consideration... and [] claim that justice requires that each individual get exactly what each is due." Olsaretti (2003b), 21. I also think this is entirely compatible with the view that desert is ideally noncomparative but our best non-ideal option is comparative desert.

empirical observation of all other relevant individuals and the total reward to be distributed (see Chap. 12 for a real-world example).[94]

3.6.5 *Brute Luck and Option Luck*

Another objection might be that this theory of desert is clear about its treatment of brute luck but less clear about its treatment of option luck. Many philosophers would argue that Sherlock and Irene had no opportunity to create a social agreement, an insurance market, or otherwise avoid these mad scientist or natural lottery outcomes. As such, this was a quintessential instance of what philosophers after Dworkin call *brute luck*.[95] Under conditions of brute luck, many argue, one looks to the empirically realized values (injured by a meteorite or not; talented or not) when measuring circumstances of chance. If these empirically realized values differ (only one individual was injured by a meteorite or talented), then the "brute luck constraint"—a pillar of moral common sense[96]—has been violated. Many philosophers believe, however, that there is another kind of luck, *option luck*, under which the relevant circumstances of chance are to be measured by expected values rather than the empirically realized values.

Option luck is said to exist to the extent that Sherlock and Irene had made a genuine, autonomous choice to enter into an indeterministic lottery. While I am open to the conclusion that Sherlock and Irene *ought to receive* certain rewards dependent upon option luck, given desert's strict sensitivity to autonomous effort and strict insensitivity to circumstances of chance, one may not *deserve* rewards that are sensitive to any kind of luck, option luck included.[97] To make my claim even stronger, desert maintains its formal structure, Eq. (3.4), even if Sherlock and Irene's genuine choice involved deliberately and knowingly choosing to enter a contract with a probabilistic outcome. Distributive desert is pre-institutional and does not disappear simply by using a convention to declare that we value some other principle(s) more than the principle of desert. Again, if the moral agent

[94] I think this formalization of vertical equity as sensitivity to the entitlement-basis but dependence upon that basis and some constant is a clearer solution to the puzzle of the "aboutness" requirement fitting with comparative desert. Cf. McLeod (2003), 127ff.

[95] Dworkin (1981b), 293; Vallentyne (2002).

[96] Freiman and Nichols (2011).

[97] Temkin (2011), 64.

has any ultimate and original control in the universe,[98] the principle of desert rewards that autonomous effort and that alone, not the outcomes that result from that effort in combination with circumstances of chance, and that is all option luck is—the combination of autonomous effort and circumstances of chance.

To see that desert and luck have no truck is to explain countless examples of desert claims in the literature. In fact, almost every single example of a separation between the winner according to the rules of the game (some might say institutional (or other) entitlement) and the deserving winner rests upon bad luck. "Perhaps the [individual] who truly deserved to win [the reward] did not in fact win because [they] pulled up lame, or tore [their] shoe, or suffered some other unforeseeable stroke of bad luck."[99] Likewise, to make an even stronger claim, desert has no basis in option luck. Consider an individual who is mugged but "is not responsible for the attack"[100] or who becomes ill with food poisoning from a hamburger through no fault of their own.[101] In each case, these authors offer the suggestion that these "innocent victims" obviously deserve some amount of compensation.

Strikingly, there is no strong distinction between brute luck and option luck in these cases. Brute luck relates to entirely unavoidable outcomes, that is, entirely independent of any factor within the individual's control. Yet, most of us do not believe that this is true of injured muscles, torn shoes, sickness, collapsing floors, muggings, or food poisoning that these authors present, by fiat, as brute luck. Although these may be rare events, few consider them independent of autonomous effort, and thus they confuse us by presenting intuitively option luck scenarios as "brute luck" scenarios. Nonetheless, we do not tell these victims that they deserve bad option-luck outcomes by genuinely choosing to walk in the neighborhood or eat at the fast-food restaurant. Instead, we feel that their identical relative responsibility in comparison to others for some outcome *Y* demands

[98] The argument is for a "thick" concept of brute luck but could be scaled back to a "thin" concept. Hurley (2003).

[99] Feinberg (1999), 74; Also, "Now suppose A is sick on the day of the examination and consequently does not perform well,..." Lamont (1994). Also, "If I apprehend a wanted man by accident (e.g., the floor collapses and I fall on top of him) I do not deserve a reward, though I may be entitled to one." Miller (1999a), 136.

[100] Lojman and McLeod (1999), 63.

[101] Feldman (1995b), 68.

deserved compensation to counteract any bad luck that diminishes their rewards—regardless of whether it was the fault of another individual or simply the universe.[102]

As is plain, one important conclusion of this rejection of option luck is that the principle of desert is not susceptible to a second form of the "harshness" objection with respect to "negligent victims" as are, allegedly, most other (brute) luck-egalitarian arguments.[103] Take Fleurbaey's iconic Bert, "an uninsured motorcycle rider who likes to feel the wind in his hair, in spite of his knowledge of the risks:"[104] a 1 in 1000 chance of a crash. When Bert crashes due to this 1 in 1000 chance, suffering severe but treatable injuries, does he have a desert claim for medical assistance (assuming such to be a distributive good as covered by this chapter)? Many in the responsibility-sensitive literature say he does not without the help of some auxiliary distributive principle.[105] Yet, even if we assume that there were good "appraisal grounds" for attaching rewards to one's autonomous effort toward playing a lottery such as Bert played, Bert is only agent responsible for their autonomous effort toward playing this particular lottery, not the empirically realized outcome thereof.[106] To claim otherwise would be to promote exactly what this literature seeks to avoid—allowing some to be "worse off than others through no fault [or choice] of their own."[107] That is to say, if desert is to offer any reward at all in such a situation (and this necessarily implies an appraisal grounds argument), then all agents who exhibited identical autonomous effort toward the choice to play this identical lottery deserve an identical reward, whether they crashed or not, via exactly the same formula stated above that we always use to measure desert. "Luck—whether it be option luck or brute luck—is irrelevant for desert."[108]

While some may wish to see more development of the separation between desert and option luck,[109] for the moment I wish to note that

[102] Kleinig (1999).
[103] Anderson (1999), 295–302.
[104] Knight and Stemplowska (2011), 9.
[105] Fleurbaey (1995a), 40–41.
[106] For a different rejection of option luck outcomes as just, cf. Cohen (2011b).
[107] Temkin (1993), 13.
[108] Vallentyne (2003), 183.
[109] For example, what if two individuals choose different indeterministic lotteries with non-overlapping outcomes?

those who disagree with me on this point of ideal philosophy may still be persuaded that my real-world methods focus entirely on brute luck, making any such disagreements moot (see Chaps. 7–11).

3.7 In Sum, This Chapter Has Argued

- *One principle of entitlement among many, a principle of desert uses autonomous effort toward* Outcome Y *as its entitlement-basis, while offering a luck-egalitarian principle in defense of its version of vertical equity.*
- *Our moral assessments that flow from agent responsibility as well as our determination of desert treat the entirety of the natural lottery in identical fashion to all other circumstances of chance as the entirety of the natural lottery is absolutely beyond the individual's control.*

PART II

Just States of Affairs

CHAPTER 4

Equal Opportunity and *Just Deserts*: Better Late than Before

For indeed any city, however small, is in fact divided into two, one the city of the poor, the other of the rich; these are at war with one another…—Plato, The Republic, Book IV

Distributive justice is the normative field of inquiry concerned with identifying which distributional procedures or outcomes of morally relevant goods are just. Chapters 2 and 3 have suggested that a distribution according to a principle of luck-egalitarian desert would be the most just—that is, a distribution insensitive to luck but exclusively sensitive to autonomous effort as a retrospective measure of agent responsibility. As a few theoretical approaches already dominate the field of distributive justice[1] and discussions of the three problems of inequality, poverty, and economic mobility, I aim to respond to those who believe that "the idea of rewarding desert is impracticable"[2] and explain how the *Just Deserts* proposal of rewarding desert interacts with these other well-defended approaches?

To begin, a rough taxonomy of the major distributive justice principles currently in the literature might list: outcome egalitarianism, sufficiency,

[1] I assess desert not as the right nor the good, nor in satisfaction of principles of solidarity, for example, Roemer (2012), 112; or democratic relationships, for example, Anderson (1999), but as a principle of distributive justice.

[2] Rawls (1999 (1971)), 274.

J. T. Dwyer, *Chance, Merit, and Economic Inequality*,
https://doi.org/10.1007/978-3-030-21126-4_4

priority (Rawls' leximin), equality of opportunity, luck egalitarianism, efficiency (welfare), desert, self-ownership and libertarianism, and a number of feminist critiques.[3] One line of argument I aim to pursue is to theoretically and concretely demonstrate the broad appeal of the *Just Deserts* proposal of luck-egalitarian desert through simultaneous, sometimes maximal, satisfaction of these disparate principles of distributive justice, such that adherents of each will have little or no reason to prefer another proposal, with the exception of proponents of (a) outcome egalitarianism.[4]

To advance the argument with a more coherent structure, allow me to defer discussion of some distributive justice principles to subsequent chapters. In Chap. 12, I will demonstrate how the *Just Deserts* proposal satisfies the more consequentialist[5] principles of outcome egalitarianism, sufficiency, priority, and economic mobility, while Chap. 13 will address feminist critiques of distributive justice. In Chaps. 4–6, however, I argue that the *Just Deserts* proposal is much closer than many might currently believe to distributive justice, all things considered, by demonstrating how *Just Deserts* satisfies the underlying needs of three remaining principles: equality of opportunity, efficiency, and liberty. In covering these three principles, I hope not only to better illustrate the principle of desert and its capacity to satisfy other dominant principles of distributive justice, but to additionally lay the foundation for the argument that the *Just Deserts* proposal may well satisfy one of the most sophisticated poly-principled accounts of distributive justice available. Namely, I set the foundation for an argument, beyond the scope of this book, that contractualists in the Rawlsian original position would in fact choose to implement the *Just Deserts* proposal. This is so given that the three elements of the two principles of "justice as fairness" speak directly to (1) liberty, (2) equality of opportunity, and (3) efficiency.[6] I further buttress this argument in Chap. 5

[3] Lamont and Favor (2014).

[4] For sophisticated discussions of non-instrumental equality as a first-order principle of distributive justice, cf. Nagel (2000); Temkin (2000).

[5] Clearly, feminist critiques of the dominant principles of distributive justice are too theoretically varied to be crudely categorized in this way as consequentialist and further they often reject the central focus on distribution as opposed to recognition, representation, or liberation from oppression. Nonetheless, I take it to be the case that a central element of most such critiques is that other distributive justice principles do not realize just distributive consequences with respect to women.

[6] Rawls (1999 (1971)), 52–53, 266.

by showing that, under certain conditions, *Just Deserts* maximally improves the lives of the worst-off individuals—where "worst off" is defined not as those with the worst outcomes but as those with the worst luck.[7]

4.1 Equal Opportunity and Just Deserts: Leveling the Playing Field

At first, equality of opportunity seems to require a process of "leveling the playing field."[8] I argue in this chapter that the *Just Deserts* proposal, by using an agnostic and *ex post* procedure, will more simply, accurately, and coherently equalize opportunity.[9] The stakes of this claim are important, for if it is true that understanding and intervening upon the "root causes" of inequality of opportunity in order to properly level the playing field before the game represent both an unnecessarily inefficient and inaccurate means to realize equality of opportunity, then the *Just Deserts* proposal can make a strong case to become a powerful complementary policy alongside a number of current equal opportunity programs in the United States.

To begin, some scholars have suggested that most discussions of equal opportunity make two assumptions. First, that jobs (and other rewards such as job-related income) ought to be distributed in accord with actual performance, that is, observed outcomes of interest. Second, that all children ought to have the "same opportunity" to develop the prerequisites pertaining to the full distribution of jobs (and possibly other rewards).[10] Thus, equal opportunity seems to rest upon a *laissez-faire outcome principle* that values performance-based differentiation and a *development principle* that values equality. As noted above, some have claimed that this development principle requires a "level playing field."[11] But what precisely

[7] With respect to the specified reward where "worst off" is defined by circumstances of chance with respect to the observed outcome of interest.

[8] Mason (2006).

[9] While equality of opportunity and desert may seem at first an unlikely match, note that Olsaretti proposes that desert have a "fair opportunity requirement." Olsaretti (2003a), 202; Olsaretti (2004), 24.

[10] Harding et al. (2005), 134; Fishkin names these the "fair contest" and "fair life chances" principles. Fishkin (2014), 25–40.

[11] By this phrase I demarcate that I am not speaking about what Rawls names "formal equality of opportunity" and Atkinson names "competitive equality of opportunity," which simply allow all players access to the "biased" playing field. Rawls (1999 (1971)), 62; Atkinson (2015), 10–11.

does it mean to have a level playing field, or more to the point, what is a theoretically sound and measurable definition of ***equality of opportunity***?

> Imagine an honest jinni appears to twelve individuals desperately stranded in the desert and says, "You will all die of dehydration today without my help. My help is this: You each are capable of genuine, autonomous choice. Ten of you shall each have ten wishes with which to exercise this choice. With each wish you may either drink exactly one liter of water or travel exactly one kilometer in any compass direction. To the oldest among you, I give only four wishes, each worth exactly two liters of water or two kilometers of travel. To the youngest among you, I also give ten wishes but, unfortunately, you shall die if you have not reached safety by your eighth wish. For each hour in which an individual registers no choice, that individual automatically drinks water. I guarantee that no individual shall die until some time after that individual's wishes have been exhausted (except the youngest among you). After today, I will never again reveal myself to you." Which, if any, of the stranded individuals had equal opportunity?

To understand equal opportunity, it would be useful to first define opportunity. Opportunity for *Outcome Y* is the distribution of *Outcome Y* conditional upon circumstances of chance where *Outcome Y* jointly depends upon circumstances of chance and autonomous effort and the distribution's variance is positive.[12] In other words, given circumstances of chance are known to exhibit a certain value, one may, and may not, realize certain values of *Outcome Y*—one's opportunity is the plural set of values of *Outcome Y* that one may realize solely by exhibiting autonomous effort. Let us unpack this.

First, note that opportunity, and thus equal opportunity, must be defined for a specific *Outcome Y* (e.g., liters of water from the jinni or surviving the next ten hours)—there is no such thing as equal opportunity (or a level playing field), ***simpliciter***. Second, the shape of the distribution of opportunity is exclusively determined by circumstances of chance—some observed outcomes of interest are, and are not, available to be realized by the individual. For example, due to circumstances of chance, no one reading this has been given the ***opportunity*** to storm the Bastille in the French Revolution. Neither has our youngest individual stranded in the

[12] More formally, we could write, Opportunity for *Outcome Y* is $P(Y = y|CC = CC_i)$ where $y = f(CC_i, \alpha\epsilon_i)$, $Var(P(Y = y|CC = CC_i)) > 0$.

desert been given the opportunity to consume ten liters of the jinni's water, nor has the oldest been given the opportunity to consume exactly an odd number of liters. Third, two individuals exhibit equality of opportunity if and only if both individuals have access to one, identical distribution of *Outcome Y* determined by circumstances of chance—that is, their circumstances of chance exhibit an identical value with respect to *Outcome Y*. While ten of the individuals exhibit equal opportunity for consumption of the jinni's water, this equality is not shared with the youngest member even though they too have ten wishes on the same terms for they will not survive to make a ninth or tenth wish—they cannot consume nine liters. Fourth, we may define ***robust equality of opportunity*** as the case in which all individuals in the population have access to one, identical distribution of *Outcome Y*—that is, each individual in the population exhibits circumstances of chance that exhibit an identical value with respect to *Outcome Y*. Such robust equality of opportunity does not exist in our jinni story. Lastly, as the observed outcome of interest (*Outcome Y*) jointly depends upon only two things in the universe, circumstances of chance and autonomous effort, and we have conditioned upon circumstances of chance (filtered cases to focus upon the subset of cases in which circumstances of chance take the value in which we are interested), *Outcome Y* is exclusively sensitive to autonomous effort.[13] That is to say, any outcome within the plural shared opportunity set is unreservedly and absolutely available to be empirically realized by each individual and any *differences* between any two individuals are exclusively dependent upon different autonomous effort.[14]

As this last statement may not be immediately intuitive, or even resisted, allow me to explain. When the mad scientist pressed Irene and Sherlock into a lottery, did they have equal opportunity for the lottery winnings? No, lotteries offer individuals equal *probability*, not equal opportunity.

[13] Circumstances of chance and autonomous effort jointly produce observed outcomes of interest and, if represented as a directed acyclic graph, these three elements form a simple collider. Pearl (2016), sec. 2.3.

[14] By this I want to set aside Cohen's distinction between opportunity and access (as opportunity implies access) and Segall's distinction between opportunity and outcome (as opportunity implies outcome) pace Segall (2013), 8, 35, once we recognize that opportunity for *Outcome Y* is, nothing more and nothing less than, the empirical distribution of *Outcome Y* conditional upon circumstances of chance where *Outcome Y* jointly depends upon circumstances of chance and autonomous effort and the distribution's variance is positive. Stated differently, a lottery is not an opportunity. Pace Segall (2013), 99, 138, 182–183.

The outcomes of the former are exclusively ***dependent*** upon circumstances of chance (e.g., the flipping of a coin) while the outcomes of the latter are exclusively ***sensitive*** to autonomous effort—while circumstances of chance may have determined that there are only 11 possible outcomes of water consumption for our stranded group, which of those outcomes becomes the observed outcome of interest for a particular individual is purely a result of autonomous effort. This distinction between probability and opportunity is not merely one of convenience—we level the playing field before we *play a game* (not play a lottery), we seek *performance-based* differentiation (not chancy differentiation). Equal opportunity holds agency over choices, and thus agent responsibility for those choices, at its core. Equal opportunity now reveals itself to be, not the product of two disparate principles (equitable development and performance-based outcomes), but the same drive as *Just Deserts* to practice horizontal and vertical equity of rewards upon the proper fundamental entitlement-basis, responsibility. The one difference is that equality of opportunity concerns the outcome itself, liters of water or winning the job candidacy, while *Just Deserts* is exclusively concerned with *rewards* as highlighted in Chap. 3.

- *Distributive justice based on a principle of equal opportunity realizes a state of affairs such that, for all individuals in the population, there is one distribution of the outcome,* Outcome Y, *and the individual's allocation of the outcome within that distribution is exclusively sensitive to autonomous effort alone.*

4.2 Forewords, Afterwords, and the Words Between

Shifting temporarily to considerations of public policy from the perspective of non-ideal philosophy, many scholars and policymakers find a distributive justice principle of equality of opportunity attractive because, as we saw above, it seeks to rectify the injustices of circumstances of chance by offering a level playing field for some *Outcome Y*. This allows each individual to, as it were, "choose" their empirically realized outcome in the same manner as every other individual. The weakness of "equal opportunity" policy implementation that seeks a level playing field, however, is that it has tried to realize robust equality of opportunity using the more difficult of two plausible approaches. I hope to show in this section why adherents of equal opportunity would be at least as well, if not better, served by the *Just Deserts* proposal.

Many of the current equal opportunity public policies within the United States (including Job Corps, Upward Bound, Head Start, and others) are in fact anti-poverty policies that grew out of the War on Poverty from the mid-1960s and operate according to the following logic: increasing human capital for the bottom of the labor market will increase mean earnings (decrease poverty), reduce the dispersion of earnings (decrease inequality), and reduce the intergenerational inheritance of advantages such as earnings (increase economic mobility).[15] Fully consistent with our control principle, many individuals support these policies as a means to the fulfillment of the American Dream, understood to mean that we live in a "highly mobile society where individuals succeed or fail irrespective of their initial circumstances at birth."[16] On the face of it, such longstanding equal opportunity policies, as well as more recent proposals,[17] may appear similar to the *Just Deserts* proposal. There is a significant difference, however.

Equal opportunity (as opposed to equality of opportunity as discussed above) states that, "Our main strategy—be we right or left—for fighting income inequality under capitalism should be to assure a *fair initial distribution* of physical and human capital themselves."[18] Once we have initially "leveled the playing field," according to this line of thinking, we have established equal opportunity and the game can begin, let the chips fall where they may. This strategy is known as an *ex ante* intervention—public policy observes an unfair "before," intervenes on this "before" in the name of equal opportunity, and then allows individuals in the fair "after" to exercise their freedom in any way they wish.[19] Distributive justice is then measured in the eyes of the equal opportunity theorist by observing *ex ante* leveling procedures rather than outcomes. Not only is this standard theory for equal opportunity public policies, but much of the luck-egalitarian literature also takes this "starting gate" perspective through

[15] Harding et al. (2005), 133.
[16] Mazumder (2005), 81.
[17] Alstott and Ackerman (1999); Darrick and Darity (2010).
[18] Freeman (1997).
[19] Roemer (1998).

the use of auctions,[20] veils of ignorance,[21] and other interventions[22] upon the population such as inheritance taxes, educational investments, and affirmative action.

Despite significant efforts, the equal opportunity strategy so conceived has unfortunately accomplished only moderate success due to the difficulties that accompany any attempt to "initially level the playing field" or create a "fair initial distribution of opportunity," difficulties that the *Just Deserts* proposal easily overcomes. Nonetheless, progressives, philanthropists, politicians, researchers, and others most often pursue *ex ante* interventions, utilizing what I would call a socio-medical framework in order to realize equality of opportunity. By socio-medical I highlight two things: (1) exactly as a doctor treats sick patients and not healthy patients, the equal opportunity tendency is to focus on the poor and a pathology of poverty as the social disease rather than inequality of opportunity itself, (2) exactly as a doctor pursues a differential diagnosis in order to address the "root causes" of disease, the tendency is to address a lack of skills or public education spending as "root causes" rather than address the merely "apparent symptoms"—inequality of opportunity for the observed outcome of interest.

What is wrong with this approach? As it turns out, we do not need to address "root causes" of observed outcomes when the fundamental concern is rewards. If we shift the problem from inequality of opportunity for an observed outcome of interest to inequality of opportunity for a reward, we can solve this problem (level the playing field if you wish) *after* we have observed outcomes rather than before. That is, rather than address "root causes," we undertake the simpler task of changing the relationship between outcomes and rewards. Ultimately, for *Just Deserts* and I think equality of opportunity too, the entitlement-basis must be autonomous effort and the entitlement must be reward, but how observed outcomes of interest fit into that relationship is of little concern. They are only our primary concern if we rigidly force outcomes themselves to be rewards. The *Just Deserts* proposal's direct focus on *ex post* rewards, rather than outcomes, makes it a great complementary public policy toward the realization of equality of opportunity for at least five reasons that I will only

[20] Dworkin (1981a,b).
[21] Rawls (1999 (1971)).
[22] Vallentyne (2002).

briefly explore: ***saturation***, ***autocorrelation***, ***preservation***, ***foundation***, and, perhaps most importantly, ***computation***.

One explanation for the limitations of current equal opportunity policies (and when I say "equal opportunity" I always mean *ex ante* intervention) is saturation. Two common foci for equal opportunity policies such as the federal Job Corps program in the United States are—borrowing from ***human capital models*** of "root causes"—skills and education. Human capital models suggest that equalizing education and skills will lead to equalized productivity and, therefore, equality of opportunity for income or employment in the labor market. Thus, public sector sponsored employment and training programs (active labor market (ALM) policies) such as job training and job subsidies try to connect various segments of the unemployed, underemployed, and otherwise economically marginalized populations to better skills and better employment.[23] If the labor market segment applicable to these marginalized workers is in fact already saturated (able to meet aggregate demand), however, any attempts to squeeze more laborers with similar skills into formal market work may have unintended negative consequences that deviate from equality of opportunity such as fiscal substitution of one worker for another, inflation disturbances,[24] and rejection by employers who may prefer fewer high-wage workers to more low-wage workers.[25]

A second explanation for the limitations of equal opportunity policies to help individuals realize the American Dream is autocorrelation—by which I mean, that which we observe today is most similar to that which we observed yesterday. Employers and employees do not bargain each morning over a new daily contract. Instead, contracts are for projects, months, even years so that the labor market is more akin to highly viscous fluid dynamics rather than an ideal frictionless sorting mechanism. Likewise, potential employees subject to an ALM intervention today are most likely to carry all the same latent variables of the human capital models, sometimes referred to as "soft skills," that employers used yesterday to make hiring decisions. Thus, some ALM programs[26] emphasize soft skills for equal opportunity policies, borrowing from ***behavioral models***

[23] Heckman et al. (1999).

[24] Assuming there is a true non-accelerating inflation rate of unemployment.

[25] Schor and Leete-Guy (1994); Schor (1991).

[26] For example, Quantum Opportunity Program and National Guard ChalleNGe Program.

of "root causes." Behavioral models suggest that equalizing personality traits, cultural roles, and scripts—essentially the skills of acquiring and maintaining a job rather than the productive skills themselves of the human capital model—will lead to equalized hireability and, therefore, equality of opportunity for income or employment in the labor market. Given the strength of autocorrelation, however, these policies find it difficult to teach an old dog new tricks against the grain of childhood role formation,[27] cultural scripts,[28] neighborhood effects,[29] and genetically inherited behavioral phenotypes,[30] not to mention the largely non-transferable physical phenotypes used by employers such as skin color, masculinity, and beauty.

A third explanation for the limitations of equal opportunity policies to "initially level the playing field," that may be seen with respect to equal opportunity policies such as the Upward Bound or Talent Search programs (both under the federal TRIO program in the United States, focusing on increasing disadvantaged children's college matriculation and graduation), is that of preservation. As the intervention seeks to raise the outcomes of the disadvantaged, this spurs action by the advantaged to maintain rank and thus their rewards (rather than lose their reward to the target of an equal opportunity intervention).[31] Unfortunately, both economically productive as well as unproductive rent-seeking behavior ("directly unproductive activities") may satisfice to maintain rank.[32] Such countermoves are possible because equal opportunity policies typically fail to utilize *comprehensive interventions* that take account of all individuals, instead choosing to isolate the disadvantaged alone as the treatment population.[33] Equal opportunity interventions upon a portion of the

[27] Duncan et al. (2005).

[28] Kohn and Schooler (1983, 1982).

[29] Sharkey (2009).

[30] Groves (2005).

[31] If this type of countermove with respect to job security behaves similarly to minimum wage ripple effects—in which changes to the wages at the bottom of the wage distribution lead to changes in the wages of those above them—we would see labor market participants taking responsive counteraction to maintain their job rank up to 20 percentile points higher on the wage distribution. Wicks-Lim (2008).

[32] One may consider the self-segregation of wealthy white flight an example of the latter. Sjoquist (2000).

[33] Cf. the recommendations here, Bourguignon et al. (2007).

population are improper equal opportunity interventions as unpredicted, and unpredictable, counteractions of competitors explicitly serve to maintain rank and reward.

A fourth explanation for the limitations of equal opportunity policies is foundation—that they rely upon a moral principle that is in fact incompatible with the goal of equality of opportunity. As Richard Freeman has suggested, perhaps the weakness of the above policies is that intervention upon adults and adolescents is not sufficiently *ex ante* to realize equality of opportunity for income or employment in the labor market, therefore society ought to intervene upon the young.[34] Thus, an early intervention program such as the federal Head Start program appears far more true to equal opportunity in that, rather than trying to raise individuals *above a line*, the idea is to give disadvantaged children enough of a "head start" such that their future outcomes are *in line with the rest of the population*. Yet, Head Start policies improperly attempt to use the principles of priority, sufficiency, charity, or compassion to realize a principle of equal opportunity.[35] These alternative principles of distributive justice are rooted in the responsibility to make the minimum necessary aid, however, and only distantly related to equality of opportunity.[36] Thus, although it seems true that early interventions are more effective and efficient than later interventions, decades of social programs targeting the poorest children (and by extension their parents, especially mothers) have been unable to substantially generate an equal opportunity society.

Finally, and conclusively, equal opportunity policies exhibit a challenge of computation—they involve unnecessary mathematical and statistical steps and estimations, attenuating the possibility of accurately realizing the goal.

[34] Freeman and Reich (1999).

[35] In fact, the 1999 federal evaluation of the Head Start program did not even use a control group (remedied in 2010 with a control group of Head Start-eligible disadvantaged children, but again without an understanding of the distribution of the full population or the long-term effects of the intervention). Zill et al. (1999); Puma et al. (2010).

[36] Anderson says the same about "compassion," with which I agree, but mistakenly argues that luck-egalitarianism expresses an attitude of "pity" which must be wrong as pity, too, fails to demand equal opportunity. Anderson (1999), 307.

> Imagine that we had ascertained that males age 15 in 1975 had higher weekly wages at age 30 in 1990 if they were training to enter the Transportation sector as opposed to Finance.[37] If one sought to realize equal opportunity for weekly wages at age 30 among young males age 15 in 1990, one might nudge some disadvantaged youth toward the Transportation sector only to find out that the 3% wage advantage in 1990 became a −43% wage disadvantage in 2005 (further exacerbated in our counterfactual story by nudging more individuals into the Transportation sector's labor supply). Here, each youth received equal *expected probability*,[38] two degrees removed from equality of opportunity. This is because we failed to appropriately intervene upon the true causal mechanism leading to weekly wages at age 30 which may in fact require continuous interventions from age 15 to 30.

On the one hand, even from the perspective of ideal philosophy in which we are omniscient over all circumstances of chance and autonomous effort, if there are any coin tosses of pure luck between the time of the *ex ante* intervention and the observed outcome of interest, then *ex ante* interventions may only ever realize equal probability, not equal opportunity. While on the other hand, from the perspective of non-ideal philosophy in which we are ignorant of some circumstances of chance and autonomous effort, the *ex ante* intervention must use incomplete knowledge of the past to predict and intervene upon the future. Note that it is not complete *ex post* knowledge in the future that simplifies things, it is that equivalently incomplete knowledge *ex post* is better than *ex ante*.

To be clear, however, I do not suggest that we eliminate *ex ante* equal opportunity programs in favor of *Just Deserts*, simply that they have some limitations for which *Just Deserts* offers an appropriate complementary strategy. At their best, such programs may increase labor force participation, attachment, resilience, and even economic growth.[39] Further, James Heckman is certainly correct when stating that "the investments we make today in disadvantaged young children promote social mobility [and]

[37] BEA—Bureau of Economic Analysis (2015).

[38] Stemming from Dworkin, some scholars seek an "envy-free" *ex ante* solution. As may be seen immediately, if the social planner with all the information cannot accurately measure *ex ante* opportunity in a dynamic economy, it hardly seems fair to trust the individuals' feelings as a better guide when they presumably lack even more information and, by definition, exhibit various information asymmetries dependent upon circumstances of chance. Dworkin (1981a,b).

[39] Bredgaard and Daemmrich (2012).

create opportunity."[40] Yet neither of these strategies holds much promise for realizing robust equality of opportunity in the absence of a *Just Deserts* policy.

4.3 Hindsight Is 20/20

The *Just Deserts* strategy for realizing robust equality of opportunity is thus to utilize one precise *ex post* intervention rather than a number of modestly effective *ex ante* interventions. Whereas *ex ante* interventions occur before measurement of the observed outcome of interest, *ex post* interventions occur afterwards. This is not a revolutionary idea and it serves as the basis of anti-poverty programs such as the Earned Income Tax Credit, which currently receives bipartisan support in Congress and elsewhere for increasing the marginal returns to formal market labor for workers with very low income and children. Importantly, *Just Deserts* avoids the five problems of equal opportunity programs mentioned above via an *ex post* intervention as I will briefly discuss below.

First, the *Just Deserts* proposal avoids the problem of saturation by refusing to subject the most economically disadvantaged members of society to further pressure and competition by eschewing policies that create greater competition for low-wage jobs. Our only mandate is to reward individuals based upon autonomous effort and let the economy change as it will. Extra pressure on the most marginalized members of the labor force through saturation is neither the means to the American Dream nor to the most efficient economy.

Second, the *Just Deserts* proposal avoids the problem of autocorrelation by breaking the correlation between soft skills and economic distribution. Policy interventions to change or regulate[41] low-advantage individuals' culture, habits, dress, speech, and other behavioral codes of conduct are no longer desirable as equal opportunity tools. As we shall simply reward individuals based upon autonomous effort, this allows all individuals to behave as they will, including all the parental partiality that high-advantage parents may desire. To be explicit, *Just Deserts* tells parents that, without regret and without reference to other principles of justice, they may justly

[40] Heckman (2014).
[41] Abramovitz (1996).

"read bedtime stories to their children."[42] The *Just Deserts* proposal is thus in favor of a wide diversity of cultural forms and parental styles and investments,[43] celebrating the United States' unique melting pot status and the value of liberty.

Third, the *Just Deserts* proposal avoids the problem of preservation by adjusting economic distribution after the fact. Rather than targeted *ex ante* interventions to combat sclerotic labor market rank ordering of workers, only to watch all other actors respond with productive and rent-seeking countermoves to maintain rank order and reward, *Just Deserts* utilizes comprehensive, unavoidable, yet entirely just, *ex post* interventions that map individual rewards to individual autonomous effort and agent responsibility for the observed outcome of interest.[44]

Fourth, the *Just Deserts* proposal avoids the problem of foundation by explicitly, clearly, coherently, and exclusively utilizing the principle of desert (allowing, of course, for combination with other principles of distributive justice at a later stage). By completely eliminating priority, sufficiency, charity, or compassion from its framework and reserving those principles for secondary public policies only, the public will support the moral goodness and justice of a principle of distribution that actually realizes robust equality of opportunity, that is, a state of affairs in which relative success and failure no longer depend upon circumstances of chance but, importantly, are strictly sensitive to hard work.

Fifth, the *Just Deserts* proposal avoids the problem of computation by freeing us from the *ex ante* requirement that we identify and understand the causal mechanisms underlying the observed outcome of interest in order to intervene upon the correct policy levers. That is to say, the *Just Deserts* proposal may remain ignorant of how specific elements of circumstances of chance actually cause inequality of opportunity yet always be as accurate,

[42] Segall (2013); Mason (2006).

[43] Following a principle of equal opportunity, one might ban private education and childcare, radically desegregate schools, and pay teachers to focus on equalizing children in mandatory universal childcare from ages 0–18. *Just Deserts*, on the other hand, simply rewards adults according to merit and lets them invest in their children as they wish. I believe the second option will be eminently more palatable to a far greater number of contemporary Americans than the first.

[44] This allows us to ignore the difficult ethical debates about legitimate and illegitimate public restrictions on the intergenerationally preservative behaviors of high-advantage parents, for example, Swift (2005).

and almost certainly more accurate, than an *ex ante* intervention, thus constituting a more effective method in terms of logic, measurement, and efficiency.[45] In engineering parlance, *feedback* beats *feedforward* every time.[46]

To conclude, the chief limitation inherent in *ex ante* equal opportunity interventions is that they unnecessarily treat observed outcomes themselves as rewards. As I hope is clear, however, our fundamental moral intuition does not concern itself with outcomes and thus does not require that "no one exhibits a *lesser outcome* through no fault [or choice] of their own" but instead that no one is ever "worse off [vis a vis reward] than others through no fault [or choice] of their own."[47] The problem with seeking equality of opportunity for observed outcomes is that by the time you have estimated "opportunity," it is too late to intervene upon the circumstances of chance that generated the unequal opportunities in the first place. All is not lost, however. Autonomous effort is a moral behavior we wish to reward, and thus once you have measured its value, it is never too late to reward it with its *Just Deserts*. We can see more clearly now that *Just Deserts* are *ex post* rewards that, in the nomenclature of robust equality of opportunity, offer all individuals access to one, identical distribution of reward within which individual allocations depend solely upon the vector of responsibility characteristics, that is, autonomous effort.[48]

- *Distributive justice based on a principle of desert uses an* ex post *intervention that eschews costly interference and monitoring of the low and high extremes of the economy, the labor market, and parental partiality; is comprehensive and unavoidable; relies not at all on charity; and is mathematically simpler and thus more accurate, less contentious, and flexible enough to instantaneously adjust to a dynamic economy.*

[45] Having said this, I would still expect *ex ante* policies to outperform our current distribution policy in terms of inequality, poverty, and economic mobility, pace Anderson (1999), 300.

[46] "For example, any attempt to steer a ship to its final destination by setting the course at the point of departure and hoping that it will hit its mark using only that information—what engineers call *feedforward*—will fail." Molander (2016), 82.

[47] Temkin (1993), 13.

[48] Given that there is only one mathematical distribution of autonomous effort for all moral agents in the universe, as long as there are no probabilistic lotteries between the time of an *ex ante* intervention and an *ex post* intervention, identically informed *ex ante* equal opportunity and *ex post* desert realize identical outcomes. Ramos and Van de Gaer (2012).

4.4 In Sum, This Chapter Has Argued

- *Distributive justice based on a principle of equal opportunity realizes a state of affairs such that, for all individuals in the population, there is one distribution of the outcome,* Outcome Y, *and the individual's allocation of the outcome within that distribution is exclusively sensitive to autonomous effort alone.*
- *Distributive justice based on a principle of desert uses an* ex post *intervention that eschews costly interference and monitoring of the low and high extremes of the economy, the labor market, and parental partiality; is comprehensive and unavoidable; relies not at all on charity; and is mathematically simpler and thus more accurate, less contentious, and flexible enough to instantaneously adjust to a dynamic economy.*

CHAPTER 5

Efficiency and *Just Deserts*: Economists' Big Trade-Off

Now that I have described the ways in which the *Just Deserts* proposal more fully realizes the core underlying need of the principle of equality of opportunity than *ex ante* equal opportunity itself, I would like to discuss how it may satisfy proponents of another principle of distributive justice, efficiency.[1]

At first, *efficiency* seems to require a *laissez-faire* market economy. I am going to argue in this chapter that the *Just Deserts* proposal, by imposing a carefully designed endowment tax, may realize a perfectly efficient economy under a broad class of conditions and, under real-world constraints, may surpass our current economy in terms of efficiency and welfare. The stakes of this claim are important, for if it is true that one of the most powerful arguments against redistribution rests upon a false dilemma between efficiency and redistribution, then the *Just Deserts* proposal can make a strong case to become a first among equals policy, able to realize both efficiency and equity in the United States.

5.1 Efficiency and Just Deserts

To begin, a distributive justice principle of efficiency is attractive to many because it seeks the maximum aggregate welfare of a population

[1] Of course, some have argued that "the principle of efficiency and the principles of justice are completely distinct and mutually irreducible." Sadurski (1985), 111, 267–275.

J. T. Dwyer, *Chance, Merit, and Economic Inequality*,
https://doi.org/10.1007/978-3-030-21126-4_5

of individuals.[2] Modern economists tend to see the ideal as a Pareto-optimal distribution of resources which has the property that no individual may be made better off without making another worse off. It is often assumed by non-economists that this technically efficient outcome may only be realized through an ideal *laissez-faire* market economy. Distributive justice is then measured in the eyes of the efficiency theorist by observing market procedures rather than outcomes. Can *Just Deserts* redistribute while satisfying a Pareto-optimal criterion? I hope to show in this section why adherents of efficiency would be at least as well, if not better, served by the *Just Deserts* proposal.

Anti-inequality, anti-poverty, and pro-economic mobility policies often ask us to pay the economic costs of so-called egalitarian redistribution in order to implement such policies. Atkinson recently outlined 15 "fresh proposals" to tackle inequality, yet, the terms of the debate continue to be "revenue from proposed taxes and the costs of social transfers" as we face an inescapable dilemma between the twin economic principles of efficiency and equity.[3] Arneson even states with great skepticism, immediately after consideration of efficiency:

> So it seems that either the theory of justice, if it requires that individuals should get what they deserve, must be utterly in conflict with the market, or the theory of justice, if it is to be in principle tolerant of the market economy, must not include as a fundamental requirement that each person should get what she deserves.[4]

Is it then the case that the efficiency of a market economy requires that the most desirable rewards (e.g., income) be offered to the most desirable inputs of land, capital, and labor (e.g., fields, plows, and farmers)? If true, then it would seem we are confronted by economics' "big trade-off" between efficiency and equity[5] and that those who exhibit a perfect efficiency preference[6] may be less satisfied by a *Just Deserts* proposal than a *laissez-faire* economic system of rewards.

[2] Rawls (1999 (1971)), 58–62.

[3] Atkinson (2015).

[4] Arneson (2007), 266.

[5] Okun (1975).

[6] Although economists are accustomed to thinking of the "big trade-off" between efficiency and equity, there are of course other social welfare functions. My belief is that very,

5.2 Economic Rents and Efficiency

There are a number of challenges to the above conclusion that ought to be kept in mind. First, even if *Just Deserts* does distort the economy, it is an empirical question whether that distortion results in net welfare gains—we might distort the economy by taking $100 of every $1,000,000 earned by Scrooge (who derives very little welfare therefrom) and giving that to Tiny Tim (who derives great welfare therefrom). Second, *Just Deserts* should not distort the economy as a strict principle of desert conforms to economists' first-best lump-sum endowment tax under a broad class of conditions. Third, under all other conditions, one may still choose a *second-best principle of desert* and, again, apply lump-sum endowment taxes to satisfy a perfect efficiency preference. Fourth, recent research has argued that both inequality as well as inequality of opportunity, two things *Just Deserts* significantly reduces, are generating economic drag on our current economy.[7] Fifth, as I shall cover in more detail in Chap. 10, a proposal such as *Just Deserts* can lower the cost of any distortionary tax regime (such as our own current fiscal system) even if the proposal is imperfect.[8] Perhaps economists no longer need to worry about the "big trade-off" and, for once, individuals can actually have it all.

Consider the following illustrative example. An entrepreneur has a field, some plows, and what we will stipulate is a perfect labor market. At the market-clearing wage, w_{10}, the curious result is that ten farmers each supply one unit of labor for a total of ten units. Although they each receive an identical market-clearing wage for an identical observed outcome of interest, $farmer_1$ realizes the greatest net welfare from the exchange, then $farmer_2$, and so on. How might this be possible?

In standard, neoclassical economic analysis of prices, the intersection of aggregate supply and demand curves is the singular price at which the market clears. This is true of all goods meeting the necessary assumptions, including labor of a given quality and intensity, that is, an observed outcome of interest. Note, however, that the canonical slope of the curve representing the supply of labor is not zero. As for all other goods with elastic supply, the higher the price offered on the market, the greater the

very few individuals have a desert neutral social welfare function but I hope to convince them below as well.

[7] Marrero and Rodríguez (2013).

[8] Logue and Slemrod (2008), 849; Also, cf. Stern (1982).

supply that is provided. If the entrepreneur raises wages, more farmers want to supply labor. The key point to notice is that supply (and demand) are made up of incremental units and, thus, some labor units are supplied before others. In our example, $farmer_1$ is first to supply one unit of labor, then $farmer_2$, and so on.

We then must ask, why is the supply of labor elastic (positively sloped) for any observed outcome of interest—that is, production of 100 widgets—that is, why does $farmer_1$ supply labor before $farmer_2$ and so on? Economists typically point to the heterogeneity of *tastes* and *talents* among individuals.[9] Some individuals prefer to work for non-profit institutions, others prefer prestige and a title or flexible working hours, and still others simply have greater talent for the job. Economists since Adam Smith have postulated that each individual compares the "whole of the advantages and disadvantages of the different employments" to find the occupation with the highest net advantages and, thus, to which they may apply the least autonomous effort for the given wage.[10] For example, $farmer_1$ may love plowing in the hot sun while $farmer_{10}$ may prefer colder climates. Thus, $farmer_1$ would have taken this employment opportunity for a lesser wage than w_{10}. Similarly, $farmer_2$ may find plowing in accord with the market-clearing outcome easy or intuitive while $farmer_{10}$, lacking a talent for plowing, may struggle mightily to reach an identical observed outcome. Thus, $farmer_2$ would also have taken this employment opportunity for a lesser wage than w_{10}. From our luck-egalitarian desert perspective, circumstances of chance have benefited $farmer_1$ and $farmer_2$ to a measurably greater extent than $farmer_{10}$ and allow them to earn an identical wage for an identical observed outcome in return for dissimilar quantities of autonomous effort.

This crucial dissimilarity is one important element that sets labor apart from land and capital[11] as an exchange of labor always includes the latent

[9] For an attempt to philosophically carve out space for payment based upon differential compensation, cf. Dick (1975). Note, however, that the mistaken view of tastes and talents as qualitatively different (rather than seeing both as circumstances of chance upon which labor supply is dependent) lead to a partial theory of desert.

[10] Smith (1976 (1776)), 111.

[11] On labor market as distinct from other markets, cf. Diamond (1982); Solow (1990).

variable known only to the moral agent, autonomous effort.[12] As Atkinson has put it, "the employer cannot, realistically, fully monitor the work effort of individual members of the labour force."[13] Of course, we should further add the converse truth that the employer cannot realistically measure every element within each individuals' vector of circumstances of chance. Thus, in our illustrative example, although all ten farmers are paid the market-clearing wage, w_{10}, for one unit of outcome each, farmers one through nine have all received economic rent, more technically, inframarginal rent.[14]

An economic rent is ***a payment over and above the amount necessary to bring a factor input into production.*** To state this more prosaically, economic rent is a free lunch for the recipient of that payment. In our example, $farmer_1$ receives the most rent, $farmer_2$ the second highest amount of rent, and so forth until $farmer_{10}$ receives absolutely zero economic rent—the market-clearing price is exactly the price needed to bring this marginal unit of labor into production.

While most economists would say that all laborers in the real world receive economic rent (by supplying more than one unit of labor), which types of laborers receive the most economic rent, that is, the largest free lunch? As aggregate demand is further shifted outward or as aggregate supply is more inelastic (steeper slope), those who would theoretically supply the first units of labor receive greater economic rent. This suggests that, in terms of ***unmerited*** inequality, the individuals who receive the greatest quantity of inframarginal economic rent (free lunch) are those individuals who exhibit the least autonomous effort to achieve the first market-clearing outcome, especially those individuals to whom circumstances of chance have given great taste or great talent for high-skill, high-training, or high-demand occupations.

An important result of the preceding discussion is that we have begun to undermine the instrumental performance-based rewards argument that rewards such as income should be distributed according to outcomes. Paying laborers for outcomes rather than autonomous effort is to pay individuals unequal economic rents which are, by definition, ***unnecessary***

[12] Thus, some scholars argue that education serves as a screening mechanism for employers' ignorance through the job competition, paper chase, and sheepskin models. Cf. Thurow (1975).

[13] Atkinson (2015), 251.

[14] Kaufman and Hotchkiss (2000), 410–414.

payments for observed outcomes. Thus, to the extent that unequal infra-marginal rents may be traced to circumstances of chance, the *Just Deserts* proposal will reduce the variance of such rents among all individuals in the population.

- *Distributive justice based on a principle of desert implements greater equality of economic rents or, more prosaically, free lunches.*

Economists will be quick to point out that the current story pertains to a rather restricted set of conditions, a single unit contract in which each farmer's second unit of outcome was more expensive than w_{10}. However, under more theoretically robust and realistic scenarios, many readers might expect that by reducing $farmer_1$'s wage from w_{10} (e.g., via taxes), $farmer_1$ would reduce output. This plausible substitution effect—an exchange of production/consumption for leisure or vice versa due to altered prices—is a classic consequence of *ad valorem* or unit *income taxes* that distorts the economy by distorting prices and, accordingly, leads to inefficiency, deadweight loss, and excess burden.[15] Such substitution only occurs, however, when the tax changes the income received on their marginal unit of product. Surprisingly, economists are in robust agreement that there are taxes that maintain efficiency and avoid deadweight loss and it is to such taxes that we turn next.

5.3 Lump-Sums and Endowments

One solution that mainstream economists have espoused for over a century to avoid distortionary substitution effects even under conditions of an ideal market is a lump-sum endowment tax.[16] Such a tax adjusts the absolute tax liability of each individual according to their endowment. This is a particular implementation of what optimal tax theorists discuss as vertical equity, "the appropriately unequal tax treatment of unequals,"[17] in which the entitlement-basis is endowment and the entitlement is an absolute transfer of resources. The lump-sum method is supported by economists

[15] Efficiency requires that production is on the production possibilities frontier and that each individual's marginal rate of substitution is identical to the marginal rate of transformation for all pairs of commodities.

[16] For justification of an endowment tax, cf. the first president of the American Economic Association as well as more modern treatment. Walker (1888); Bradford (1984).

[17] Lambert (2001), 175, 183.

because it is perfectly non-distortionary within an ideal market—meaning there are no changes among the relative prices of all market goods (including leisure) and thus no deadweight loss or inefficiency—and, thus, any one of the multitude of Pareto-efficient allocations may be achieved with appropriate lump-sum taxes and transfers.[18]

Yet why use an endowment tax when any unavoidable lump-sum tax meets this efficiency criterion? "[B]oth a head tax system and a tax regime that raised revenues solely by taxing commodities for which individuals exhibited inelastic demand (e.g., insulin and chemotherapy) might attain [optimal tax theory] efficiency but would on most reasonable accounts fail politically and morally."[19] Likewise, the *laissez-faire* principle of distribution is simply a lump-sum tax where all individuals share an identical tax liability of $0. Rather than tax chemotherapy and insulin, or pursue the *laissez-faire* mapping, the *Just Deserts* proposal seeks to secure its place as economists' first-best tax system: one that is not only maximally efficient, but also just, that is, satisfies the economic principle of equity.[20] Yet, how is a lump-sum tax connected to *Just Deserts*?

The connection comes via the concept of endowment, economists' term for what I have named circumstances of chance and what social scientists and those in the humanities might name *privilege*. Classically, that which we define as nature is an endowment: lakes, trees, coal, oil, oxygen, soil microbes, pollinators, and so on, but it is also true that certain human qualities are endowments, including personal tastes and talents. More technically, endowment is defined as *all potentially productive assets* the individual has at their disposal for which they have not labored or exchanged labor.

> Imagine that you are enjoying a sunrise from a clearing as you hike through a "natural endowment forest" and you feel an intense desire to eat an apple while enjoying this sunrise when your friend returns from the forest with two apples and asks, "From the strictly economic point of view, how much would you pay me right now for one delicious apple?" What is your reply?

[18] Atkinson and Stiglitz (1980), 343.

[19] Ben-Shalom and Stead (2010), 1520.

[20] In addition to equity and efficiency, many would add simplicity as a third goal of any system of taxation. I believe *Just Deserts* is orders of magnitude simpler than our current system. Simon (1977).

The question about "one delicious apple" is deliberately vague because the strictly economic reply is as follows, "Even if consuming an apple were my only means of survival, assuming an ideal market for such apples, I would pay you absolutely nothing for it and not a penny more. I would pay you handsomely, however, for your shipping, handling, and delivery of the apple in question."

This story demonstrates that we ought to pay to each their due—to the transporter, payment for transportation, and to the apple tree, payment for apple production. It would in fact be a completely unnecessary payment, about which economic rents I have said much above, to pay the transporter a 100% profit for apple production[21] on which they expended absolutely zero resources, incurred zero costs, and, furthermore, exhibited absolutely zero autonomous effort. Although the textbook example of economic rent consists of unnecessary payment received by landowners, we now see the damning consequences for all other endowments, including individual tastes and talents for which the individual has not themselves labored. To pay individuals for their endowment is to pay them 100% profit for a circumstance of chance for which they are not at all agent responsible. Contrary to the well known dictum of economics, "There is no such thing as a free lunch," the receipt of unnecessary payments for tastes and talents due to chance, and chance alone, is exactly that—a perfectly free lunch. As such, the *Just Deserts* proposal shall seek to reward all individuals as if they counterfactually possessed an identically valued free lunch.

Beyond natural endowments and personal endowments, we have not even mentioned social endowments: the whole of the physical, technical, and political infrastructure that enables a modern market economy with large firms that express market needs for legal briefs and artistic sculptures and other valuable goods. One ingenious argument by Gar Alperovitz and Lew Daly recommends so-called redistribution on precisely these grounds, that the modern market economy is a massive social endowment over and above the endowment given in the *state of nature*, and each individual thus shares entitlement to this social endowment through a principle of equality.[22] This argument serves to illustrate a third analytic facet of the vast size of endowments relative to the individual's contribution to final observed outcomes while helping us to also realize the untenable position

[21] That is, 100% of payment for apple production is profit.

[22] Alperovitz and Daly (2008).

of "noncomparative desert" for economic reward under the conditions of non-ideal philosophy.[23]

Absolute, or noncomparative, desert demands that we ignore endowment and make deserved rewards exclusively ***dependent*** upon autonomous effort. While logically possible, I find this an implausible basis for a public policy of economic reward as it seems to demand an extra-historical and omniscient knowledge of a table of correspondence between 7 units of autonomous effort and 45 units of value and 12 units of autonomous effort and 83 units of value, across all time and space, universally applicable to every moral agent who has, or ever will, exist. To my mind, we have three choices: either (1) twenty-first-century Parisians in fact "deserve" more than seventeenth-century Parisians (having realized a secular increase in autonomous effort, they deserve to live more than very "poor, nasty, brutish and short" lives),[24] (2) their deserts are equal and one population is farther from true, absolute, desert than the other, or (3) desert is always relative to the currently relevant population of moral agents.[25] While (2) and (3) both strike me as plausible, only (3) strikes me as feasible as a public policy and that is where I focus my energies.

To return to lump-sum endowment taxes, it turns out that under some rather broad conditions, a lump-sum endowment tax mapping of reward is identical to a luck-egalitarian mapping based upon the principle of desert. For example, if we were to *ex post* intervene upon individuals' rewards via some treatment (or transfer) of the observed outcome of interest because it is the case that the reward is isometric to the observed outcome of interest—for example, the observed outcome of interest is money income and the transfer and reward are also measured in money—then each individual's reward will also fit the function: $R_{iY} = f(t_i, CC_i, \alpha\epsilon_{iY})$ where t_i represents the treatment (or transfer). This treatment, it must be noted, does not reflect a change to our generalized formula but rather it is an element of the vector of circumstances of chance that we highlight because it is one over which policymakers have control. As such, the *pre-intervention value of this treatment*, t_i, was equal to zero for all individuals.

[23] Cautiously, given our informational limitations, "there is nothing that can be said about, for example, the [precise] income level that should be attached to being [precisely this] hard-working." Matravers (2011), 147.

[24] Hobbes (1991 (1651)).

[25] This is Brad Hooker's "oil fields" critique of "noncomparative desert," writ large. Arneson (2007), 280; Also, pace Sher (2014), 33.

Table 5.1 Luck-egalitarian mapping (homogeneous goods), given that $R_{iY} = (t_i + CC_i) * \alpha\varepsilon_{iY}$

	$\alpha\varepsilon_{iY} = 1$	$\alpha\varepsilon_{iY} = 2$
$CC_i = 2$	$t_i = +1$ $R_{iY} = 3$	$t_i = +1$ $R_{iY} = 6$
$CC_i = 4$	$t_i = -1$ $R_{iY} = 3$	$t_i = -1$ $R_{iY} = 6$

Fleurbaey has powerfully argued that there are two important conditions now possible: (1) ***homogeneous goods*** (all individuals value one unit of treatment in identical fashion to some quantity of units of circumstances of chance) and (2) ***heterogeneous goods*** (not all individuals exhibit an identical exchange rate between treatment units and circumstances of chance units). To clarify this with an example, let us assume that the reward function is $R_{iY} = (t_i + CC_i) * \alpha\epsilon_{iY}$.[26] This is an example of a reward function under conditions of homogeneous goods where treatment and circumstances of chance exhibit a functionally identical relationship to autonomous effort (in this case, a multiplicative relationship).

The key fact of this luck-egalitarian mapping of desert (see Table 5.1) is that all individuals in the same row exhibit an identical treatment while, simultaneously, all individuals in the same column exhibit an identical reward. To be explicit, this is the definition of a lump-sum endowment tax that simultaneously realizes robust equality of opportunity and no economic distortions.

On the contrary, let us now assume that the reward function is $R_{iY} = t_i + (CC_i * \alpha\epsilon_{iY})$.[27] This is an example of a reward function under conditions of heterogeneous goods where treatment and circumstances of chance fail to exhibit a functionally identical relationship to autonomous effort (in this case, treatment is related additively while circumstances of chance are related multiplicatively).

The key fact of this luck-egalitarian mapping of desert (see Table 5.2) is that, due to heterogeneous goods, there is no possible reward mapping able to realize a state in which all individuals in the same row exhibit an identical treatment while, simultaneously, all individuals in the same column exhibit an identical reward. Stated differently, Fleurbaey's liberal reward principle

[26] Fleurbaey (2008), 18.
[27] Fleurbaey (2008), 32.

Table 5.2 Luck-egalitarian mapping (heterogeneous goods), given that $R_{iY} = t_i + (CC_i * \alpha\varepsilon_{iY})$

	$\alpha\varepsilon_{iY} = 1$	$\alpha\varepsilon_{iY} = 2$
$CC_i = 2$	$t_i = +1$ $R_{iY} = 3$	$t_i = +2$ $R_{iY} = 6$
$CC_i = 4$	$t_i = -1$ $R_{iY} = 3$	$t_i = -2$ $R_{iY} = 6$

(lump-sum endowment tax) and compensation principle (robust equality of opportunity) are now at odds. This is precisely because these are two conditionally incompatible principles of horizontal equity—equal transfer for equal luck vs. equal reward for equal responsibility. Given that luck-egalitarian desert always satisfies Fleurbaey's compensation principle (equal reward for equal responsibility), luck-egalitarian desert is not equivalent to any lump-sum endowment tax (equal transfer for equal luck) under conditions of heterogeneous goods.

Thus, this points toward an important question for the *Just Deserts* proposal as a public policy of distributive justice in accord with the principle of desert. In Chap. 11, I discuss whether the *Just Deserts* proposal may in fact operate under conditions of homogeneous goods. At this juncture I simply wish to state that this is entirely an empirical question and its answer depends, in part, upon the specific public policy one chooses to implement. Second, assuming our best current public policy operates under conditions of heterogeneous goods, although there may be substitution effects and thus distortions and deadweight loss from a principle of desert that is not identical to a lump-sum endowment tax, it is still an empirical question as to whether net welfare is positive or negative. Third, assuming the answer is net negative according to neoclassical economics, it is an open, empirical question whether this assessment would become positive once we accounted for the value to individuals of realizing the distributive justice principle of desert for all individuals in the population.

- *Distributive justice based on a strict principle of desert, under broad conditions to be empirically determined, is perfectly non-distortionary and identical to economists' first-best tax: a lump-sum endowment tax.*

5.4 Lump-Sum Endowment Taxes: Introduction

Although most economists view a lump-sum endowment tax as the optimal tax system, some distributive justice scholars and economists simultaneously assert that it is neither feasible nor desirable.[28] For example, Daniel Shaviro writes, "[t]he idea [of endowment taxation] deserves greater prominence and acceptance, even though we will never see, and probably do not want to see, a literal, direct endowment tax."[29] The *Just Deserts* proposal must confront these objections and I will focus my discussion here in Chap. 5 on desirability and offer a rebuttal of feasibility objections in Chap. 11.

To fix ideas, Murphy and Nagel suppose that a lump-sum endowment tax would require knowledge of "potential annual earnings" which they define as maximal earnings. Second, they suppose that the tax might be so severe "that [an individual] may be condemned by his training to only one feasible line of work."[30] As we will see, both assumptions are mistaken and seem strangely at odds with their otherwise forceful defense of a robust philosophical understanding of taxes and transfers as an integral core of any economic system of distribution.[31]

> Imagine that a corporate lawyer, Laurel, wishes to produce some sculptures but the market for their sculptures exhibits very low demand. Unfortunately, taxed $200,000 on $500,000 in potential annual earnings, Laurel finds that in order to pay their high tax bill, the time for sculpture is reduced almost to zero. Finding no other suitable means to acquire $200,000 in earnings to pay the tax (i.e., produce $200,000 of something for which others have a market-expressed need) while leaving greater time for sculpture, Laurel is condemned by training to practice corporate law and produce very few sculptures.

[28] Murphy and Nagel (2004), 121–125.

[29] Shaviro (2002), 125.

[30] Murphy and Nagel (2004), 123.

[31] For a rejection of Murphy and Nagel's misplaced distinction between an endowment tax and other taxes on grounds of freedom, cf. Stark (2005); A similar, concise assessment: "By arguing that the endowment tax would enslave the highly endowed, critics of the endowment tax are subjecting it to a moral standard they do not apply to contemporary policies that apply similar standards but are considered politically and morally legitimate." Benshalom and Stead (2010), 1526.

There are a few oddities about this story. First, a tax upon ***maximum potential earnings*** is not the same as a tax upon endowment as these are by definition distinct and separate concepts.[32] More specifically, a decomposition of maximum potential earnings reveals two elements: circumstances of chance (i.e., endowment) as well as maximum autonomous effort Thus, Murphy and Nagel and other scholars of endowment taxes[33] have mischaracterized an endowment tax from the beginning as a tax on "maximum potential outcomes" rather than endowment alone which has helped to fuel a specious limited autonomy, or "slavery of the talented,"[34] objection.

The kernel of truth in this objection, however, is that any lump-sum endowment tax under conditions of heterogeneous goods is unable to satisfy Fleurbaey's compensation principle: a principle of horizontal equity that requires equal reward for equal responsibility (or robust equality of opportunity). Yet, a lump-sum endowment tax may always realize weak equality of opportunity—a mapping in which all the individuals exhibiting at least one value of autonomous effort realize identical reward irrespective of their varying circumstances of chance. When realizing merely weak equality of opportunity, then, one must choose which specific value of autonomous effort will exhibit this quality and it is the choice of "maximum potential earnings" as our reference point or benchmark that causes unnecessary problems for individuals like Laurel who exhibit high-endowment.

To clarify why lump-sum endowment taxes cannot satisfy responsibility-sensitive reward under conditions of heterogeneous goods, assume that a

[32] It is perhaps Mirrlees' foundational scholarship that suggested "maximum potential earnings" as the correct referendum. Mirrlees' groundbreaking work suggested that the tax base should be an "[individual]'s income-earning potential" and, unlike endowment tax proponents, that "the most reliable indicator of [their] income-earning potential is [their observed] income." Mirrlees (1971), 175.

[33] Sugin (2011); Mirrlees (1971).

[34] "The talent slavery objection is aimed at an endowment tax which defines endowment as one's maximum wage rate multiplied by the maximum number of hours one could work..." Note also that an *ex post* calculation of endowment, separated from autonomous effort, dismisses David Hasen's objection that "the system does not produce ... [earnings] capacity." Zelenak (2006).

"lump-sum endowment tax" has the following generalized form and may be uniquely identified by the vector, $\{\epsilon_A, \epsilon_i\}$:

$$T_i = [Endowment_A + \epsilon_A \sigma(\alpha\epsilon_{Endowment_A})] \\ -[Endowment_i + \epsilon_i \sigma(\alpha\epsilon_{Endowment_i})] \quad (5.1)$$

where T_i is the absolute transfer for individual, i (negative amounts are debits; positive amounts are credits); $Endowment_A$ is the mean endowment of our population; ϵ_A is the effort reference-point coefficient with respect to mean endowment; $\sigma(\alpha\epsilon_{Endowment_A})$ is the functional value of 1 marginal standard deviation of autonomous effort for an individual at the mean endowment with respect to the observed outcome of interest; $Endowment_i$ is the individual's endowment; ϵ_i is the effort reference-point coefficient with respect to individual endowment; and $\sigma(\alpha\epsilon_{Endowment_i})$ is the functional value of 1 marginal standard deviation of autonomous effort for *this particular individual's level of endowment* with respect to the observed outcome of interest.

If we assumed that "maximum potential earnings" meant exhibiting positive 2 standard deviations of autonomous effort in combination with one's endowment (setting ϵ_i to a value of 2 for the unique lump-sum endowment tax, {0,2}) and transferred lump-sums according to this "maximum potential earnings" reference point, then all individuals who actually exhibited positive two standard deviations of autonomous effort from the mean would hold the same absolute post-intervention *reward* (i.e., $R_{iY} = Outcome\ Y + T_i$). That is, weak equality of opportunity would hold for at least these individuals irrespective of the functional value of their circumstances of chance. Note that the "lump-sum maximum earnings tax," {0,2} is different from what I believe is the canonical lump-sum endowment tax, {0,0}. In this latter case, only those individuals who put forth mean autonomous effort would hold identical reward under conditions of heterogeneous goods.

In order to clarify the above, an illustration will be beneficial. Take the population mean outcome of interest in Barry's math exam to be a score of 100 and that we were going to reward students with a score that represents desert, that is, the reward is isometric to the observed outcome. Assume that low-endowment individuals who exhibited autonomous effort equal to ±1 standard deviation from the mean ended up with observed outcomes of 45 or 55 (i.e., 50 ± 5 or 50 ± 10%) while identical high-endowment

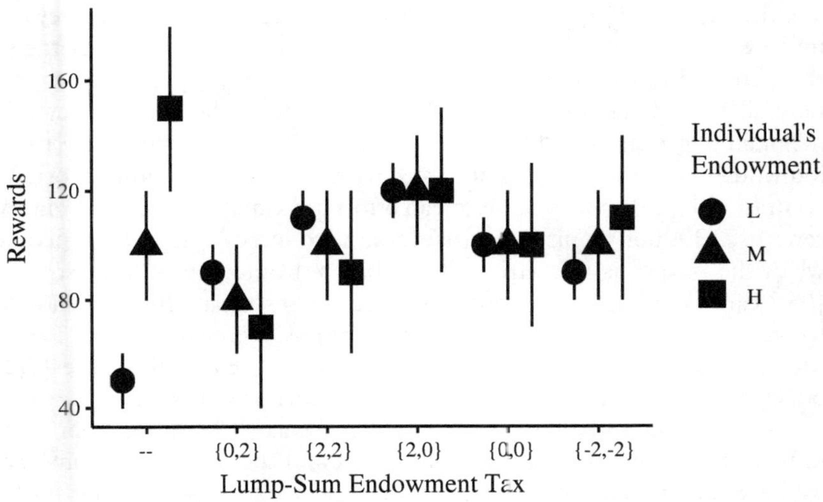

Fig. 5.1 Rewards by lump-sum policy, by endowment and effort (assuming heterogeneous goods)

individuals exhibited 135 or 165 (i.e., 150±15 or 150±10%). One standard deviation of autonomous effort is thus worth a ratio of 3:1 (i.e., 15 points:5 points) for high-endowment individuals in comparison to low-endowment individuals. More formally, as in Table 5.2, $R_{iY} = t_i + (CC_i * \alpha\epsilon_{iY})$.

To illustrate, Fig. 5.1 shows the original distribution alongside five lump-sum endowment tax policies. The central shape on each vertical line segment indicates outcomes for individuals exhibiting mean autonomous effort, while the top and bottom ends of the vertical line segments indicate outcomes for individuals exhibiting high or low autonomous effort (i.e., +1 and −1 standard deviation from the mean), respectively. As may be seen, our bivariate lump-sum endowment tax specification, $\{\epsilon_A,\epsilon_i\}$, allows us a great deal of control over the final mapping. While we cannot change the range of outcomes received by individuals within a specified level of endowment, we can change the relative positions of the ranges among levels of endowment (L = Low, M = Medium, H = High). For example, the use of a lump-sum endowment tax {0, 2} causes all high effort individuals to receive identical rewards, 100, yet high-endowment individuals who exhibit less than high effort are now the worst off among all individuals exhibiting identical autonomous effort. This policy also decreases aggregate reward under conditions of heterogeneous goods and a reward that is isometric to the observed outcome of interest. Adjusting to a {2,2} policy, we simply raise all individuals' income by 20 with respect to the {0,2} policy and maintain aggregate reward, granting weak equality of opportunity to all individuals who exhibit +2 standard deviations of autonomous effort. In contrast, the {2,0} policy causes mean effort individuals to receive identical rewards, 120, but requires external rewards to increase aggregate income when the reward is isometric to the observed outcome of interest. The {0,0} canonical lump-sum endowment tax causes mean effort individuals to receive identical rewards, 100, and maintains aggregate reward. Lastly, the {−2, −2} policy appears to be the symmetric reflection of the {2,2} policy across both the axes of autonomous effort and endowment.

As noted above, the lump-sum endowment tax {0,2} differs from {0,0} in that, if the observed outcome of interest and the reward are isometric, we have diminished the aggregate reward held by the population—not a desirable property for an economic tax. In fact, all isometric endowment taxes that do not have identical values for ϵ_A and ϵ_i exhibit aggregate reward that is either lesser or greater than the amount of pre-tax reward itself. While it is tempting to multiply the {0,2} reward of all individuals in the population so that post-tax reward is equal to pre-tax reward, this is not possible without ceasing to be a lump-sum tax and, thus, incurring economic inefficiency. In addition, adjusting the {0,2} reward with a uniform additive (or subtractive) correction so that post-tax reward equals pre-tax reward just is the {2,2} reward. As I hope is already clear, future scholarship on lump-sum endowment taxes must specify whether the tax under discussion is a {0,0}, {2,2}, or some other lump-sum endowment tax as each bivariate specification behaves differently.

Assuming that Murphy and Nagel actually wish to discuss the effect of a {2,2} lump-sum endowment tax on Laurel, we must note that while this {2,2} policy at first appears to penalize the "talented," this objection inappropriately focuses only on high-endowment individuals who exhibit low autonomous effort. In fact, after a lump-sum endowment tax as illustrated in Fig. 5.1, high-endowment individuals who exhibit more autonomous effort than ϵ_i will receive the *greatest reward* among all individuals in the population exhibiting identical autonomous effort. That is to say, it is always high-endowment individuals who will populate *both the bottom and the top* of the post-lump-sum distribution of the reward under the illustrated conditions of heterogeneous goods and a balanced vector lump-sum endowment tax such as {2,2}. Furthermore, this illustration undercuts the "slavery of the talented" objection to some extent by helping us to see that, even with the {2,2} tax, it's still possible that high-endowment, low-effort individuals are at least as well off as low-endowment individuals exhibiting identical effort.

As the lump-sum "maximum potential earnings" tax {2,2} and the canonical lump-sum endowment tax {0,0} appear to be cut from the same cloth, do we have any good reasons to prefer certain values for $\{\epsilon_A, \epsilon_i\}$? Given that far fewer individuals will receive identical rewards for identical effort with $\epsilon_i = 2$, I would rather select $\epsilon_i = 0$ in $\{\epsilon_A, \epsilon_i\}$ as this represents the simultaneous mean, median, and mode of normally distributed autonomous effort. Recall that all moral agents participate in one sole distribution of autonomous effort that is independent of all circumstances of chance. Thus {0,0} seems an intuitively fair point to initially select for our balanced vector lump-sum endowment tax that we will analyze in Chap. 12.

In sum, a strict principle of desert requires use of the luck-egalitarian mapping of desert which, under conditions of homogeneous goods, is identical to the canonical lump-sum tax {0,0}. Under conditions of heterogeneous goods, there are two simple options: (1) one may apply the strict principle of desert and evaluate the deadweight loss or (2) one may compromise with the distributive justice principle of efficiency and continue to use the canonical lump-sum tax {0,0} with no deadweight loss.

5.5 In Sum, This Chapter Has Argued

- *Distributive justice based on a principle of desert implements greater equality of economic rents or, more prosaically, free lunches.*
- *Distributive justice based on a strict principle of desert, under broad conditions to be empirically determined, is perfectly non-distortionary and identical to economists' first-best tax, a lump-sum endowment tax.*

CHAPTER 6

Liberty and *Just Deserts*: Slaves, Dynasties, and Moral Agents

Now that I have described the ways in which the *Just Deserts* proposal realizes the core underlying need of the principle of efficiency, I would like to discuss how it may satisfy proponents of another principle of distributive justice liberty.

Attractive accounts of liberty often require a process of consent based upon a right of self-ownership, "where such a right consists of robust and stringent rights of control over oneself: one's mind, body, and life."[1] I argue in this chapter that the *Just Deserts* proposal, by allowing such property rights in oneself in addition to property rights to all of the income that one can gain from one's autonomous effort, can simply, accurately, and coherently maximize liberty. The stakes of this claim are important, for if it is true that libertarianism has unnecessarily and improperly extended liberty to mean property rights to all of the income that one can gain from certain portions of one's endowment, then the *Just Deserts* proposal can make a strong case that distributive justice does not infringe upon individual liberty.

A distributive justice principle of liberty is attractive to many because it protects the individual from (a large class of) outcomes dependent upon others' autonomous effort to which the individual did not offer consent. As the reader might fear that the *Just Deserts* proposal runs roughshod over individual liberty in an effort to redistribute, there are two

[1] Otsuka (2003), 2.

J. T. Dwyer, *Chance, Merit, and Economic Inequality*,
https://doi.org/10.1007/978-3-030-21126-4_6

potential objections to *Just Deserts* from the principle of liberty that I would like to address in this chapter. First, many modern liberals are perfectly comfortable with taxes but reject lump-sum endowment taxes as described in the last chapter—allegedly this constitutes illegitimate coercion or force in a way that typical income taxes do not. Second, although few are committed to the moral monism of exclusively valuing liberty as the one ethical principle of any value, libertarianism seems to reject all taxes in principle and has a growing following as systemic inequality simultaneously reaches its most exaggerated levels. Libertarians generally argue that, today, only outcomes agreed to by valid consent may produce distributive justice. Distributive justice is then allegedly measured in the eyes of the libertarian by observing a process that excludes certain kinds of taxes rather than by observing the distribution itself.

I hope to show in this section why liberals and libertarians would be at least as well, if not better, served by the *Just Deserts* proposal as it best fulfills a liberal impulse that each person be the unalloyed master of his or her place in the social distribution—that each individual freely decides whether they will be the poorest or richest member of society.[2]

6.1 Lump-Sum Endowment Taxes: Liberal Critique Rejected

Let us now assess the liberal's argument: that a lump-sum tax might restrict liberty by condemning certain individuals to only one feasible line of work and thus percentage income taxes must be preferred over lump-sum endowment taxes. This claim states, for example, that due to their high-endowment of $300,000, Laurel's only means of paying the lump-sum tax is by working as a corporate lawyer while they would prefer in the absence of the tax to produce sculptures.[3]

As discussed in Chap. 5, a fundamental problem with this presentation is that it misunderstands the content of endowment. As mentioned, autonomous effort is mutually exclusive, exhaustive, and independent of endowment where endowment is all potentially productive assets for which the individual has not themselves labored or exchanged labor—that is, exhibited autonomous effort. Not only does Laurel's endowment

[2] Sadurski (1985), 123.
[3] For this view of liberty, cf. Sugin (2011).

encompass their talent for labor with a high production value (i.e., corporate law), Laurel also exhibits tastes that depend upon circumstances of chance, including their relative distaste for corporate law and their taste for sculpture. As endowment encompasses both tastes and talents relative to earnings for which Laurel has exhibited zero autonomous effort, the liberal's objection above falls apart. That is to say, one cannot claim that Laurel has an exceptional talent for working as a lawyer, exceptional distaste for such work, and simultaneously claim that they have a high-endowment of $300,000. A properly conceptualized endowment tax sees that Laurel's exceptional talent is nullified to some extent by Laurel's exceptional relative distaste for law as compared to sculpture, and thus Laurel's tax liability is far less than $200,000 because their endowment is far less than $300,000. Thus, it is not possible for an endowment tax to "condemn" Laurel to work as a lawyer solely in order to pay the $200,000 tax liability.[4]

Perhaps the liberal might counter that it is not that Laurel has exceptional distaste for the law, it is that Laurel has extraordinary taste for leisure. This again misunderstands endowment by narrowing its content. Laurel's endowment includes Laurel's complete vector of circumstances of chance—clearly including all tastes and talents on which earnings depend, including the taste for leisure. If it is true that Laurel exhibits extraordinary taste for sculpting sand castles and has very little taste for consumption via monetary exchange or for production of goods others find valuable,[5] this constitutes a very important part of Laurel's endowment that will, to some extent, nullify Laurel's high talent for corporate law.

The liberal might ask, "Does the endowment tax not condemn Laurel if Laurel was *originally* endowed with great talent and great taste for work as a lawyer up until their graduation from law school, but now they exhibit great distaste and little talent for work as a lawyer?" The fundamental question from the perspective of *Just Deserts* is the following: is Laurel agent responsible for such change? If Laurel is not responsible to even the slightest extent for this change, having befallen ill luck at the hands of a mad scientist's experiment, then circumstances of chance are entirely object responsible for this change. This would constitute a direct

[4] My criticism applies equally to "Lovely" and "Lonely." Van Parijs (1995), 64.

[5] Note in all cases, pace Sher, that it is irrelevant whether "most people" have a set of tastes or distastes, but it is Laurel's endowment (tastes and talent) that is "morally significant." Sher (1987), 108.

and unmitigated modification of Laurel's endowment and, thus, Laurel's tax liability—while Laurel previously exhibited a tax liability of $200,000, perhaps they now owe $20,000 due to the mad scientist's intervention. However, to the extent that Laurel was agent responsible for this change, Laurel's endowment—and thus, tax liability—does not change.

Some may find this element of the principle of desert too harsh—perhaps Laurel holds a moral belief that self-harm, or self-sacrifice, with respect to their endowment as a corporate lawyer is the right thing to do as they "laudably" work as a nearly penniless sculptor? Are we to "condemn" Laurel into violating their conscience? While this hardly seems like condemnation—I think few would pity the saint for their life of penury if they had taken a genuinely autonomous vow of poverty—I want to offer middle ground for those still convinced by the harshness objection.

Recall that our lump-sum tax has two variables of interest, ϵ_A and ϵ_i. Thus, rather than allocate to Laurel a reward of −$180,000 via a tax liability of $200,000, we may implement the *Just Deserts* Lump-Sum Endowment Minimum Reward, Balanced Vector $\{\epsilon_A, \epsilon_i\}$ model (such that $\epsilon_A = \epsilon_i$), reducing ϵ_A, ϵ_i in such a way that the minimum reward among the entire population is an allocation equal to a minimum threshold of reward (a "universal basic income"), for example, $1000.[6] Thus, we see that there is no reason to agree that Laurel (or any other individual, whether low or high endowment) is "condemned" to a particular occupation when that argument rested upon an inappropriate specification of a {2, 2} lump-sum endowment tax and a misunderstanding of the immense capaciousness of endowment itself as all productive capacity dependent upon circumstances of chance. Of course, it is still an empirical question whether the population finds that it ought to eschew the canonical {0,0} lump-sum endowment tax so that the individuals with greater than mean endowment can consume their free lunch.

- *By adjusting the variables of interest that determine the behavior of a lump-sum endowment tax,* $\{\epsilon_A, \epsilon_i\}$, *one may satisfy the liberal objection*

[6] Pace Anderson, the principle of desert is strictly devoid of paternalism but there is nothing forbidding us from supplementing a principle of desert with one of sufficiency. Anderson (1999); One may notice this solution resembles that of Fleurbaey, "Min Egalitarian-Equivalence." Fleurbaey (2008), 115.

by guaranteeing that no empirically observed choice of autonomous effort is foreclosed.

6.2 Liberty and Just Deserts: Dynasties and Agents

While liberals may be comfortable with some taxes, conservative libertarians seem to argue that all taxes constitute unjust takings that infringe the liberty of the individual. For example, Robert Nozick famously suggested that the full sum of distributive justice would be circumscribed by "justice in transfer"[7] which covers transfers of resources or "holdings" (1) from unowned to owned, (2) from owned by one individual to owned by another, and (3) from owned by an individual back to unowned again. Following Nozick, one's rights to ownership and use are either full or null, according to whether the relevant transfer was just. The principal type of just transfer between individuals is transfer by valid, mutual consent.[8] As such, taxes without consent are illegitimate infringements of liberty. Viewed from the perspective of one single transfer, this appears a simple, intuitively plausible requirement that, in principle, should be easy to measure and verify.

Although there is already a rich literature that seriously engages Nozick's position,[9] I would like to explicitly do so from the perspective of *Just Deserts*. Nozick argues against so-called redistribution' suggesting that any distributive "patterning [of resources] requires continuous interference with an individual's actions and choices."[10] First, what might Nozick mean by "continuous interference?" Second, and far more troubling, what might Nozick mean by "an individual?"

To fix ideas, let us assume that Tommy Thief acquires unjust takings of $1000—violating justice in transfer—from Ricardo Robbed that are never justly unwound. Tommy later exchanges that $1000 for a new timepiece

[7] Technically, Nozick states three axioms but I find them equivalent to one. Putting it in more economic terms, it is singularly by looking at flows that we can determine whether stocks are just. Nozick (2013), 151.

[8] Taking a more extreme stance than Nozick, Hayek states that the distribution of economic resources via market mechanisms is not even a subject of justice. "There can be no distributive justice where no one distributes." Hayek (1978), 58.

[9] Gibbard (1976); Grunebaum (1987); Cohen (1995); Roemer (1996).

[10] Nozick (2013), 166.

under mutual consent with the watchmaker and we want to know if this transaction represents justice in transfer or not. Nozick clearly states that the answer is no. Despite the fact that the process between Tommy and the watchmaker involved mutual consent, the watchmaker is not entitled to the $1000 because Tommy was not entitled to the $1000. Just as Tommy is not entitled to the timepiece, neither is the watchmaker entitled to the hat purchased with those unjust takings, and so on. That is to say, *prima facie* just transfers are not in fact just if any link in the historical chain of transfers was not just. Perhaps surprisingly, this means that in short time, given enough market exchanges under a specific transactions velocity of money (and goods), each participant in the economy holds some resources derived from Tommy's unjust takings. Unless the libertarian has some way to hermetically isolate unjust takings that have not been "unwound" to Ricardo, the facts of modern money creation[11] probabilistically guarantees that the dollar value of Tommy's unjust takings circulating within the economy will actually be greater than $1000.

If we made the simple assumption that an identical proportion of each individual's currently held resources stems from Tommy's unjust takings, we would conclude that the rich and the wealthy currently control, although they are not entitled to such control, a greater absolute dollar value of resources stemming from Tommy's unremedied takings than do the poor and impecunious. Yet, even this proportional rule is likely wrong given that we have not lived in the simple economy Nozick has in mind for over 5000 years—we live in a financial economy in which the tendency of assets, whether derived from Tommy's ill-gotten gains or not, is ever greater inequality.[12]

Finally, the wealthy are knowingly unable to present an impeccable pedigree for their holdings given that our history is replete with "robbery, genocide, and slavery"[13] among other unjust takings. Note that this critique does not even attack conservative libertarian intuitions about consent as based upon abstract models far from representative of actual imperfect markets in which nominal "consent" looks like one party, perhaps unjustly, taking advantage of the other. It simply notes that justice in transfer has often been the exception, not the rule—thus, it would be

[11] McLeay et al. (2014).
[12] Fernholz and Fernholz (2014); Molander (2016), Ch. 4; Nash (1950); Piketty (2014).
[13] Roemer (1996), 207.

highly presumptuous to claim an infringement of rights *today* based upon the mere fact (rather than the content) of redistribution. For these reasons, conservative libertarians face the uncomfortable prospect that it might not be the case that the wealthy need protection from potential continuous interference, but that they overwhelmingly enjoy the benefits of ongoing continuous interference in the form of a failure to unwind all transactions dependent upon Tommy's theft.

The greater problem, however, is that not only do Tommy, Ricardo, and the watchmaker live different lives due to unjust takings, but unjust takings have an amazing persistence through the generations for all of their descendants. The inequality of unmerited holdings today flows directly from inequality of unjust holdings from past generations. Expanding our scope, it seems reasonable to assume that not only does unjustified wealth inequality persist intergenerationally, not only does this lead to capital income inequality, but that these advantages translate, to some extent, to unequal labor income inequalities. Although this extent may in fact be small, it will be useful to highlight some recent relevant research both for this line of argument as well as the next section.

For an individual of today's generation whose labor income is 50% of the mean, the best contemporary research suggests it will take five further generations (125 years) before the earnings of their lineal descendants—great-great-great-grandchildren—will substantially approach the societal mean.[14] This critique grows more trenchant once we note that this earnings estimate is derived from recent economic data. If we assume that today's economy allows more economic mobility and more transfers in justice than economies of 125 years ago (c. 1900), this suggests that present distributive inequality is anchored in an even greater number of generations in the past and, thus, in centuries-old unmerited inequalities based to an even greater extent upon unjust takings than this prospective estimate would suggest.

Furthermore, this five-generation gap concerns contemporary individuals whose ratio of earnings are 1:2, but the present earnings distribution contains individuals between whom lies many times this difference. Thus, if the power of chance continues to inhibit economic mobility at today's estimate, it will take 16 generations (400 years) for the average S&P 500

[14] Bowles et al. (2005b); Mazumder (2005).

worker's descendants to mingle as economic equals with the descendants of their CEO given the current income ratio between them of 1:300.[15]

Given our discussion of wealth and, to some extent, labor income, one might easily suggest that the individuals with the greatest amount of freedom today are in a robust sense simply those individuals with the good luck to have won such rich, lucky, and even successfully unjust ancestors in the natural lottery. Thus I describe a libertarianism that cannot implement "rectification" (i.e., redistribution to just holdings) as a dynastic system of distributive justice—an "inheritance society"[16]—in that it perfunctorily calls the present distribution of resources just in the face of good evidence that it exhibits unmerited inequality based upon more than five generations of unjust takings and insufficient title.

- *Libertarian justice in transfer is an unworkable system in the presence of ubiquitous violations of consent and allows today's individuals to retain the unjust holdings of their forebears over at least the previous five generations.*

6.3 Agents and Liberty

I also stated that libertarianism has a contentious understanding of the individual. Recall that there are only two vectors in the whole universe from the perspective of the moral agent, the mutually exclusive, exhaustive, and independent vectors of circumstances of chance and autonomous effort. Now if liberty refers to the moral freedom of autonomous effort, then there is literally no transfer to or from the individual that may logically enhance or diminish "liberty" given that autonomous effort is always independent of all circumstances of chance. If liberty instead refers to the freedom to realize any observed outcome in one's opportunity set, it is again not possible for any other agent to take that away. Recall that equality of opportunity is not the same as equality of probability—opportunity is a distribution of an observed outcome of interest that is unreservedly and absolutely available

[15] I have used 300 as a ratio of S&P 500 CEO pay to average worker pay, 0.6 as the coefficient of intergenerational income elasticity (assumed such, perhaps unrealistically, to be constant across the distribution from mean to tails), and a range of the mean ±10% as "similarity." Cf. Davis and Mishel (2014); Mazumder (2005).

[16] Piketty (2014), 351.

to be realized by the individual's autonomous effort alone as in the case of the jinni.

Given the above, perhaps the libertarian wishes to forbid any (negative) intervention upon the individual's circumstances of chance that make up their endowment toward any and all observed outcomes of interest—that is, forbid others from altering the shape of one's current opportunity set. This prohibition also strikes me as untenable. As discussed earlier, endowment encompasses any and all potentially productive assets for which the individual has not labored or exchanged labor. Conservative libertarians should feel little support for *absolute* rights to *all* of the things (e.g., natural resources, talents, tastes, and the products thereof) for which one has neither labored nor exchanged labor as they have little to do with liberty, *per se*. Endowment, properly defined, includes the natural endowment, Alperovitz and Daly's social endowment, the individual's body, tastes, and talents, as well as all other gifts the individual has ever received. While one might have an intuition that it is easy to draw a line of exclusivity around each individual's endowment such that there is zero overlap between the endowments of different moral agents, it is just the opposite. Many things that are beyond one individual's control are beyond many, or all, individuals' control, and this is just as true of the potentially productive circumstances of chance that make up one's endowment. If intervention upon one individual's *entire* endowment were forbidden, every other individual would be forbidden from autonomous effort.

The conservative libertarian might concede that they do not seek ownership rights for each individual over their entire endowment, but merely of each individual over their own talents, tastes, and body. *Just Deserts* is more than happy to agree so long as the ownership rights are one's of control and not full rights in the market value of such circumstances of chance. Each individual may use (or not use) their talents, tastes, and body in whatever manner they see fit, but the economic value of the products of such use may justly be brought under a rewards system for distribution across some or all individuals. Let's turn to Locke to make this more persuasive to the conservative libertarian as "libertarians inherit the concept of self-ownership from Locke."[17]

[17] Olsaretti (2004), 91.

- *The elements of each individual's endowment are not exclusive as, prior to autonomous effort, all individuals share an identical endowment, simply from different relative positions.*

While there has been ample ink spilled over John Locke's writing on "Property" in the Second Treatise on Government,[18] allow me to offer a *Just Deserts* reading in order to redefine liberty (without, of course, implying that Locke held this view).[19] Locke states, "yet every man has a property in his own person... The *labour* of his body, and the *work* of his hands, we may say, are properly his [Dwyer's italics]."[20] First, there is no doubt that one is full owner of one's labor, that is, one's autonomous effort. Second, Locke grants each individual property in his person, that is, his body. While those sympathetic to *Just Deserts* might feel a temptation to grant to each individual whatever portion of their body derives from autonomous effort (or something less than full self-ownership),[21] it is important to recognize that full self-ownership neither undercuts *Just Deserts* nor suffices to support conservative libertarians. Thus, *Just Deserts* supports full ownership, recognizing "that even *full* self-ownership on its own does not guarantee that agents have any effective freedom or any entitlement to their products [Vallentyne's italics]."[22] As we are agents who cannot exist nor produce without natural resources, ownership of artifacts turns upon ownership of natural resources (or more broadly, endowment). Here, Locke makes the claim that "there must of necessity be a means to appropriate" the fruits of nature. That means is of course labor. For Locke, work is the mixing of labor and natural resources, and it joins the individual and the artifact. While mixing one's tomato juice in the ocean does not make one owner of the seas,[23] mixing one's labor with natural resources does generate property rights in at least some of the artifact for Locke. Yet, how much of the artifact is not so simple.

[18] Locke (1997 (1689)), secs. 25–51.

[19] For example, Locke famously finds liberty even in the absence of autonomous effort. Locke (1690), bk. II, chapter XXI.

[20] Locke (1997 (1689)), sec. 27.

[21] Also, cf. Steiner (2009).

[22] Vallentyne (2000), 5.

[23] Nozick (2013), 175.

> Imagine that the world is composed of (1) a forest of apples that gives exactly 12 identical apples to each visitor, (2) a road to the forest with houses alongside, (3) that apples may only be consumed in one's own home, and (4) that walking to and from the forest is the only labor or autonomous effort in the world. Ricardo Robbed walks 400 meters to the endowment forest and receives 12 apples. Tommy Thief lives 1000 meters away from the forest, however, and thus it costs Tommy twice as much autonomous effort to realize the same consumption. One day, rather than walking 400 extra meters, Tommy simply waits to rob Ricardo of his apples outside of Ricardo's house. What has Tommy Thief gained and what has Ricardo lost?

Although Ricardo has "mixed" his autonomous effort with the apples by walking to and from the forest, this does not make the entirety of the apples Ricardo's property and private right nor is such appropriation necessary to incent Ricardo's apple gathering. Instead, Ricardo may only claim that they own the added value of the labor that is now part of and annexed to the product.[24] That is, any attempt to legitimate the appropriation of the entire artifact, or any portion of the artifact not derived from the individual's labor, is unwarranted. Thus, the only thing Ricardo has lost is the labor—the autonomous effort—required to walk to the endowment forest and return with apples. Likewise, Tommy has not gained ownership over the apples but, at the very least, has profited by the difference in labor (autonomous effort) between walking the full distance and robbing Ricardo (taking possession of Ricardo's added value without Ricardo's consent). At this point, each individual has full self-ownership and, when one is entitled to "mixing" their self with a portion of their endowment, Locke is happy to say one retains ownership of one's labor by obtaining some portion of the added value generated in artifacts.

Thankfully, Locke did not leave us without a means to calculate one's added value nor does Locke condone Tommy's theft. Lockean liberty means not merely ownership of one's labor and its transformation into added value but that others may not reduce one's share of product below what one would derive from a precise luck-egalitarian portion of endowment.[25] This may seem to be an unusual reading of liberty, yet Locke clearly states that "this labour [autonomous effort] being the

[24] "For on reflection it is seen that no labor really 'produces' any material thing, but only adds to its value..." Sidgwick (1999), 51; for a similar suggestion, cf. Brody (2000), 35–36.

[25] Otsuka (2003), chap. 1.

unquestionable property of the labourer [moral agent], no [individual] but [this individual] can have a right to what that is once joined to, *at least where there is enough, and as good, left in common for others* [Dwyer's italics]." To what, I ask, can one join autonomous effort? The only answer is endowment, that is, potentially productive circumstances of chance.

If one is willing to place great weight on "and as good," one could argue that the Lockean proviso, "enough, and as good," matches a luck-egalitarian formulation that helps us to determine the portion of apples to which each individual is entitled. "Enough, and as good" does its work, not by reference to observed outcomes of interest (e.g., apples gathered, honey gathered, water gathered) but to the functional value of endowment itself. Importantly, when individuals' shares in usufruct are derived from functionally identical values of endowment, each moral agent is fully free to be the poorest or richest member of society. That is to say, when one must leave "enough, and as good" functional value of endowment for others, the distribution of reward is perfectly responsibility-sensitive and identical to the *Just Deserts* proposal. Through this particular version of "libertarianism,"[26] each individual is thus maximally free to be the absolute "master of [their] place in the social distribution"[27] of the maximum value (see Chap. 5) of economic resources.

- *From the perspective of desert, the Lockean proviso may lead naturally to luck-egalitarian usufruct in which each is maximally free to hold the maximum allocation within the distribution.*

Despite the apparent ease with which Locke's language fits a luck-egalitarian distribution, Nozick wishes to make a small alteration to the Lockean proviso that allegedly leads to a significant consequence. Nozick suggests that appropriation of natural resource endowment may (via labor) be in accord with justice as long as *no one is worse off* than they would have been were it unowned. The basic intuition at work here is that if a rule of appropriation transfers more reward to those whose personal endowment is most productive, then everyone will be better off as those hyper-endowed individuals will produce more than they would under the "enough, and as good" proviso. It is plausible that by "lifting the enough, and as good tax"

[26] Vallentyne (2000), 8–10.
[27] Sadurski (1985), 123.

from the hyper-endowed and by making everyone *better off*, that liberty is enhanced in two dimensions.

Crucially, however, this proviso is an *indeterminate* rule of appropriation that is often interpreted by conservative libertarians and their opponents as a rule that unnecessarily favors the hyper-endowed. This interpretation, however, is not the only way to apply Nozick's proviso. For example, everyone would be better off paying a tithe to a king under strong property rights than a world absent exclusive property rights[28]—clearly, this does not make monarchies just. Further, as we already know from Chap. 5, by making Ricardo full owner of his entire inframarginal economic rent, the Nozickean proviso does not leave Tommy *best off*.[29] Ricardo would and will gather precisely as many apples whether or not he appropriates his inframarginal economic rent. Yet, by granting Ricardo ownership over his greater amount of inframarginal rent, Tommy must pay the apple *transporter* for apple *production*, unnecessary payments that generate unnecessary inequality and make Tommy unnecessarily worse off. In sum, anyone attracted to Nozick's proviso can always make Tommy better off (while maintaining Pareto optimality) by choosing a precise definition of the proviso that transfers some of Ricardo's inframarginal rent.

One might object here that we have forgotten about consent. It would seem that Tommy can't consent to purchase apples from Ricardo for $100 and then come back the next day with the government and rightfully take back $10. To me, it's highly plausible that an integral part of the consent given relates to the distribution of functional endowment. That is to say, Tommy cannot give such Nozickean "consent" because "consent consists in the transfer of rights that individuals possess in a state of nature rather than the expression of approval."[30]

To conclude, we may at one and the same time allow Tommy and Ricardo robust rights of non-interference over, and full self-ownership in, their own persons—in order to grant each individual's "basic liberty protecting the integrity of the person,"[31] prevent unjust imprisonment,

[28] Gibbard (2000), 25–26.

[29] Of course, a judgement of "worse off" always depends upon the chosen comparator and there are other comparators beyond the Lockean proviso. Lamont (1997), 29.

[30] Otsuka (2003), 120.

[31] Rawls (1999 (1971)), 89.

forbid slavery, and so on—without granting them ownership of their respective functional endowment, that is, inframarginal economic rents. The conservative libertarian has asked liberty to do too much—attempting to push a natural right claim (to one's own labor and its derived added value in artifacts, including bodies)[32] to a much bigger claim on inframarginal rents. Given the indeterminate nature of Nozick's proviso, I think the burden of proof is on inegalitarian libertarians to provide substantive arguments for this claim.

- *The Nozickean proviso fails to note that the Pareto-optimal production frontier does not require full property rights in products derived from "mixing" one's labor with endowment and that such a rule of appropriation always needlessly harms the hypo-endowed and buyers by granting hyper-endowed individuals strictly unnecessary payments for inframarginal rent.*

To conclude Part II, while three process-oriented principles of distributive justice recommended three different processes necessary for a just distribution, I have shown in the last three chapters that one process—that of distribution according to rewards proportional to luck-egalitarian desert—may satisfy all three principles: equal opportunity, Pareto-optimal efficiency (conditionally), and liberty. If equal opportunity sets itself an unnecessarily difficult *ex ante* task while desert makes it simpler and more accurate *ex post*; if efficiency claims all taxes reduce output and welfare while desert enables us to use strictly non-distortionary lump-sum endowment taxes; if liberty claims that lump-sum and possibly all taxes are prohibited while desert shows how flexible lump-sum taxes are, that the foundation of liberty is plausibly luck-egalitarian, and that the hypo-endowed are worse off under the Nozickean proviso than with the *Just Deserts* proposal, and that it is only under desert that each is free to choose their place in the distribution of reward; it then remains to show that the *Just Deserts* proposal is not mere philosophy, but a viable public policy.

[32] Cf. Pojman and McLeod (1999), 5.

6.4 In Sum, This Chapter Has Argued

- *By adjusting the variables of interest that determine the behavior of a lump-sum endowment tax,* $\{\epsilon_A, \epsilon_i\}$, *one may satisfy the liberal objection by guaranteeing that no empirically observed choice of autonomous effort is foreclosed.*
- *Libertarian justice in transfer is an unworkable system in the presence of ubiquitous violations of consent and allows today's individuals to retain the unjust holdings of their forebears over at least the previous five generations.*
- *The elements of each individual's endowment are not exclusive as, prior to autonomous effort, all individuals share an identical endowment, simply from different relative positions.*
- *From the perspective of desert, the Lockean proviso may lead naturally to luck-egalitarian usufruct in which each is maximally free to hold the maximum allocation within the distribution.*
- *The Nozickean proviso fails to note that the Pareto-optimal production frontier does not require full property rights in products derived from "mixing" one's labor with endowment and that such a rule of appropriation always needlessly harms the hypo-endowed and buyers by granting hyper-endowed individuals strictly unnecessary payments for inframarginal rent.*

PART III

Just Public Policies

CHAPTER 7

Economy and Desert

All good distributive justice proposals must allow for clear translation into policy. While some might believe that principles of distributive justice are not necessarily our best "rules of regulation" in the real world, they may still usefully guide our policies in both content and consequences.

Having argued for distributive justice as *Just Deserts* with respect to the control principle, in which each individual's allocation is exclusively sensitive to their autonomous effort, there are still unanswered questions within this luck-egalitarian desert-based account of distributive justice. While Chaps. 2 and 3 focused on what Knight has termed the "basal grounds"[1] of responsibility and desert as well as the *sensitivity prong* of the "appraisal grounds" of responsibility and desert, here we turn toward the *correspondence prong* of the "appraisal grounds." First, Chap. 7 will explore the question: what is the proper observed outcome of interest for which we might "deserve" a distributive justice reward? Second, Chap. 8 will explore the question: what is the proper *reward* for autonomous effort toward the observed outcome of interest? Third, once we have addressed the correspondence prong of the "appraisal grounds," we need to answer two last questions about the "basal grounds" of responsibility and desert. Chapter 9 will explore the question: who counts as an individual eligible for such rewards? Finally, Chap. 10 explores the question: which circumstances

[1] Knight (2011).

J. T. Dwyer, *Chance, Merit, and Economic Inequality*,
https://doi.org/10.1007/978-3-030-21126-4_7

of chance do we need to observe in order to precisely measure this autonomous effort toward the observed outcome of interest?

Each of these chapters thus helps translate our formalization of a theory of desert from Chap. 3 (see Eq. (3.4)) into concrete concepts that we can measure and use in Chap. 11. Here the argument takes a turn from the perspective of ideal philosophy to that of non-ideal philosophy—we are interested in using prudential and/or moral grounds, under assumptions of limited but sufficient information[2] and power, to identify the best public policy implementation of an economic system of reward based upon a distributive justice principle of desert. Desert statements, unlike rule statements which are simply true or false, require arguments about values, moral principles, and controversial moral appraisals. Desert itself cannot tell us what is right or good. For our purposes, distributive desert tells us only how to reward individuals with respect to previously defined values.

7.1 Economy and Desert

While one could of course attempt to apply luck-egalitarianism to determine the deserved outcomes of individuals within institutions such as the criminal and civil justice systems[3] (what Aristotle called retributive justice)[4] as well as the healthcare system,[5] I focus the *Just Deserts* proposal as a public policy of distributive justice on one particular institution, albeit one with a large circumference, the economy. While I will not provide a grand theory of correspondence, I draw heavily upon the intuitions and arguments in the existing literature in the hopes that I at least make a strong *prima facie* case that distributive justice requires rewarding a specific autonomous effort with a specific reward.

[2] We want a theory that is "feasible and fair," in which we have "sufficient information" to make a "reasonable approximation" of the "relative effort levels of individuals across an entire economy." Wolff (2003), 223–224.

[3] While the current criminal justice system imposes negative consequences in order to (1) protect society from this individual, (2) prevent this individual and others from committing future crimes, and (3) punish this individual for their wrongdoing, a *Just Deserts* system would only affect the punish component, although likely in very interesting ways. Cf. Matravers (2011); Feinberg (1970f), 215.

[4] Although, for an account of retributive justice as distributive, cf. Sher (1987), 76–82.

[5] Although criminal justice and health may more naturally elicit an impetus toward observed outcome egalitarianism (less crime and illness) over an *ex post* distribution of desert. Cf. Segall (2009).

To begin, the *Just Deserts* proposal needs to explicitly decide upon an observed outcome of interest for which an individual's autonomous effort toward that outcome would possess a certain merit, one that society feels would correspond with moral deservingness of some economic reward. In seeking this outcome of interest, recall that many philosophers have previously understood desert as a three-part relation of the form, *i* deserves *R* because of *q*, where *i* is the moral agent, *R* is the reward, and *q* is the "desert-basis" quality possessed by *i*.[6] While Aristotle argued that society ought to distribute economic rewards with respect to a desert-basis of virtue-excellence, *arete*, the contemporary distributive justice literature has typically focused elsewhere,[7] tying economic rewards (the currency of distributive justice) to three distinct concepts, all revolving around economic labor[8]: *value contributed*,[9] *effort expended*,[10] and *costs incurred*.[11]

It should be noted, however, that recent economic scholarship on equality of opportunity and responsibility-sensitive distributions have taken a different direction from philosophers. Instead, they seek to define so-called effort as connected to "human capital accumulation choices and labor supply decisions" by measuring (1) years of education and (2) hours of formal market labor as the twin outcomes of interest upon the basis of which inequalities may be understood as legitimate.[12] In other words, economists have argued that individuals must exert autonomous effort along two dimensions: toward hours and education. Thus, in our *Just Deserts* proposal, we must decide whether the observed outcome of interest is best represented by philosophers' or economists' suggestions.

I argue that philosophers have the upper hand. To understand why, let us first examine why contemporary philosophers of distributive justice rejected Aristotle's desert-basis, virtue—a desert-basis tentatively shared by Arneson as "conscientiousness" to pursue the right and good, or *subjective*

[6] Lamont (1994), 45–46.

[7] "What people deserve on the basis of virtue is not money but happiness." Hurka (2003), 59.

[8] Lamont and Favor (2014); Lamont (1994).

[9] Miller (1976), Miller (1989); Riley (1989).

[10] Sadurski (1985); Milne (1986).

[11] Dick (1975); Lamont (1997); For a fascinating and persuasive alternative account, notably attractive for its focus on autonomy, cf. Sher (1987), chap. 3.

[12] Cf. Pistolesi (2007); Lefranc et al. (2009); Aaberge et al. (2011); Almås et al. (2011).

virtue.[13] Contemporary philosophers have focused on economic labor for two *instrumental reasons*, expanding upon liberalism's foundation of property rights by labor found in the writings of John Locke[14]: (a) many market measurements are both more precise and more objective than virtue measurements in that (a1) all observers may ensure they are using the same unit of measure with inter-observer reliability and (a2) one may ignore differences between agents who do, and do not, exhibit "moral motives for their performances;"[15] and, secondly, (b) offering rewards to labor (but not virtue) aligns with Pareto-superior outcomes which, by definition, benefit all individuals. Further, philosophers argue that we ought to reward economic labor for one *intrinsic reason*, again following Locke: (c) our moral intuitions, no doubt aided by our intuitions of cause and effect, prefer "fitting" ends for acts of production. Intuitively, it seems "fitting" to reward a laborer with the end-product, or value, of their labor. That is to say, labor is a means of directly conferring value onto an object insofar as the product is the valued aim and purpose of the agent (or the principal on whose behalf the agent labors) and it is this object and its value that is the most fitting reward for labor.[16]

To further buttress philosophers' arguments, let us add arguments more easily noted once one begins the attempt to construct viable public policies of desert. Instrumental reason (a) broadly concerns measurement, yet philosophers' suggestions as well as economists' suggestions are both (a1) subject to precise, objective measurement and (a2) ignore motives. Philosophers' suggestions, however, (a3) exhibit far greater differentiation—thus allowing for a much more finely grained match between rewards and autonomous effort. Both years of education and hours of labor needlessly assume that individuals may only realize ~20 or ~4000 precise amounts of the observed outcome of interest while philosophers' suggestions may take on many more values.

More devastatingly, years of education (as a means of measuring effort toward human capital accumulation) and hours of formal market labor (as a means of measuring effort toward labor supply) are poor and inappropriate outcomes of interest as each fails to meet instrumental reason (b) as no

[13] Arneson (2007), 272ff.

[14] Lamont and Favor (2014).

[15] Miller (1999c), 134; Also, cf. Hurka (2003), 58.

[16] Sher (1987), 53–68, 99–103.

one actually rewards individuals in the real economy for their education or their hours, *simpliciter*. We do not reward the doctor who mends a child's broken arm for their education directly, nor for their hours directly, but we instead reward the doctor for combining both elements along with others in order to mend a broken arm. To state it more bluntly, to reward individuals for years of education incents unproductive investment in "years of education" just as rewarding individuals for hours of labor incents unproductive "work hours."

We may now see clearly that any rewards for *intermediary* observed outcomes of interest will always be second-best according to (b) because they will necessarily distort markets as individuals will put more autonomous effort into the intermediary outcomes than into the final observed outcomes of interest we actually desire and value. This is an even more powerful objection to years of education than hours of labor as the two second-degree observed outcomes of interest for economists are not hours and education but hours and productivity, that is, hours and the wage rate. That is to say, education is in fact at least a third-degree observed outcome of interest.

Furthermore, with respect to intrinsic reason (c), there may seem to be an immediate and intrinsic connection between productivity (human capital) and outputs just as there is between hours (labor supply) and outputs. Yet we must be clear that it is solely their combination, productivity times hours, that is truly intimately and intrinsically connected to the observed outcome of interest—and it is only the added value from autonomous effort that we would pay for if we did not wish to pay for the worker's endowment.

Finally, (a4) just as with *ex ante* equal opportunity policies, economists' twin observed outcomes of interest generate a difficult problem of computation. While philosophers must measure the individual's autonomous effort toward one observed outcome of interest, economists recommend measuring so-called effort for two observed outcomes of interest. Yet, how ought we reward this multivariate vector of autonomous effort? If Ann exhibits autonomous effort toward human capital accumulation at the 75th percentile but only exhibits autonomous effort toward labor supply at the 50th percentile, should she receive an identical reward to Bob who only exhibits autonomous effort toward human capital accumulation at the 50th percentile but exhibits autonomous effort toward labor supply at the 75th percentile? Even with an understanding of the function, *product = f(years of education, labor supply)*, there is no easy answer to this question that does not reduce to an exclusive focus on the final product. For these reasons, it is the final observed outcome of interest, and only the final observed outcome of interest, that should become part of the *Just Deserts* proposal.

7.2 Fixed Outcome

Of our three suggestions—value contributed, effort expended, or costs incurred—which will we use as the *Just Deserts* measure? As noted in Chap. 2, we cannot measure autonomous effort directly. Effort expended would thus be doubly incoherent: circularly measuring the extent to which one's autonomous effort depended upon one's autonomous effort and selecting an observed outcome of interest that cannot be observed.

From among our closely related remaining two contenders, we must choose value contributed. There is no good instrumental or intrinsic reason to sadistically reward those who choose occupations for which they have no taste or talent and, furthermore, incent a less productive economy that explicitly rewards inefficiencies.[17]

Having settled upon value contributed as the proper measure, now we must specify how the *Just Deserts* proposal will in fact measure this concept. First off, I should note that from the perspective of non-ideal philosophy, it may be impossible to measure the value contributed by an individual's economic labor. Although we might use a number of observed outcomes, including wealth, income, and others, none of these is quite specific enough to align with our other reasons for rewarding value contributed. For example, greater measures of wealth may be held for many other reasons, including gifts and reduced consumption. Income, also, is too broad a measure, including capital gains, the sale of assets, retirement withdrawals, and a number of other items extraneous to our core concept.[18] Instead, the economist's measure of value contributed from economic labor is

[17] While this is too quick, I ignore this for reasons of time and space. Further, Olsaretti has examined costs incurred at length. Olsaretti (2004), 49–55.

[18] Thus "wages, capital income, and all public cash transfers" is far too broad for a principle of desert. Aaberge et al. (2011); This is even more true for "labor, business, [and] capital [income, plus] realized capital gains, as well as.. unemployment insurance, sickness pay, parental leave payment, and pensions." This is because it is not the use of these compensation benefits but the value of these benefits to those who do and do not use these benefits that counts. For an overexpansive measurement of total market income in Sweden, cf. Björklund et al. (2011).

total employee compensation.[19] Thus, the *Just Deserts* proposal measures the autonomous effort exhibited toward value contributed by utilizing compensation as our non-ideal observed outcome of interest.[20]

- *Distributive justice based on a principle of desert rewards individuals in a manner that is exclusively sensitive to the autonomous effort they have exhibited toward the desert-base, total employee compensation.*

Having decided upon compensation as the best observed outcome of interest to use as a proxy for value contributed, we need to establish a few other details. In order to make proper measurements, comparisons, and allocations of *Just Deserts* among individuals according to vertical equity as stated in Chap. 3, we must use a ratio measure of compensation as opposed to an interval, ordinal, or nominal measure. Given the centrality of sensitivity within a principle of desert, it would be of little use to know that moral agent, *i*, deserved the sixth largest reward or that they deserved a reward greater than 20% of the population. This requirement for a ratio measure thus eliminates compensation-rank or compensation-percentile as the proper outcome of interest despite the fact that ordinal compensation may under certain conditions increase the stability of our non-ideal measurements of value contributed over long periods of time. Second, we may not use family compensation,[21] household compensation,[22] or the compensation of any *group* of individuals as our observed outcome of interest references only the individual moral agent who may exhibit autonomous effort and thus "deserve" a reward based upon their

[19] While earnings accounted for 98.6% of compensation in 1929, today they represent only 68.4% of compensation. As might be expected, employees with higher earnings have not only greater absolute values of benefits but greater percentage values of benefits within total compensation. Thus, the ideal *Just Deserts* policy would use total employee compensation as the outcome of interest. Unfortunately, the best dataset for the *Just Deserts* proposal does not include dollar values of benefits, so we make do with a second-best model in Chap. 12 that measures labor income. Kaufman and Hotchkiss (2000), 422; BLS—Bureau of Labor Statistics (2014); Total employee compensation should not be confused with "differential compensation." Cf. Dick (1975).

[20] Under ideal circumstances, I think we would use the compensation offered within an ideal market rather than actual compensation within an actual market. To see the practical difficulties to which this is the ideal solution, cf. Sidgwick (1999), 54–55.

[21] For example, Mazumder's recent work uses "family income." Mazumder (2001a).

[22] Lefranc et al. (2009); Marrero and Rodríguez (2013).

agent responsibility.[23] Third, we are technically interested in measuring the *present expected value* of individual total employee compensation, that is, the expected money value of wages and benefits at the time of the economic labor so compensated. That is to say, if an employer offers to pay a defined benefit pension or stock options to certain employees, each employee has been paid not in the future pension payments or option proceeds themselves but in the present expected value of such compensation at the time of labor performed. Similarly, received unemployment insurance payments do not count as compensation as we have already counted the compensation from which the premiums were deducted to pay for the insurance. Likewise, vacation days and sick days are not to be counted as compensation as, again, that has already been counted in one's salary—whether the employer pays $100 for 100 widgets and 10 vacation days or $100 for 100 widgets and 50 vacation days, the total compensation is an identical $100 for 100 identical widgets. To repeat, the present expected value of individual total employee compensation is measured by how much someone else in a market system valued an observed outcome connected to this one individual's economic labor at the time of labor performed.[24]

7.3 In Sum, This Chapter Has Argued

- *Distributive justice based on a principle of desert rewards individuals in a manner that is exclusively sensitive to the autonomous effort they have exhibited toward the desert-base, total employee compensation.*

[23] This is to say, no group, whether that be a "family," "sex," "ethnos," and so on, may "deserve" a reward, although they may be entitled to such through other ethical principles. While Rawls' minimax solution applies to groups, he says nothing about intragroup distributions, which I take to be a shortcoming. Just as an adequate poverty measure must be sensitive to not only the average "poverty gap" but also the distribution of resources among the impoverished, so must we seek a just distribution of resources among the members of each statistically distinct group. Cf. Sen (1976).

[24] Note that the measure of compensation required for a *Just Deserts* proposal is not technically the same as compensation as portrayed by the Bureau of Labor Statistics. These statistics are interested in the total compensation per hour of *work* while we are interested in the total compensation per year of *time*. For more details on total employee compensation survey data collected by the Bureau of Labor Statistics, cf. BLS—Bureau of Labor Statistics (2015).

CHAPTER 8

Measure for Merit

This disposition to admire, and almost to worship, the rich and the powerful, and to despise, or, at least, to neglect persons of poor and mean condition, though necessary both to establish and to maintain the distinction of ranks and the order of society, is, at the same time, the great and most universal cause of the corruption of our moral sentiments.—Adam Smith, Theory of Moral Sentiments, 1759, I.iii.3

8.1 Measuring Justice: De Gustibus Non Disputandum Est

The theory of desert from Chap. 3 may be used to answer the question of proper reward in myriad ways as there are plausibly a great diversity of "appraisal grounds" arguments for a correspondence between certain rewards and certain observed outcomes of interest.[1] As the proper observed outcome of interest for an economic reward is best measured by present expected value of total employee compensation as a proxy for value contributed, which measure of economic reward best corresponds to this observed outcome of interest as an appropriate deserved reward?

Thinking now of practicable public policy, distributive justice concerns itself not with discrete economic goods as they are, but with distributions of

[1] Knight (2011), 155.

J. T. Dwyer, *Chance, Merit, and Economic Inequality*,
https://doi.org/10.1007/978-3-030-21126-4_8

some "fundamental substantial good."[2] Thus, we are uninterested in just allocations of liters of water, minutes of solitude, letters in one's first name, romantic affection, religious travel expenses, or the infinite other commensurable, non-fundamental goods,[3] including the three most commonly cited public policy arenas for distributive justice, that is, education, health, or jobs. Distributive justice is therefore only interested in one fundamental good (more technically, any non-fungible or incommensurable goods that may exist and only to the extent that they are incommensurable). Stated differently, no one may step up to the bar of justice and justly claim that they deserve better reading skills, liver function, or vacation benefits if the fundamental good is already justly distributed. Equally important, however, is that there is no requirement that desert covers absolutely everything—that is, one might deserve a scholarship but not shoes just as one might deserve one fundamental good but, perhaps, not another. The two fundamental goods most often suggested by theorists of distributive justice are *welfare* and *resources*,[4] occupying pride of place in the "mental state" and "objective list" categories of fundamental goods.[5] Below I briefly sketch the rationales behind each but ultimately conclude that a public policy of distributive justice ought to use a money metric resourcist definition of Cohen's *advantage* by which we can best capture both welfare and resources as well as Sen's proposed capabilities (or midfare).

8.1.1 *Welfare*

The argument on behalf of welfare as the proper fundamental good, the appropriate "currency of justice," rests principally on the intuition that welfare is what we ultimately care about.[6] Note, however, that even if this were true, this may still not be the right argument with respect to correspondence to value contributed—the chosen observed outcome of

[2] Christiano (2007).

[3] Cf. Knight (2009), chap. 4.

[4] Sen has suggested a third: capabilities. Roemer briefly raises five criticisms, the most important being an assumption that there is no "universally correct or unique answer to the distribution question." Thus, I focus on welfare and resources but return to capabilities in a brief concluding note. Roemer (1996), 188–193.

[5] Hirose (2014).

[6] Although note Cohen's claim that the "egalitarian distributor need not distribute according to what sensible people care about." Cohen (2011d), 100–101.

interest. If one individual has produced for another individual a precise quantity of value (and an unknown quantity of welfare), why should we think that the laborer then ***deserves a precise reward*** of welfare rather than of value? Hurka has even claimed that if an individual "does not derive joy from his earnings, that is no concern of economic [distributive] desert."[7] For Hurka, moral desert has a correspondence between the intrinsic values of virtue and happiness, while distributive desert has a correspondence between the instrumental values of work and income.[8]

Setting this first argument aside, however, a more immediate problem with welfare-based distributions is that of valid measurement. Many philosophers and economists are, as a consequence, uncomfortable with what is known as *cardinal interpersonal utility comparisons*,[9] stating that "epistemic and practical obstacles"[10] may rule out attempts to distribute welfare. Although it may seem obvious that the welfare gains to the citizens of Rome from an intact Rome "outweighed" the gains to Nero's welfare from a burned Rome,[11] there may be no way to validly measure units of welfare in one individual, let alone across individuals. Due to this weakness, Rawls, Dworkin, and other scholars of distributive justice have rejected welfare as the reward of choice.[12]

As you may disagree with economists' understanding of Nero (and Adler has offered some sophisticated arguments in favor of interpersonal welfare comparisons),[13] let us offer a few other arguments that might hold even under ideal conditions where the measurement objection is overcome. The literature has offered objections on the grounds of sour disposition, expensive taste, and other-regarding welfare. Before we reject welfare as our reward on these grounds, however, note that these three objections do not properly account for circumstances of chance.[14] If an element of one's

[7] Hurka (2003), 58.

[8] Hurka (2003), 57–59.

[9] This is not the case, however, for all components of welfare economics or social choice theory, and there is a difference between cardinal and ordinal comparisons as well, for example, Rawls' difference principle rests upon ordinal comparisons that allow us to identify representative individuals within groups and rank their welfare levels across groups.

[10] Cohen (2011a), 96.

[11] Sen (1970), 99.

[12] Rawls (1999 (1971)); Dworkin (1981a,b).

[13] Adler (2011), chap. 3.

[14] Arneson (1989), 83–84.

circumstances of chance is the bad luck of a sour disposition, the bad luck of expensive taste, or the bad luck of a jealous, envious, altruistic, or sadistic personality, we cannot fault the individual and hold them blameworthy and accountable for factors beyond their control. Thus, in each case we must offer extra recompense to those whose tastes are most difficult to please and reward other-regarding vice over virtue—not a promising outcome for a principle of distributive justice.

Sen has made a more powerful objection to welfare as the proper reward by considering the possibility of malformed subjective perceptions (more popularly known as Aesop's fox's "sour grapes") such as one might find in the "battered slave, tamed housewife, broken unemployed, [and] hopeless destitute"[15] who no longer want what they have learned they cannot have. The problem suggested by Sen is that if we choose to reward individuals with welfare, it seems very plausible that such a policy might be counterintuitively required to expend all of the means to realizing welfare on oppressors (who now have costly welfare functions) rather than the oppressed (who now, through no fault or choice of their own, have very cheap welfare functions). These problems of idiosyncratic, subjective, and possibly exogenous welfare functions remain, in John Roemer's words, "the Achilles heel ... of any *welfarist* approach to distributive justice."[16]

8.1.2 Resources

If welfare receives mixed reviews, then what can we say in favor of resources from a public policy standpoint? First, and as already noted, by resources we do not mean six loaves of bread and 19 liters of water for each individual, still less do we attempt to reward individuals with other individuals' bodies, tastes, or talents—dividing beauty, mathematical acumen, and walking stamina among the population.[17] By resources we mean money-value[18]: a perfectly fungible unit of value by which an individual may consume, save,

[15] Sen (1987), 11.

[16] Roemer (1996), 245. Also note that in this instance, Roemer means by endogenous that one's welfare might be "determined *inter alia* by the resources one receives or expects to receive."

[17] The *Just Deserts* proposal has no interest in rectifying the injustice of unequal sightedness by taking eyes from the sighted and giving them to the blind. Nozick (2013).

[18] Here I assume that money-value is identical to purchasing power–it is the use of one's money that matters, not its denomination.

invest, and accomplish any project of their desire and choosing. Second, as opposed to welfare, economists and all others will agree that resources possess an observable market value—you may disagree with the market price to be sure, but it still offers an objective measure orders of magnitude less costly to ascertain and more accurate than any measure of subjective welfare.

Based upon market exchanges, resources embody public agreement as to values generating both an audit trail[19] for measurement and a foundation of intercomparability among different individuals. When the mad scientist in Chap. 2 offered Sherlock and Irene their natural lottery endowments, $990,000 and $10,000 of lifetime income, it was clear and self-evident that (a) Sherlock and Irene had a *different* quantity of resources, (b) Sherlock had a *greater* quantity of resources, and (c) Sherlock's quantity of resources amounted to a precise *ratio* of Irene's quantity of resources (i.e., 99:1). As an objective measure, note that it is unimportant how much the individual subjectively values their individual allocation or the allocations of others. Furthermore, no matter how oppressors or other circumstances of chance alter the welfare or resource functions of the oppressed, the resource view does not drive the oppressed into blissful poverty via adaptive preferences.

Lastly, as mentioned above, resources may be the best fit with respect to the "correspondence grounds" of desert. If one individual has produced for another individual a precise quantity of money-value (and an unknown quantity of welfare), there is a strong intuitive connection to distributing a reward in the same currency, money-value.

8.1.3 Capabilities

While most philosophers have focused on the relative advantages of distributing either welfare or resources, I should note that Sen proposed that the correct reward is *capabilities*, an approach further developed and expanded upon by Nussbaum.[20] Sen suggests that we are more interested in what a person may do (capabilities) rather than their potential consumption (resources) or what they feel via realized consumption (welfare). While there is some attraction to this idea, the principle of desert demands that we go beyond what we ultimately care about to make an "appraisal"

[19] Cf. "the public audit constraint" of feasibility. Wolff (2003), 229.

[20] Sen (1985); Nussbaum (2001); and Nussbaum (2013).

argument that some fundamental good properly corresponds to value contributed in the way that rewards ought to correspond to desert. This poses a problem as it appears there is no single fungible capabilities unit that encompasses all capabilities. Nonetheless, Sen tries to squeeze capabilities in between resources and welfare in what some philosophers have named "midfare"[21]—that which is posterior to having goods and anterior to having utility.[22]

Sen is of course correct to highlight the question of which particular outcomes (or rewards) ought individuals have the choice/opportunity/freedom/capability to realize. While Sen has argued that midfare (doings or beings) is a superior choice to welfare in that it avoids the consequences of adaptive preferences, what is its superiority to resources as our reward?

> Imagine that we offered Helen and Fiona equality of opportunity to eat almonds but, due to early malnutrition, Helen cannot easily digest almonds and must eat twice as many almonds to receive identical nutrition, strength, energy, and muscle power as Fiona. Here Sen suggests that justice demands that we give Helen more resources (almonds) than we would have in the absence of a midfare analysis. Is Sen correct?

One potential means to encompass Sen's objection in favor of midfare as well as powerful arguments in favor of welfare is to follow Cohen's suggestion that we adopt the placeholder "advantage" as we try to discern the constituent parts that make up the currency of distributive justice. The currently best defended potential rewards are resources, midfare, and welfare. Although the empirical portion of this book, Chaps. 11 and 12, will focus more narrowly on what we typically consider to be money resources as economic reward, I want to use Cohen's concept of "advantage" to sketch how *Just Deserts* could incorporate both midfare and welfare as well. Notably, we might instead consider that these three rewards (resources, midfare, and welfare) are simply three important classes of resource: (1) external, transferable resources such as almonds and money, (2) (plausibly non-transferable) midfare conversion factor resources such as digestive enzymes and literacy levels that turn (1) into midfare (doings and beings), for example, almonds into muscle power and money into an informed reading of the newspaper, and (3) (plausibly non-transferable)

[21] Cohen (1993).
[22] Sen (1985), 11.

welfare conversion factor resources that turn (2) into welfare, for example, muscle power and reading the newspaper into well-being. Taking Sen's objections seriously, the distribution of economic reward ought to then account for differences in non-transferable *capacitative* and *consumptive* circumstances of chance, that is, the circumstances of chance involved in the production of midfare and welfare, respectively.[23]

In this way, if Fiona and Helen exhibited value contributed of $100 and $50, *Just Deserts* first accounts for productive circumstances of chance to ascertain, for example, that they exhibited identical autonomous effort toward value contributed. *Just Deserts* could then account for the money-value of capacitative and consumptive circumstances of chance held by Fiona and Helen in order that they each held an identical aggregate value of external, transferable resources and non-transferable capacitative and consumptive resources, thus, identical "advantage" includes the money-value of all economic resources. In this way, perhaps I can capture the interest of proponents of all three "currencies" of distributive justice.[24]

Unfortunately, it must be noted that measurement of capacitative and consumptive circumstances of chance is not susceptible to the same methods the *Just Deserts* proposal used to measure productive circumstances of chance. Nonetheless, insofar as there are objective measures of, for example, depression and a market to escape and/or avoid depression, this consumptive conversion resource factor has a market value. Similarly, one may say the same of literacy as a capacitative conversion resource factor. In this way, each individual could deserve a reward of the total value of all economic resources (external, capacitative, and consumptive resources as our best public policy measure of Cohen's advantage) that is strictly sensitive to their autonomous effort toward value contributed.

- *Distributive justice based on a principle of desert favors the money-value of all economic resources as the reward linked by "appraisal grounds" to total employee compensation where all economic resources may include*

[23] Note that this is a point on which Cohen wished to press Dworkin, "...since people are made differently, both naturally and socially, not only (a fact to which Dworkin is sensitive) in their capacities to produce, but also (the fact to which [Dworkin] is insensitive) in their capacities to obtain fulfillment." Cohen (2011a), 90.

[24] As Roemer has argued, "With a suitably general conception of what resources are, these two conceptions [equality of resources and equality of welfare] cannot be distinguished." Roemer (1986).

external resources, midfare conversion factor resources, and welfare conversion factor resources.

8.1.4 Income and Wealth

To be clear, when I say the market value of all economic resources[25] is the proper reward subject to a public policy of distributive justice, not only does this *Just Deserts* proposal overturn the more frequently discussed unmerited income inequality, but it also upends unmerited wealth inequality, a far more severe inequality among individuals.

Quite simply, wealth inequality currently constitutes an important contemporary injustice perpetrated by unmerited circumstances of chance. It is currently estimated that the combined wealth of the globe's richest 1% will overtake that of the other 99% in 2016.[26] Surprisingly, these numbers are nearly unchanged in an analysis of the United States alone. While Saez and Piketty have estimated that *income inequality* in the United States rewarded the top 10% of income recipients with 50% of all income in 2012,[27] Saez and Zucman's estimate of *wealth inequality* suggests that the wealthiest 10% in the United States own 77% of all wealth. Furthermore, the wealthiest 0.1% of the population (160,000 families) controlled wealth nearly equal to that of the bottom 90% (145 million families) in 2012, 22% and 23% of total wealth, respectively.[28] While the *Just Deserts* proposal may not lead precisely to Americans' surprisingly egalitarian ideal of wealth distribution (true across income brackets, political ideology, and sex)[29]—with the top 20% controlling only 1/3 of wealth—it will remove all unmerited wealth inequality whereby the distribution of the full stock of economic reward will for the first time in history be exclusively sensitive to autonomous effort rather than circumstances of chance.

In conclusion, I should note that one of the limitations of the dataset that I will use for my simulation in Chap. 12 is that I am only able to focus on the *Just Deserts* distribution of the external, transferable

[25] Minus the returns to land (rent) and capital (interest) one held at the beginning of the *Just Deserts* year and did not subsequently gift, sell, or otherwise transfer. This ensures a market for the efficient use of land and capital.

[26] Hardoon (2015).

[27] Saez and Piketty (2003).

[28] Saez and Zucman (2014).

[29] Norton and Ariely (2011).

resources from labor income as there is no wealth supplement for the particular years of interest for my analysis nor are there any measurements of total compensation, nor of capacitative or consumptive conversion factor resources. Nonetheless, I should note that Sen's other work on non-ideal theory suggests he might support *Just Deserts*' use of external, transferable resources as a significantly comprehensive reward which can measure and solve an enormous and clinically significant injustice today rather than obstruct *Just Deserts* until the perfect distributive policy of all "advantage" comes along the day after tomorrow.

8.2 In Sum, This Chapter Has Argued

- *Distributive justice based on a principle of desert favors the money-value of all economic resources as the reward linked by "appraisal grounds" to total employee compensation where all economic resources may include external resources, midfare conversion factor resources, and welfare conversion factor resources.*

CHAPTER 9

The Individual Moral Agent

Who or what counts as an individual moral agent, deserving of an economic reward? In answer to this question, we may usefully borrow from a field of economics research known as earnings dynamics. Typically, the earnings dynamics literature has focused its attention on father-to-son intergenerational earnings elasticity that requires measures on multiple generations of individuals in order to ascertain how earnings change from father to son—in other words, how far the apple falls from the tree. It is this research that allowed us to say in Chap. 6 how many generations must pass before descendants of average employees of S&P 500 firms mingle as equals with descendants of their CEOs. The models used in this research to connect fathers' earnings to sons' earnings typically include a persistent, permanent, or lifetime component—that is, these researchers are interested not in the relationship between a father's earnings at age 42 and a son's earnings at age 27, or vice versa, but in the relationship between father's and son's lifetime earnings. One difficulty for such models is that the estimate of the father's and son's lifetime component seems to require measures of earnings for the entire lifetime of both the father and the son, a feat of considerable data capture that, to my knowledge, no nationally representative survey has yet accomplished.[1]

[1] Even in Sweden, such administrative income data is readily available to researchers beginning only in 1968. Cf. Björklund et al. (2011).

J. T. Dwyer, *Chance, Merit, and Economic Inequality*,
https://doi.org/10.1007/978-3-030-21126-4_9

Faced with this obstacle and very limited data, the first intergenerational mobility researchers utilized one year of empirical earnings for each individual as a proxy or surrogate measure for fathers' and sons' lifetime earnings components. The results of these early studies suggested that sons' earnings were indeed dependent upon fathers' earnings, one plausible outcome of the natural lottery, but only weakly so.[2] With the development and continuation of the Panel Study of Income Dynamics beginning in 1968, the best intergenerational earnings[3] data readily available to scholars of the US economy, Gary Solon demonstrated that better estimates of the lifetime component of both fathers' and sons' earnings could be derived from averages of multi-year earnings as proxies for lifetime earnings that reduced the noise of transitory one-year earnings shocks.[4] Other research showed that multi-year estimates composed of mean empirical earnings data from an individual's fifth decade (40–50 years old) was a further improved proxy of lifetime earnings.[5] The result was that these updated models, by utilizing empirically more robust proxies for "lifetime earnings," overturned prior findings of weak dependence in favor of sons' earnings showing moderate to strong dependence upon fathers' earnings—especially in the United States.[6]

There are a few notable problems that remain. First, even among the most recent research, many of these models remove individuals from the analysis, a choice that is impermissible for a *Just Deserts* proposal. For example, had these father-son models actually been used for *ex ante* equal opportunity purposes, they would have nothing to say with respect to the dependence of female earnings on circumstances of chance and autonomous effort because women had been removed from the analysis.[7]

[2] Sewell and Hauser (1975); Behrman and Tarbman (1985); Becker (1988).

[3] For the present, I focus on lifetime compensation. Wealth is of course subject to the same joint distribution dependent upon chance and merit. While there is disagreement, economists' average estimate is that 50% of capital accumulation in the United States stems from gifts or bequests, not autonomous effort. Murphy and Nagel (2004), 116; Beckert (2008).

[4] Solon (1992).

[5] Baker and Solon (1999); Mazumder (2001b).

[6] "The most firmly established result in this area of research is that intergenerational reproduction [i.e., elasticity of earned incomes] is lowest in the Nordic countries and highest in the United States (with a correlation coefficient two-thirds higher than in Sweden)." Piketty (2014), 484.

[7] Cf. Pistolesi (2007); Lefranc et al. (2009); Aaberge et al. (2011); Björklund et al. (2011).

Our economy has changed drastically in many ways,[8] one of which is that many more women are today contributing greater value in the formal labor market,[9] and there is no reason to believe the economy will cease to be a dynamic system.[10] Not only must we include women in our distributive justice proposal, we must include all moral agents (every person who is *compos mentis*) as we hold each and every individual responsible for their autonomous effort. In fact, it would be highly detrimental to realizing distributive justice if those whose pecuniary self-interest conflicted with such a distribution were able to manipulate the distribution of economic reward by removing themselves or their connections from the jurisdiction of the *Just Deserts* proposal.

Second, while previous earnings dynamics research has simply removed measurements of zero annual earnings from multi-year proxy measures,[11] this too is not possible for a *Just Deserts* proposal. Although the likelihood of misleading models was estimated to be high if measurements of zero earnings during a five- or ten-year period, for example, during the individual's fifth decade, were given full weight as a representative proxy of the individual's lifetime earnings,[12] years with zero compensation are equally important to the *Just Deserts* proposal as years with positive compensation and may not be discarded.

Third, as mentioned above, some intergenerational earnings dynamics models require proxy measurements of sons' earnings during the ages of 40–50, or potentially full measurements of lifetime earnings at retirement, but the *Just Deserts* proposal, however, may not wait until individuals retire to enact distributive justice.[13] Distributive justice is not a gold watch received on one's last day of work, but is something to be "continuously" implemented. For this reason, the *Just Deserts* proposal ignores proxies and

[8] Atkinson (2015), 18.

[9] Such changes are in fact interesting drivers of household inequality as high-earning men and high-earning women began to marry since the 1980s. Schwartz (2010).

[10] As mentioned in Chap. 4, this dynamism is a key feature in the argument for *ex post* equality of opportunity.

[11] Almås et al. (2011).

[12] For a discussion of the difficulties of estimating lifetime income, cf. Benus and Morgan (1975).

[13] In contrast to Aaberge et al., we are not interested in measuring "permanent income" once an individual is eligible for retirement, but the dynamic measure of endowment—a quantity that exists when one is age 10, 35, 42, or 88. Cf. Aaberge et al. (2011).

uses the actual cumulative sum total of lifetime compensation measured on a rolling annual basis. This original method offers us maximal information for an annually implemented policy with universal scope that is sensitive to a dynamic economy and is possible not because of new administrative data sources, but because distributive justice requires knowledge of cumulative, *dynamic endowment.*[14]

To better fix ideas, imagine that for Average Joe at age 35, the present value of the sum total of compensation he has received throughout his lifetime for formal market labor amounts to $400,000. Comparing Joe to those most similarly situated, we have precisely measured his *lifetime* autonomous effort as identical to the population mean and reward Joe accordingly. The following year his annual compensation is $0, thus we again observe a new sum lifetime total of $400,000 lifetime compensation for Joe at age 36. A proper comparison after this second year reveals that Joe has now exhibited less than mean lifetime autonomous effort and we reward Joe accordingly. As is clear here and will be discussed further below, the proper measure is not individuals' annual compensation,[15] but lifetime compensation.

- *Distributive justice based on a principle of desert applies to all moral agents capable of agent responsibility for the desert-basis, that is, present value of dynamic lifetime compensation, including those with zero lifetime compensation, and is updated with a new measurement of the desert-basis at each new time period.*

9.1 One Life To Live

This now exposes a further assumption of a *Just Deserts* proposal, an important addition to the economic distributive justice literature. Although there are other interesting philosophies of identity,[16] I think that most readers share a second fundamental moral intuition: that the moral agent persists

[14] Note that I have very much rejected the claim that "An efficient ability tax cannot contend with a dynamic endowment." Sugin (2011), 252.

[15] Almås et al. (2011).

[16] Parfit (1971).

throughout their lifetime.[17] It would trouble us to intervene upon an individual either *ex ante* or *ex post* if there were not some morally relevant diachronic persistence[18] to the moral agent receiving the intervention over the relevant time period. Thus, we believe that Sherlock at age 55 is more than merely intimately connected to Sherlock at age 30, rather, the elder Sherlock may justly be held accountable for the autonomous effort, or agent responsibility, of the younger. If this is the case, then what we are truly after, allowing methodological concerns to follow from ethical foundations,[19] is a just distribution of resources across the entire lifetime of the moral agent.[20] This follows the intuition that "it seems undeniable that a lifetime is a morally significant unit."[21] Nonetheless, due to its dynamic nature, the *Just Deserts* proposal allows any individual who started out with low effort to rocket back to the top—all they have to do is exhibit more autonomous effort, which by definition is independent of any circumstances of chance such as past poverty.

The lifetime unit, however, raises some unforeseen complications. Younger individuals have obviously shorter lifetimes and thus lesser dynamic endowments than their elders. It is no less a circumstance of chance that one individual may be 30 years old while another may be 60 years old. Based on autonomous effort, should the younger individual have access to the sum total of all economic resources, even those produced by the older individual before the younger was even a moral agent?[22] If yes, exactly as in the case of all other circumstances of chance on which observed outcomes depend, this would mean that labor market entrants and retirees

[17] Note, however, that Fleurbaey presents an extremely interesting discussion of second chances, that is, how to manage new moral agents within the same "person." Fleurbaey (2008).

[18] Sher connects this "persistence" or stability over time to our status as deliberating agents. Sher (1987), chap. 9.

[19] Without wishing to commit fully to methodological or ontological individualism, the *Just Deserts* proposal is certainly individual-centered. Cf. Robeyns (2005).

[20] cf. Holtug and Lippert-Rasmussen (2007), 10ff.; Daniels (1996), 259–264; Nagel (1991), 69; Dworkin (1981b), 304–305; Rawls (1999 (1971)), 56.

[21] McKerlie (2007), 172. Stated differently, there is no such thing as, and thus no problems raised by, intrapersonal desert. The *Just Deserts* proposal is, however, quite open to the possibility that someone might generate a conceptually compelling, empirically driven method to discount autonomous effort that belonged to "another" moral agent in a prior period of the same lifetime. Cf. Fleurbaey on "second chances." Fleurbaey (2008).

[22] For a relevant discussion of age and inequality, cf. Paglin (1975); Danziger et al. (1976).

with identical lifetime autonomous effort would possess identical amounts of post-intervention resources despite their very different labor market compensation. Stated differently, seniority is a significant factor of dynamic endowment. The justice of a model that treats age as a circumstance of chance is that Irene, who died unexpectedly young, received (although almost certainly did not consume) her $1 million in lifetime reward in spite of this untimely fact. The risk is the plausible moral hazard. Once a young individual has consumed their lifetime supply of resources at age 30, I'm not sure how many would be so fully committed to desert as to withhold further resources until that individual increase their lifetime autonomous effort?

In the models I share with you in accord with the *Just Deserts* proposal in Chap. 12, I will thus share age-based models that both (a) treat age as strictly a circumstance of chance and (b) temper this condition by treating age as a unique and dynamic circumstance of chance that we expect each moral agent will pass through during the course of a full life expectancy. Specifically, the former gives all individuals a share in the total sum of all economic resources while the latter subtracts from the reward the total sum of employee compensation earned by their contemporaries before some relative point in time. For example, one might remove from Joe's possible reward any lifetime compensation earned by Joe's contemporaries before Joe's 25th birthday (see Chap. 12 for a real-world example).

Using an individual's lifetime as the proper moral unit raises a second complication that, unfortunately, has no plausible *ex post* resolution. Even among the same birth cohort, some individuals may die much younger than others. Although we have accounted in some ways for the brute luck of death by accounting for "life expectancy," as I said early in Chap. 2, death remains one of the elements of chance that a *Just Deserts* proposal is powerless to eliminate. For example, life expectancy at birth for males in 2010 in McDowell County, WV, is 21.1 fewer years than for females in Marin County, CA, (63.9 and 85.0 years, respectively).[23] These life expectancy disparities are further compounded in part because lower income (probabilistically lower dynamic endowment) individuals have shorter average life spans than higher income (probabilistically higher dynamic endowment) individuals. Not only does the current market economy reward circumstances of chance to a significant degree, but even a

[23] Wang et al. (2013).

progressive safety net program such as the social security system, designed in part to mitigate such unmerited inequality, is in fact regressive due to different life expectancies.[24] These life expectancy facts of the natural lottery should strike us as a further injustice to be remedied by distribution. It is not simply the case that the natural lottery gave some individuals a larger allocation of resources each year of their lifetime, but in addition, these same lucky individuals live a greater number of years over which to consume and control these resources. Given these complications, the *Just Deserts* proposal ought to incorporate a life expectancy coefficient. In this way, 65 years of one individual's lifetime reward may be identical to 85 years of another's even in models that do not treat age as strictly a circumstance of chance.

As a last minor note, although wealth inequality is much greater than income inequality and the aggregate capital stock is greater than aggregate annual income (on the order of 4–7 times greater),[25] the latter is not true for lifetime income. If the average individual has lived half a lifetime and an average lifetime is 60 years, then aggregate lifetime income to be distributed in any 1 year is equivalent to 30 years of aggregate annual income. It is of course true that the vast majority of that income has already been consumed, but this accounting exercise further highlights the magnitude of the *Just Deserts* proposal.[26]

- *Distributive justice based on a principle of desert understands the moral agent as persisting across a lifetime and recognizes that circumstances of chance include both age and life expectancy.*

9.2 In Sum, This Chapter Has Argued

- *Distributive justice based on a principle of desert applies to all moral agents capable of agent responsibility for the desert-basis, that is, present value of dynamic lifetime compensation, including those with zero*

[24] Pointing to the need for endowment-based policies rather than universal policies such as an increased official retirement age. Coronado et al. (2000).

[25] Piketty (2014).

[26] Even if for extra-desert reasons, we put capital income or even both capital income and capital under a different distributive justice regime.

lifetime compensation, and is updated with a new measurement of the desert-basis at each new time period.
- *Distributive justice based on a principle of desert understands the moral agent as persisting across a lifetime and recognizes that circumstances of chance include both age and life expectancy.*

CHAPTER 10

The Natural Lottery Alone

10.1 The Natural Lottery Alone

Although the *Just Deserts* proposal logically requires less scientific effort than *ex ante* equal opportunity policy interventions as argued in Chap. 4, we still need data on what economists name endowment, philosophers term circumstances of chance, and social scientists term privilege. One suggestion is that, "In actual practice, the society in question shall decide through some kind of political process, what it wishes to deem 'circumstances,'" a conclusion drawn because Roemer "[did] not have a theory which would enable [him] to discover exactly what aspects of a person's environment are beyond [their] control."[1] The *Just Deserts* proposal has such a theory and thus postpones this "political process,"[2] attractive as it may be, until after implementing a baseline that no skeptic can refuse. This baseline is reached via a simple, administratively efficient process that wastes as few resources as possible while generating precise measurements of each individual's autonomous effort toward our outcome of interest.

[1] Roemer (1998), 8.

[2] The dangers of a political process, rather than finding a starting point that all can agree on, is both a misspecification of circumstances as well as effort, often by treating years of education and hours of labor as "Effort." Fleurbaey (1995b); Almås et al. (2011); Lefranc et al. (2009); Pistolesi (2007).

J. T. Dwyer, *Chance, Merit, and Economic Inequality*,
https://doi.org/10.1007/978-3-030-21126-4_10

The *Just Deserts* proposal's theory of circumstance selection is the following: it is absolutely certain that all phenomena prior to or at the time of the individual's birth constitute factors entirely beyond their control, pure circumstances of chance. Thus, we use only measurements of such phenomena in order to generate our precise, indirect measurement of autonomous effort. This entirely avoids the conundrum as to what extent various outcomes in the chain of outcomes we call life were dependent upon the individual's autonomous effort.[3] For example, while Laurel's education and/or professional legal training is strongly correlated with lifetime compensation, attempts to directly ascertain or estimate the full extent to which one individual's education or training is in turn dependent upon autonomous effort is, using any other method than I have just recommended, a political and methodological minefield. While this pre-birth natural lottery requirement is a severe restriction on our allowable circumstances of chance, I nevertheless defend it and show in Chap. 12 that it more than suffices to eliminate a significant quantity of unmerited inequality.

To reveal some of the power of this method, let us suppose that we follow contemporary earnings dynamics research, and we find that lifetime compensation depends to some extent upon one's father's lifetime compensation.[4] However, a skeptic of such a model might say: is it possible that the father's lifetime compensation is in some manner dependent upon the autonomous effort of the child? Note that if the father's compensation were dependent upon a circumstance of chance related to the child, a circumstance of chance related to another individual, or upon another individual's autonomous effort, the skeptic's objection would have no force. Yet the skeptic demands that we reject the possibility that the father's lifetime compensation is dependent to any extent upon the child's autonomous effort—a possibility that would vitiate our entire theory of desert. Can the *Just Deserts* proposal meet this challenge?

[3] "Among our inequalities some are initial inequalities or inequalities of birth. Others arise only during the course of our lives. It is next to impossible to determine how many of the second inequalities are morally deserved." Spiegelberg (1999), 151; Spiegelberg (1944).

[4] Aaberge et al. use father's annual earnings in one year when son was 16–18 years of age as a circumstance of chance. Interestingly, they suggest that their model was not sensitive to such a one-year point estimate when fathers were different ages as a substitution of "years of education," although not "pre-birth years of education," yielded similar results. Cf. Aaberge et al. (2011).

Our theory from Chap. 2 has clearly specified pathways to measure autonomous effort. Observed outcomes are dependent upon two mutually exclusive, exhaustive, and independent components: circumstances of chance and autonomous effort. To be explicit, one individual's autonomous effort may not be directly dependent upon the autonomous effort of another individual.[5] Thus, the only dependency pathway of a post-birth parental outcome dependent upon a child's autonomous effort looks like the following: (1) a child-related outcome (Outcome #1: score on Barry's math exam) is jointly dependent upon child-related circumstances of chance and the child's autonomous effort; (2) the parent's posterior outcome (Outcome #2: parent's lifetime compensation) is jointly dependent upon parent-related circumstances of chance—including, to some extent, the child's outcome #1—and the parent's autonomous effort; (3) the observed outcome of interest (Outcome #3: child's lifetime compensation) is dependent to some extent upon Outcome #2 (parent's lifetime compensation). If this is the case, we must account for the fact that this outcome of interest, Outcome #3, was dependent upon the child's autonomous effort by two different pathways (directly and indirectly). Not only does this lead to a convoluted mathematical process in an attempt to isolate the child's autonomous effort, it cannot avoid the skeptic's objection. Each such post-birth estimate of the child's autonomous effort on the math exam or anything else will continue to run into the skeptic's objection that we have confused the *explanans* and *explanandum* by not properly disentangling cause and effect along both the direct and indirect pathways. This forces us into an infinite regress backward in which perhaps the math score is indirectly dependent to some extent upon the child's autonomous effort on a reading test at age four, which is itself indirectly dependent to some extent upon the child's autonomous effort on some other earlier outcome, *ad infinitum*.

The *Just Deserts* proposal avoids this convolution and possible mathematical pleonasm by restricting all information to pre-natural lottery circumstances of chance—the individual's dynamic birth-endowment.[6]

[5] Cf. "But if we fully understand Reid's notion of agent causation we can see, I think, that no event or agent can cause someone to agent-cause some change." Rowe (1987).

[6] Thus, we may not even use "number of siblings" as a circumstance, rather we must use "pre-birth number of siblings" until the skeptic acquiesces or is ignored. For "number of siblings" based research, cf. Aaberge et al. (2011); Nor may we use the outcomes of IQ tests taken at the age of 18, cf. Björklund et al. (2011).

This pre-birth information is immune to the skeptic's concerns and, furthermore, already captures an enormous amount of the post-birth information of interest—one's educational attainment, work hours, place of residence, and so on, likely all depend on the natural lottery. That is to say, if the only circumstances of chance which our skeptic will accept as pure brute luck are constituted by the natural lottery,[7] our measurements of autonomous effort toward lifetime compensation will show no improved accuracy by including the individual's autonomous effort toward intermediary outcomes. This is because such estimates rest, ultimately, upon the same natural lottery—the only thing the skeptic accepts as a circumstance of chance. Of course, it should be noted that this severe informational restriction is only a fortified starting point against the skeptic and I would be willing to relax this condition in the hope that better, and more sophisticated, models of endowment's contribution to lifetime compensation can be agreed upon by bona fide interested parties (e.g., including post-birth parent's lifetime compensation, post-birth neighborhood data, etc.).

- *Distributive justice based on a principle of desert utilizes only pre-birth circumstances in its models to measure autonomous effort toward the observed outcome of interest.*

10.2 Feature Selection

Now that we have restricted the relevant circumstances of chance to those prior to, or at the time of, the natural lottery, how is it that researchers select among the restricted set of circumstances to arrive at the "best model" of the generalized functional relationship?

$$Y_i = f(CC_i, \alpha\epsilon_{iY}) \tag{10.1}$$

That is, given that we are operating in the realm of the non-ideal, how do we decide to include some circumstances but not others? To use a political process is again, not only unnecessary, but likely to lead to purposeful

[7] The skeptic has in some sense, to speak anachronistically and somewhat imprecisely, forced us to consider Arneson's "canonical moment" between Vallentyne's "initial brute luck" and "later brute luck" as birth. Vallentyne (2002); Arneson (1990).

elimination of useful features and possible selections of superfluous and confounding measurements. To avoid this, I suggest that good-faith parties might publicly agree on a method of model selection and thus bind ourselves to follow certain principles.

First, we must begin with currently existing administrative data[8] linking each individual in the population to their lifetime compensation and circumstances of chance. For example, cutting-edge research has recently demonstrated the feasibility of such linking techniques through the use of administrative federal income tax records of 40 million children and their parents to understand the geographical variance of intergenerational mobility in the United States[9] as well as through the use of administrative Social Security Administration Summary Earnings records matched to Survey of Income and Program Participation data.[10] To stress my point, even if the only currently existing administrative data were the outcome of interest and "grandmother's maiden name," we would not wait for better data but would proceed immediately to use this circumstance of chance to realize *Just Deserts.*

Of course, datasets are never clean and without missing values. In cases where data is missing, data must be provided by valid administrative documentation or, as a last resort, imputed. Rather than standard imputation techniques, however, I propose a *Just Deserts* imputation policy. For each missing value in the dataset, we assign the individual the value of the minimum observed circumstances of chance (as valued by the function) for that variable plus 20% of the range (the distance between minimum and maximum) in the first year of implementation, the new minimum plus 40% of the new range in year two, adding 20% each year. Thus, at 5 years after policy implementation, missing values receive the maximum functional value for that variable, and they receive 400% of the maximum functional value at 20 years. As an example, if father's compensation were a relevant variable and missing for the first ten years of implementation for Average Joe, we might replace that missing value with $5000 in year one, $40,000 in year five, $100,000 in year nine, and so on, until the individual

[8] It should be noted that economists' suggested measure, hours of formal market labor, fails this criterion as well. First, many survey respondents simply tick off 2000 as "full-time, full-year" when answering this survey question, but more importantly, no administrative source currently has formal labor market hours data.

[9] Chetty et al. (2014).

[10] Mazumder (2001a,b).

in question, Average Joe, documented that their father's compensation was actually $112,500. Immigrants and their immediate descendants pose a special, although not insurmountable, data problem that may require imputation or valid administrative documentation from other jurisdictions. While this may seem to impose large costs on the *Just Deserts* proposal, we will see how utterly simple our models may be and yet still realize significant reductions in inequality and poverty and achieve maximal increases in economic mobility and equality of opportunity.

- *Distributive justice based on a principle of desert must use administrative data as its foundation.*

If our currently existing administrative dataset is composed of our outcome of interest, lifetime formal market compensation, and perhaps ten circumstances of chance with reliable, accurate, administrative data, how do we identify the best current model? What makes one model better than another? Before we answer this question, I think we need to privilege a starting point if we are not to exhaustively examine every logically possible combination. I would recommend that the *first model* to be designated as "best current model" be a linear model with independent residuals[11] resulting from a stepwise feature selection algorithm to simplify the process and reduce costs by eliminating apparently insignificant variables. For example, the backward stepwise Akaike Information Criterion (AIC) algorithm might begin with all raw (untransformed) variables, assume no interactions, and, without testing all logical combinations, arrive at a culled list of raw variables which offer significant, unique associations with the greatest quantity of deviance in the sample. At this point, I would then estimate parameters via a well understood method, Multiple Linear Regression via Ordinary Least Squares, and call this the "*first model*" as well as the "best current model."

Once done, researchers and members of the public are of course free to propose alternatives that could significantly outperform the *first model* under the following test.[12] The precise, proposed alternative with all

[11] Perhaps we say that the studentized Breusch-Pagan test should have a p-value > 0.05.

[12] I would of course be happy if statisticians were able to provide a better test under the same guidelines: simple, robust, conservative estimate of value of autonomous effort and circumstances of chance.

parameters fixed is either provided *a priori* or generated from a blinded interaction with 10 random groups taken from a randomly selected 10% of the population, each containing 1% of the population as training data for k-fold cross-validation.[13] At this stage, whether *a priori* or data-derived, one must explicitly set all parameters of the model. Then we use further cross-validation on the holdout set, the remaining 90% of the population. That is, for 10,000 random selections of 1% of the population, calculate the Root Mean Squared Error (RMSE). Sort the RMSEs from smallest to largest and return the 95th centile. If that outperforms the "best current model" on this same test, it becomes the new "best current model." This ratchet algorithm can continue to improve the "best current model" until the following year's *first model.* This strategy helps avoid the delay of justice via an exhaustive examination of all models by choosing a very robust, significant model as a starting point. The strength of cross-validation is that it significantly penalizes models that "overfit"—in other words, it penalizes models that would recommend greater egalitarianism simply by adding extra variables to fit the data. Furthermore, this test should be amenable to models generated by machine learning techniques.

My hope is that this satisfies our non-ideal objectives: estimate autonomous effort while reducing administrative costs of data collection and model generation and simultaneously possessing great confidence that the *Just Deserts* distribution is *more just* than our current distribution by the greatest possible amount.

Simultaneously, we should not limit ourselves to a static set of variables in our currently available administrative data. We should also use well-structured, well-tested, and well-understood valid items from nationally representative surveys to suggest further circumstances of chance upon which individual lifetime compensation is significantly dependent. If possible, while wisely spending time and resources, we should add these circumstances to our administrative dataset in an attempt to generate a further improved model.

- *Distributive justice based on a principle of desert employs a simply defined* starting point *and then follows a ratchet algorithm that only enables improvements irrespective of the source of the model.*

[13] Guyon et al. (2010), 71.

10.3 Correlation Does Not Imply Causation: Amen

The algorithm I have sketched above is not a theoretical guarantee that we have identified the true underlying causal mechanisms at play with respect to lifetime compensation that the socio-medical search for "root causes" seeks. As social scientists work diligently to disentangle competing theories and mechanisms of chance external to the individual, they have not arrived at a final conclusion and in fact their ideas about "best models" have recently undergone significant change.

Older models of the causal mechanisms explaining the dependence of sons' lifetime earnings upon the lifetime earnings of fathers tended to be human capital models. These models looked to causal mechanisms such as the following dependent variable (DV), independent variable (IV) specification: (DV) sons' earnings simultaneously depend upon (IV1) job tenure, (IV2) cognitive skills, and (IV3) education which simultaneously depend upon (IV4) fathers' earnings (see Fig. 10.1). Newer models give much greater weight to both genetic components with respect to the human capital model itself, as well as to a behavioral model that incorporates (IV5) personality, (IV6) preferences, (IV7) identity, and (IV8) culture onto the human capital model, again, dependent to a larger extent than previously estimated upon (IV9) genetic factors.[14]

Given that our understanding of the true underlying causal mechanisms is changing, how can my simple algorithm be trusted to generate an appropriate model? Fortunately, the *Just Deserts* proposal does not need to include the "root causes" of the observed outcome of interest in order to justly distribute rewards.

> Imagine that we collect circumstantial natural lottery data about our population and we see a statistical relationship of dependence between decreased lifetime compensation and carrying an unexpressed, completely recessive gene, rG, with no observable effects, that is, the phenotypic expressions between those who do, and do not, have this gene are identical and, thus, no individual can discriminate directly upon rG or its effects without conducting specialized tests.[15] We also *correctly believe*, to be explicit, that

[14] Groves (2005), 215–217.

[15] I make no recommendation that we collect genetic data from the population, but the idea of a recessive gene offers the perfect test case as this guarantees that heterozygous carriers

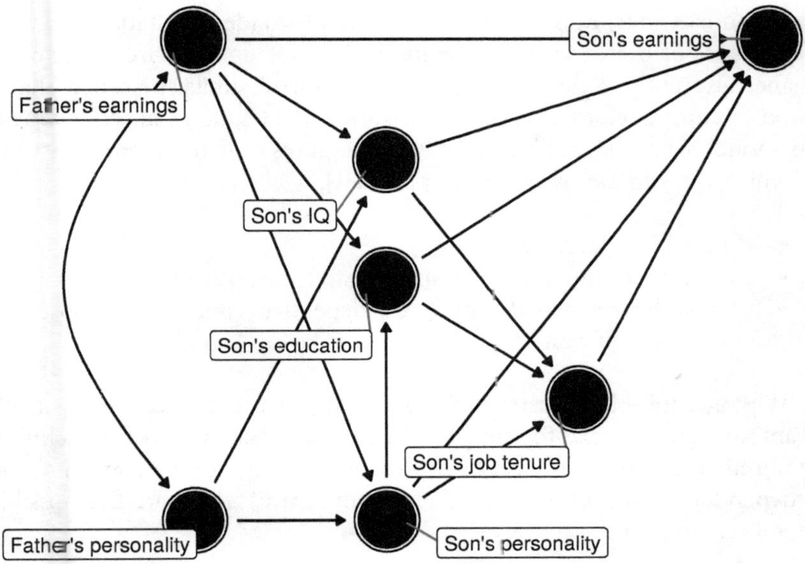

Fig. 10.1 Human capital and behavioral models of intergenerational transmission of earnings

> this unexpressed rG gene is *not a "root cause," directly or indirectly*, of decreased lifetime compensation. This is a textbook case of correlation without causation. The question is: should we compensate those members of the population who carry this recessive gene for decreased lifetime compensation (reduced dynamic endowment) solely on the evidence that, through no fault of their own, they carry an unexpressed gene with no observable consequences and absolutely no causal relationship to their decreased lifetime compensation?

As long as there is a valid statistical relationship of dependence between rG and lifetime compensation, then yes, we should unhesitatingly compensate these members of the population for their bad luck. It is not necessary for a *Just Deserts* proposal to identify true causal mechanisms, nor true

are identical to homozygous non-carriers except for the presence of an element on which no human can directly discriminate.

causes, nor even true correlations,[16] but simply to identify statistically valid *dependence* of the observed outcome of interest upon a circumstance of chance. Recently, Kyle Logue and Joel Slemrod similarly argued that a good circumstance of chance to measure and include in an endowment tax model, what they refer to as a "tag," requires only three properties (all of which the *Just Deserts* proposal provides):

- It must be observable.
- It must be immutable (at least until after observation).
- It must be *correlated* with [i.e., dependent upon] [the observed outcome of interest].[17]

Why is a full-blown causal theory of explicit causal mechanisms irrelevant and unnecessary for the *Just Deserts* proposal? Given the technical requirements of dependence, once we observe that lifetime compensation is dependent upon rG (or any other circumstance), there are five possible causal relationships:

1. Changes in lifetime compensation cause the presence or absence of rG: … → LC → … → rG
2. the presence or absence of rG causes changes in lifetime compensation: … → rG → … → LC
3. a latent, or unobserved, antecedent circumstance of chance causes both changes in lifetime compensation and the presence or absence of rG, rg ← … ← Z → … → LC
4. a combination of 1, 2, and 3, or
5. solely due to chance, our observations *incorrectly* imply one of the above relationships exists between the presence or absence of rG and changes in lifetime compensation when none in fact exists.

To be sure, the skeptic might claim that the *Just Deserts* measurements of autonomous effort are only accurate if our model includes only those circumstances of chance whose relationship to our outcome of interest falls under category (2). As we shall see, they ask too much. Given our

[16] Correlation requires two continua, but carrying the unexpressed CF gene or not carrying are "categories" or "factors," not "continua." Benshalom and Stead (2010).

[17] Logue and Slemrod (2008).

theoretically savvy selection of solely those circumstances measured prior to or at the time of the natural lottery, we may strike (1) off our list, confident in our assumption that the future does not cause the past. We use well-understood statistical techniques to avoid (5) by calculating the probability of observing this empirical dependence if (5) were in fact true, and thus the probability of a type I error. Thus, we are left with only (2) or (3) ((4) being some combination of those two possibilities). In (2), the presence or absence of rG actually causes changes in lifetime compensation and so our skeptic is satisfied. In (3), the most interesting case, the presence or absence of rG acts as a "tag" that helps us to measure another latent circumstance of chance that does possess a causal pathway to changes in lifetime compensation. Ignorant of valid measurements of that other latent circumstance (or circumstances), and cognizant of the fact that we have captured some of the extent to which changes in lifetime compensation are caused by that latent circumstance through its mutual causal impact upon both lifetime compensation and our "tag," combined with an interest in agent responsibility rather than properly calibrated interventions on our "tag," there is no good reason to reject rG from our model [18] Furthermore, George Akerlof argued that such "tags" can lower the cost of any distortionary tax regime (such as our own current fiscal system) even if the correlation is imperfect.[19]

Thus, by meeting Logue and Slemrod's three properties of a good "tag," we have addressed the three classical problems of the economic "theory of screening"[20] in which we might want to impose tax liabilities on tax units in accord with certain unobserved *qualia*, that is, an ideal or perfect observation of each individual's latent natural lottery birth-endowment.[21]

- *Distributive justice based on a principle of desert measures autonomous effort accounting for the extent to which the outcome of interest is dependent upon, not caused by, observed circumstances of chance as*

[18] We can see now that although we must reject the outcomes of an IQ test administered at the age of 18 (as well as BMI and component measures), it would be perfectly valid to use genetic information measurements made at age 0 or 18 as long as they met our three criteria. For use of IQ test outcomes, cf. Björklund et al. (2011).

[19] Logue and Slemrod (2008), 849; Also, cf. Stern (1982).

[20] Lamont (1995).

[21] Atkinson and Stiglitz (1980), 359.

all causal models and mechanisms are theoretically irrelevant to the precision of the measurement.

10.4 In Sum, This Chapter Has Argued

- *Distributive justice based on a principle of desert measures autonomous effort accounting for the extent to which the outcome of interest is dependent upon, not caused by, observed circumstances of chance as all causal models and mechanisms are theoretically irrelevant to the precision of the measurement.*

CHAPTER 11

Just Deserts

> Who shall say how far the Oedipus Tyrannus was the product of Sophocles, how much of Athens, how much of the Hellenic genius, or how much belongs to humanity?—J. A. Hobson. The Industrial System: An Inquiry into Earned and Unearned Income. 1910. Ch. 14

Before the age of data,[1] it was previously assumed obvious that the possibility of endowment taxes was vitiated by informational challenges. Skepticism reigned as some scholars suggested that the difficulties are intractable, that if we tax high-endowment individuals "more than dunderheads, we open the door to all forms of falsification: we make stupidity seem profitable—and [anyone] can [] seem stupid."[2] If we could accurately measure endowment, however, almost all economists would say that it allows for optimal taxation according to both efficiency and equity through a lump-sum endowment tax.

I will now demonstrate exactly how we may measure endowment (circumstances of chance) in order to isolate economic rewards that are deserved from those gotten by luck. The following policy implementations represent a few first-order approximations of the *Just Deserts* proposal, limited only by the survey data at my disposal, and uses one of the best

[1] For an argument that the seventeenth century managed individually tailored lump-sum taxes, for example, in the 1660 Poll Tax, cf. Hahn (1973), 106.

[2] Graaff (1957), 78.

J. T. Dwyer, *Chance, Merit, and Economic Inequality*,
https://doi.org/10.1007/978-3-030-21126-4_11

understood statistical techniques to isolate and measure the dependence of observed outcomes of interest upon circumstances of chance. The initial "best current model" behind these implementations will only improve with the use of currently available administrative government data (that eliminates sample size problems and better represents the extreme right tail of the distribution)[3] and more sophisticated modeling techniques.[4]

11.1 Compensation

Earnings, income, and compensation are different concepts. Earnings are generally wages, salaries, tips, and other employee pay (including self-employment) derived from formal market labor, while income may further include interest, dividends, retirement income, social security, alimony, child support, unemployment insurance benefits, and so on. Compensation, however, includes earnings as well as all employee benefits such as employers' contribution to social security, paid leave, supplemental pay, health insurance, retirement savings, and other.

In the model presented here, we rely on measurements of labor income[5] rather than compensation due to the restrictions of the best survey data we have.[6] As a consequence: our survey-based models will further underestimate the unmerited inequality in our society because high earners (probabilistically high-endowment individuals) receive a greater percent of their compensation in the form of benefits than do low earners who receive a greater percent of their compensation in the form of earnings.[7]

[3] Mitnik et al. (2015), 17–18.

[4] This data is restricted, not classified, and thus requires significant investments of time, resources, and background verification and analysis to be accessed. Thus it is a future project.

[5] "Labor part of farm income and business income, wages, bonuses, overtime, commissions, professional practice, labor part of income from roomers and boarders or business income." Survey Research Center, Institute for Social Research, University of Michigan (2019).

[6] Slottje et al. (2000), 350.

[7] Pollin and Wicks-Lim (2013a,b). As such, our model would allow hyper-endowment individuals to keep some unmerited compensation. Nonetheless, over time just as policy caused this shift during the Great Depression, one might sensibly predict that *Just Deserts* policy would be buttressed by policies to block the hyper-endowed from hiding their compensation.

11.2 Distributing Rewards Via the Principle of Desert

In the United States in the year 2016, let us call that particular individual with lifetime compensation (LC) of $400,000, "Average Joe," because he controls the hypothetical average LC of the population. Our task is to decompose Joe's LC into compensation that stems from unmerited circumstances of chance and compensation due to autonomous effort. How should we proceed?

To begin, recall our mathematical identity from Chap. 2 where there is some functional relationship between our observed outcome of interest, Y_i, and the mutually exclusive, exhaustive, and independent pair, circumstances of chance and autonomous effort (see Eq. (2.1)).

One extreme position with respect to this equation is to assert *a priori*, without knowing a single circumstance relevant to Joe's life, that Joe's LC depends solely and entirely upon Joe's autonomous effort:

A Priori Model #1: Joe's LC depends solely upon Joe's autonomous effort

$$LC_{Joe} = f(0, AutonomousEffort_{Joe}) \tag{11.1}$$

This ascriptive agent responsibility position is not very compelling, and we are forced to reject this dogmatic model as wholly unsatisfactory as we are certain that lifetime compensation depends, at least in part, upon circumstances of chance.[8]

At the same time, it would be just as questionable to adopt the other extreme position of hard determinism which denies, *a priori*, that Joe has even a shred of agent responsibility for his LC[9]:

A Priori Model #2: Joe's LC depends solely upon Joe's circumstances of chance

$$LC_{Joe} = f(CircumstancesofChance_{Joe}, 0) \tag{11.2}$$

[8] Technically, social scientists would see such a model as a saturated model with a dummy variable for each individual.

[9] For example, the standard federal income tax deduction for the blind may be viewed as such an expression with respect to responsibility. *26 U.S. Code § 63 - Taxable Income Defined* (2000).

This position may be even less compelling than the first to many non-philosophers as it asserts that Joe has no autonomous input that affects or changes observed outcomes in the world. This challenges a shared, core intuition and belief in the existence of moral autonomy and our normative ideal of agent responsibility, and if this position were true, Joe himself would technically be a mere circumstance and object, a Light Logan thrown about by the Strong Sam of the physics of our universe. Note that this position is a *Just Deserts* model that requires strict equality among rewards, not however on the distributive principle of equality, but based upon a principle of desert.

So we reject this second dogmatic position[10] as well and suppose, *a priori*, that our best method of approach is to attempt to empirically determine to what extent Joe's *LC* is jointly dependent upon circumstances of chance and Joe's autonomous effort. This position rejects Nagel's supposition that, "The area of genuine agency, and therefore of legitimate moral judgment, seems to shrink under [scientific] scrutiny to an extensionless point."[11] Rather than theorizing *a priori* about how much agency "seems" to exist, *Just Deserts* takes an agnostic theoretical stance and simply allows the empirical facts to dictate the extent to which Joe is agent responsible—whether fully responsible, not at all responsible, or somewhere in between. That is to say, it is absolutely acceptable and possible that the empirical data may force *Just Deserts* into one of the above rejected *a priori* dogmatic positions (a *laissez-faire* or strict egalitarian mapping), based exclusively upon the principle of desert. It is for this reason that I believe that scientific determinists and libertarian free will incompatibilists (as well as a host of compatibilists) might be drawn to the *Just Deserts* proposal—*Just Deserts* allows the best science we have at hand to dictate our best estimate of desert.

Given that Chap. 2 established that autonomous effort is not directly observable and is mutually exclusive, exhaustive, and independent of all

[10] While the fatalist sees no point to public policies, the scientific determinist does as policies change outcomes. Thus, even if the scientific determinist does not believe in agent responsibility, the *Just Deserts* proposal should still satisfy them better than our current economy as it is scientific rather than dogmatic.

[11] Nagel (1979), 35.

circumstances of chance, the only means to indirectly measure Average Joe's autonomous effort is to measure each individual's circumstances of chance and observed outcomes of interest and to then estimate the underlying lifetime compensation function. To do so, our method begins with the assumption that Joe's *LC* is absolutely independent of circumstances of chance and allows empirical evidence to push us toward the determinist position that Joe's outcome is exclusively dependent thereupon. If the hard determinist should object here, wondering why we have placed the benefit of the doubt against them, we should note that this is a logical, rather than prejudicial, process. It is not possible to prove independence of Joe's *LC* from all circumstances of chance without omniscient measurement of such—thus, we begin from an assumption of autonomous agency and use empirical evidence to increase our confidence that outcomes are in fact dependent upon some circumstances of chance, latent or not. In order to do so, as argued in Chap. 2, we must compare Joe with other individuals similarly situated.

Although the theory is agnostic as to model family and technique and open to whichever model is "best,"[12] as stated in Chap. 10 I will here use one of the most well-understood statistical techniques available to generate a precise equation that is robust enough to include all circumstances of chance for all population members *at the same time* (as argued in Chap. 2). This also has the felicitous, and theoretically motivated, result that all members of the model population will automatically participate in one sole mathematical distribution of autonomous effort. Conveniently, the core equation of this statistical technique has the following generalized form:

$$LC_{Joe}(\$400,000) = f(CircumstancesofChance_{Joe}, AutonomousEffort_{Joe}) \tag{11.3}$$

[12] Please note that I implement a particular model for illustrative purposes only and do not suggest that this would be the actual "best" model for the economy of the United States for the calendar year 2016. It may turn out that frequentist methods are surpassed by Bayesian, black-box, or neural-net methods, it may turn out that generalized additive models perform better than linear models, it may turn out that multilevel models are superior to pooled models, and so on. The important thing is simply to compare one model with another and choose the "best" model.

Using the most popular econometric method of Multiple Linear Regression via Ordinary Least Squares, we solve a linear model with the following form[13]:

$$
\begin{aligned}
LC_i &= \beta_0 \\
&+\beta_1 Circumstance(1)_i \\
&+\beta_2 Circumstance(2)_i \\
&+\ldots \\
&+\beta_p Circumstance(p)_i \\
&+\alpha\epsilon_{iY}
\end{aligned}
\tag{11.4}
$$

The Ordinary Least Squares method comprehends and contrasts all individuals at one time, while comparing individuals only to those most similarly situated, and generates the coefficients β_0 through β_p which apply to all individuals in the population through their respective circumstances. For us, however, we are uninterested in any particular coefficient, β_j, and solely focused on $\alpha\epsilon_{iY}$. Once we know Joe's values for his LC as well as Circumstance (1) through (p), the only unknown in Joe's individual equation is $\alpha\epsilon_{iY}$, or Joe's autonomous effort. I should note that we

[13] Technically, we should call this a generalized linear model with an identity-link function, but this is the most popular, and well-understood statistical model available and is often called a linear model. As an agnostic proposal, I do not mean to suggest that this is the best model family for this problem, even less that this is the best model for this problem. I merely use a linear model as a first-order approximation to elucidate the proposal's process and rules of selecting the best current annual model. Of course, given my brief discussion of decomposing birth-endowment into original resources and conversion factors, a multilevel linear model may outperform our first-order approximation. Similarly, should it turn out that Bayesian, machine learning black box, or any other method is "better" than frequentist statistics, then our adherence to the control principle demands we use such tools to make more accurate measurements of autonomous effort. Furthermore, note that some recent research suggests a more complicated model may underlie true earnings dynamics in the United States: earnings variance in the population is due to persistent factors (~50%), transitory factors (~30%), measurement error (~20%), and a random walk component (~?%). The transitory factors are serially correlated via a first-order autoregressive process (80%). Hyslop (2001); Mazumder (2001a); Although the PSID is too small, a much larger dataset of Canadian tax data has enabled researchers to further identify a random walk component, heterogeneity in age-earnings profiles, an age-based component to transitory variance, a time-varying permanent component. Baker and Solon (1999).

will not calculate the absolute value of autonomous effort, but rather its normalized value relative to the population. That is, while there is no such thing as "negative autonomous effort," an individual who puts forth less autonomous effort than their peers will receive a negative value in our formula for $\alpha\epsilon_{i\gamma}$. Thus, we have the capacity to solve the equation by treating autonomous effort as the residual[14] in our model.[15]

11.3 Generating a First-Order Approximation

While I do not currently have "restricted access" or "classified access"[16] to various government databases, I will nonetheless share a robust first-order approximation of the full *Just Deserts* proposal as applied to survey data of the US population despite the very stringent restrictions I have placed upon admissible circumstances of chance. This illustration is intended, not as the ideal truth of desert, but the necessary first step to initiate the non-ideal policy guided by a principle of luck-egalitarian desert.

11.4 Methods

Using the Panel Study of Income Dynamics,[17] not coincidentally, a fruit of the Office of Economic Opportunity and the War on Poverty,[18] I follow the algorithmic procedure described above to generate the initial "first model" of those pre-birth circumstances of chance on which Joe's *LC* significantly depend. I then improve upon that with a new "best current model," the details of which I share below. While the procedure

[14] While it does put more pressure on measurement error, this focus on residuals follows standard econometric practice, cf. Bowles et al. (2001); Card and DiNardo (2002); Fields (2003); Katz and Autor (1999); Mazumder (2001b, 2003); Roemer (2002, 2013); Björklund et al. (2011).

[15] Thus, as was argued in Chap. 2, we now formally and explicitly reject the contention of Dworkin and Fleurbaey that one's subjective perceptions—identification with behaviors/outcomes—are related to descriptive responsibility. Dworkin (1981b); Fleurbaey (2008).

[16] Administrative data will be far preferable to survey data when implementing the *Just Deserts* proposal. In the United States, this will require Internal Revenue Service or Social Security Administration (SSA) records. Cf. for a survey matched to SSA summary earnings records, Mazumder (2005).

[17] Survey Research Center, Institute for Social Research, University of Michigan (2019).

[18] Hill (1992), 4.

is unorthodox, so is our purpose—rather than focusing on the correct features and parameters of our model, we need to estimate to what extent the observed outcome of interest depends upon chance.

For all individuals providing 2016 data in the Panel Study of Income Dynamics for whom we know labor income at any time in their lives, I calculated their cumulative lifetime labor income as of 2016. I then calculated 13 variables of natural lottery outcome data to simulate natural lottery administrative data (where a large number of individuals had missing data): age, sex, race, mother's and father's birth year, mother's and father's race, mother's and father's first year of recorded labor income, mother's and father's cumulative labor income prior to the individual's birth, whether their mother was married at birth, and the average annual U3 unemployment rate in the year the individual turned 18 years old. This simulated administrative data (likely of less quality and greater missingness than real administrative data, weakening the results described here) contained 8932 unweighted individuals (Table 11.1).

Table 11.1 Descriptive statistics, simulated administrative data

Variable	*n*	Mean	SD	Median
Log cumulative labor income	8932	12.5	2.3	12.9
Age	8932	45.4	17.0	42.0
U3 annual rate at age 18	7790	6.1	1.6	5.8
Mother's birth year	7323	1949.0	15.3	1952.0
Father's birth year	5780	1946.1	15.5	1950.0
First year of labor income	8927	1995.5	15.6	1999.0
Mother's first year of labor income	7322	1977.3	10.1	1974.0
Father's first year of labor income	5780	1976.8	9.9	1973.0
Sex	8932	1.6	0.5	2.0
Race	8910	1.7	1.1	1.0
Mother's race	7178	1.6	0.8	1.0
Father's race	5775	1.5	0.8	1.0
Mother's pre-birth cumulative labor income	4960	68,288.1	118,113.7	14,448.2
Father's pre-birth cumulative labor income	3991	206,907.0	277,225.8	111,044.9
Longitudinal weight	8932	34.9	26.7	31.8

I then temporarily filtered out all individuals who were missing any of these data,[19] leaving me with 3727 unweighted respondents. I then regressed these data against the observed outcome of interest, the individual's cumulative lifetime labor income and used the backward stepwise AIC algorithm to prune variables. As this resulted in heteroskedastic residuals, I changed the observed outcome of interest to the natural log of cumulative lifetime labor income, discussed further below. This pruning on the natural log model resulted in discarding five variables, keeping age, sex, mother's race, father's birth year, father's race, mother's and father's cumulative labor income prior to the individual's birth,[20] and the U3 unemployment rate at age 18. Temporarily filtering out individuals missing any of these data, there were now 3753 unweighted respondents. Then regress these data against the observed outcome of interest and use the beta coefficients to apply the 20% functional value rule discussed in Chap. 10 to those individuals' previously missing data. At this point, there were again 8932 unweighted respondents. Then fit a prediction for all of these individuals (including observed and imputed data) and calculate the RMSE on 10,000 random samples of 1% of the individuals. The 95th centile of that RMSE was 2.99 and the fitted values were associated with 33% of the variance among observed values. This constituted the "first model" with specific parameters (Table 11.2).

Next, I tested whether I could outperform that RMSE measure with an alternative model. From the simulated administrative data (with missing values), I selected a few variables, filtered out all individuals with missing data on these variables, and ran a generalized additive model. I then applied the 20% rule to all the filtered individuals and reran a generalized additive model. The 95th centile of the RMSE on 10,000 random samples was 2.05 and the fitted values were associated with 36% of the variance among observed values. This is the "best current model" that I analyze in Chap. 12 (Table 11.3).

[19] For administrative data, one might substitute for this step a filtering out of all individuals for whom one could not, or did not wish to, use multiple imputation.

[20] Theoretical power comes at the cost of using very few years of mothers' and fathers' earliest lifetime compensation. It should be noted that the elasticity coefficient estimated from this brief number of years may exhibit attenuation bias of 10–40%. Once we have agreed that parents' compensation is not caused by children's compensation, we may improve our models even further. Cf. Mazumder (2001b). I would also like to have included neighborhood poverty rates based upon restricted-use PSID "geocodes," but did not have access. Sharkey (2009).

Table 11.2 Regression statistics, first model

Term	Estimate	Std. error	*t* statistic	*p*	
(Intercept)	−13.57	10.83	−1.25	0.21	
Age	0.15	0.01	22.10	0.00	***
U3 annual rate at age 18	−0.18	0.02	−9.29	0.00	***
Father's birth year	0.01	0.01	2.09	0.04	*
Sex (Female)	−0.54	0.05	−9.92	0.00	***
Mother's race (Black)	−0.32	0.08	−3.79	0.00	***
Mother's race (American Indian)	−0.20	0.19	−1.07	0.29	
Mother's race (Asian)	0.27	0.18	1.53	0.13	
Mother's race (Pacific)	−0.85	0.43	−1.97	0.05	.
Mother's race (other)	−0.65	0.23	−2.76	0.01	*
Mother's race (NA)	0.61	0.68	0.89	0.37	
Mother (never married)	−0.42	0.11	−3.83	0.00	***
Mother (widowed)	0.10	0.58	0.17	0.87	
Mother (divorced; marriage annulled)	−0.17	0.21	−0.82	0.41	
Mother (separated)	0.37	0.26	1.43	0.15	
Mother's pre-birth labor income	0.00	0.00	3.29	0.00	***
Father's pre-birth labor income	0.00	0.00	4.06	0.00	***

0.00 < * * * <= 0.001 < ** <= 0.01 < * <= 0.05 < . <= 0.10

Table 11.3 Regression statistics, current best model

Term	Estimate/EDF	Std. error/ref. DF	*t*/*F* statistic	*p*	
(Intercept)	12.87	0.05	258.26	0.00	***
Sex (Female)	−0.95	0.04	−26.00	0.00	***
Mother (never married)	−0.30	0.08	−3.73	0.00	***
Mother (widowed)	0.08	0.36	0.23	0.82	
Mother (divorced; marriage annulled)	−0.36	0.07	−5.08	0.00	***
Mother (separated)	0.00	0.20	0.02	0.98	
s(Age)	7.54	8.44	29.65	0.00	***
s(U3 annual rate at age 18)	1.00	1.00	0.52	0.47	
s(Mother's birth year)	3.73	4.75	2.07	0.07	.
s(Father's birth year)	5.62	6.76	6.82	0.00	***
s(First year recorded labor income)	8.08	8.77	120.83	0.00	***
s(Mother's pre-birth labor income)	3.72	4.60	5.62	0.00	***
s(Father's pre-birth labor income)	1.00	1.00	7.86	0.01	

0.00 < * * * <= 0.001 < ** <= 0.01 < * <= 0.05 < . <= 0.10

The equation of the "best current model" based upon a sample of 8927 (simulating an administrative dataset) has the following form (see Eq. (11.5); Table 11.3):

$$\begin{aligned} LC_{Joe} &= ChanceLE_{Joe} + \alpha\epsilon_{Joe} \\ \ln(LC_{Joe}) &= \beta_0 \\ &+\beta_1 Sex_{Joe} \\ &+\beta_2 Mothermaritalstatus \\ &+s(Age_{Joe}) \\ &+s(U3_{Joe}) \\ &+s(Firstyearlaborincome_{Joe}) \\ &+s(Motherbirthyear_{Joe}) \\ &+s(Fatherbirthyear_{Joe}) \\ &+s(Motherpre\text{-}birthLC_{Joe}) \\ &+s(Fatherpre\text{-}birthLC_{Joe}) \\ &+\alpha\epsilon_{Joe} \end{aligned} \tag{11.5}$$

Looking at these equations, "Chance *LC*" is Joe's *LC* that is completely dependent upon circumstances of chance over which Joe's autonomous effort has no possible influence given that they occurred before Joe's birth. As it turns out, $ChanceLC_{Joe}$ = \$400,000 and $\alpha\epsilon_{Joe}$ = \$0. This does not mean that Joe exhibited zero autonomous effort, rather this signifies that Joe put forth the population's expected value of exhibited autonomous effort. Thus, the *Just Deserts* proposal will reward Joe precisely for his autonomous effort in comparison with the rest of the population, and this reward will be identical to the reward allocated to all others who put forth identical autonomous effort toward lifetime compensation.

Yet, is it not true that Joe worked hard in school, and that he currently works hard at his job to "deserve" his pay? It is indeed true that Joe's *LC* depends unsurprisingly to a large extent upon the hours (labor supply) and wages (productivity) of labor Joe performs as well as on Joe's maximum level of education (human capital accumulation)—all things that constitute, *prima facie*, hard work. Yet, Joe may not justly claim full agent responsibility for these outcomes as they are, to some extent, also dependent upon factors beyond Joe's control. The power of the *Just Deserts* proposal is that any dependency between the observed outcome of interest and Joe's birth-endowment is captured and accounted for. Thus, we sift out Joe's natural lottery endowments from his autonomous effort and reward him precisely for the latter alone. While he does work hard, roughly half of all individuals in the population work harder, exhibiting more autonomous effort—thus, they ***deserve more*** than Joe.[21]

One should also note one peculiarity of our initial "current best model." This particular model utilizes the natural log function, ln(), to transform the outcome LC_{Joe} into $\ln(LC_{Joe})$, where $e^{\ln(LC_{Joe})} = LC_{Joe}$. We undertake this transformation because it is an extremely common transformation of economic models that avoids the heteroskedastic residuals of the initial attempt to generate an initial *first model*.[22] Further, every individual is part of the same distribution and autonomous effort is independent of circumstances of chance, thus, heteroskedastic errors fail to fit the theory.

Second, note that this natural log transformation forces our Ordinary Least Squares method to minimize percentages rather than dollar amounts when seeking the correct parameters. That is to say, because our outcome of interest is the natural log of lifetime labor income, the difference between \$200,000 and \$220,000 is treated equivalently to the difference between \$400,000 and \$440,000 when we seek to account for circumstances of chance in the data. Unfortunately, the fact that this lognormal transformation was used to realize homoskedastic residuals happens to force our particular lifetime compensation function to operate under conditions of heterogeneous goods where the function takes the form, $Y_i = (CC_i * \alpha\epsilon_{iY}) + t_i$. A marginal unit of autonomous effort multiplies economic resources while a marginal unit of *Just Deserts* transfers merely adds or subtracts.

There seem to be two choices here, both of which I will explore. One, we utilize an endowment tax that uses a strict principle of desert

[21] Roemer leans, incorrectly in my view, toward *more deserving* rather than deserves more. Roemer (1998), 78.

[22] The *p*-value of the studentized Breusch-Pagan test is $1.48e{-}24$ prior to log transformation, $1.06e{-}01$ afterward, and $1.32e{-}220$ after including only the variables chosen by the stepwise AIC procedure on the log-transformed model.

to meet Roemer's definition of robust equality of opportunity through the *Just Deserts* Luck-Egalitarian model. Two, without knowledge of the answers to the following empirical questions, we assume (a) that we cannot efficiently find an improved, principled reward function, transfers included, that operates under conditions of homogeneous goods; (b) that, *a priori*, a strict principle of desert would incur a loss of Pareto efficiency; and (c) that there is no price we would pay for a gain in justice as desert. Thus, we utilize a lump-sum endowment tax in accord with a second-best principle of desert through the *Just Deserts* lump-sum {0, 0} model. Unsure that either approach dominates the other with respect to the relevant moral agents' ethical preferences, I will share the surprising results of both choices for a more comprehensive picture of the possibilities of a *Just Deserts* proposal.

11.5 The Just Deserts Proposal

I would now like to share four specific models of the *Just Deserts* proposal and their mechanics:

- *Just Deserts*, Luck-Egalitarian (JD.LE)[23]: the lifetime compensation of all surviving contemporary individuals is to be allocated according to a unique and precise luck-egalitarian mapping with respect to each individual's autonomous effort toward individual lifetime compensation. This is the recommended model by those who normatively support only one principle of distributive justice: desert. Note that this also perfectly satisfies efficiency under conditions of homogeneous goods while always perfectly satisfying equality of opportunity and the liberty discussed in Chap. 6.
- *Just Deserts*, Age-Restricted Luck-Egalitarian (JD.AR): the lifetime compensation of all surviving contemporary individuals, minus the compensation earned prior to relative time, m_i, is to be allocated according to a unique and precise luck-egalitarian mapping with respect to each individual's autonomous effort toward individual lifetime compensation. This is the recommended model by those who

[23] One apparent weakness of our present data is that it measures gross labor income rather than net. Note that, "arguably, post-fisc [measures are] a more attractive objective, for it is a more proximate measure of consumption opportunities." Roemer (2002), 6. I would argue, however, that this is the right measure as *Just Deserts* needs to occur prior to other taxes and transfers in order to measure autonomous effort.

normatively support two principles of distributive justice: desert and seniority.

- *Just Deserts*, Lump-Sum Endowment {0, 0} (JD.LS): the lifetime compensation of all surviving contemporary individuals is to be allocated according to a unique and precise {0, 0} lump-sum endowment tax mapping with respect to each individual's dynamic endowment toward individual lifetime compensation. This is the recommended model by those who normatively support two principles of distribution under conditions of heterogeneous goods: desert and efficiency.
- *Just Deserts*, Lump-Sum Endowment Minimum Reward, Balanced Vector $\{\epsilon_A, \epsilon_i\}$ (JD.LS.MR.BV): the lifetime compensation of all surviving contemporary individuals is to be allocated according to a unique and precise $\{\epsilon_A, \epsilon_i\}$ lump-sum endowment tax mapping with respect to each individual's dynamic endowment toward individual lifetime compensation, setting the lowest post-distribution allocation to the level of sufficiency such that $\epsilon_A = \epsilon_i$. This is the recommended model by those who normatively support three principles of distribution: desert, efficiency, and either sufficiency or a rejection of certain lump-sum taxes on grounds of liberty.

11.6 *** The Just Deserts Proposal's Formulae

11.6.1 Model #1: Just Deserts *Luck-Egalitarian*

Here is the general formula (using Sherlock, S, as an illustrative example) for the preferred *Just Deserts* proposal, a strictly luck-egalitarian principle of desert without any age restrictions:

1. First, at the end of time period, t, calculate the present value of Chance Lifetime Compensation for each individual according to the "best" model with respect to the sum of lifetime compensation for all contemporary individuals:
   a. $LC_i = f(ChanceLC_i, \alpha\epsilon_{iY})$

2. Solve for luck-egalitarian circumstances of chance (CC_{LE}) where the population is constituted by Sherlock (S), Joe (J), and Irene (I):

$$\sum_{i \in N} LC_i = \sum_{i \in N} e^{[\ln(CC_{LE})+\alpha\epsilon_{iY}]}$$
$$\$360{,}000 = e^{[\ln(CC_{LE})-0.128]_S} + e^{[\ln(CC_{LE})+0]_J} + e^{[\ln(CC_{LE})+0.118]_I}$$
$$\$360{,}000 = [CC_{LE} * 0.88]_S + [CC_{LE} * 1]_J + [CC_{LE} * 1.125]_I$$
$$\$360{,}000 = CC_{LE} * 3.005$$
$$CC_{LE} = \$119{,}800 \tag{11.6}$$

3. Solve for Sherlock's *Just Deserts*:

$$R_{iY} = e^{[\ln(CC_{LE})+\alpha\epsilon_{iY}]}$$
$$R_{SY} = e^{[\ln(CC_{LE})-0.128]}$$
$$R_{SY} = [CC_{LE} * 0.88] \tag{11.7}$$
$$R_{SY} = [\$119{,}800 * 0.88] = \$105{,}424_S$$

4. To make things simpler for the more complex Age-Restricted distribution, note that Sherlock's reward above is the luck-egalitarian circumstances of chance times 0.88, what we might call the individual's Autonomous Effort Coefficient (AEC)[24]:

$$AEC_i = \frac{LC_i}{ChanceLC_i} = \frac{\$220{,}000_S}{\$250{,}000_S} = 0.880_S \tag{11.8}$$

5. Calculate each individual's Autonomous Effort Share (AES):
   a. $AES_i = \frac{AEC_i}{\sum_{i \in N} AEC_i} = \frac{0.880_S}{3.005} = 0.293_S$

[24] Pace Roemer, note that this solves the problem of what units to use for autonomous effort. As our "best model" suggested, it cost identical autonomous effort to increase *LC* by 10%, regardless of Chance *LC*, this is a proper comparative unit of measure of autonomous effort. Had our "best model" suggested it cost identical autonomous effort to earn $1000 more in *LC*, regardless of Chance *LC*, then we would have used a unit (*LC*—Chance *LC*) instead. Roemer (2012), 179.

6. Calculate each individual's Pre-*Just Deserts* allocation (PJD):
   a. $PJD_i = AES_i * \sum_{i \in N} LC_i = 0.293_S * \$360{,}000 = \$105{,}424_S$
7. Calculate the Quarter-Century Annualized Growth Rate of Mean Compensation (QCAGRMC):
   a. $QCAGRMC = [\frac{AnnualCompensation_{\mu,t}}{AnnualCompensation_{\mu,t-25}}]^{1/25} - 1$
8. Calculate each individual's Lifetime Expectancy Coefficient (LEC):
   a. $LEC_i = (1 + QCAGRMC)^{\text{Lifetime Expectancy}_i - \text{Lifetime Expectancy}_\mu} = 1.1_S$
9. Calculate each individual's Longevity-Adjusted Pre-*Just Deserts* (LAPJD):
   a. $LAPJD_i = \frac{PJD_i}{LEC_i} = \frac{\$105{,}424_S}{1.1_S} = \$95{,}840_S$
10. Finally, calculate each individual's *Just Deserts*, making a proportional adjustment for accounting purposes:
    a. $JD_i = \frac{\sum_{i \in N} LC_i}{\sum_{i \in N} LAPJD_i} * LAPJD_i$
    b. $JD_S = \frac{\$360{,}000}{\$95{,}840_S + \$119{,}800_J + \$134{,}775_I} * \$95{,}840_S = \$98{,}462$

11.6.2 *Model #2:* Just Deserts *Age-Restricted Luck-Egalitarian*

Here is the general formula for our second model:

1. First, at the end of time period, t, calculate the present value of Chance Lifetime Compensation for each individual according to the "best" model with respect to the sum of lifetime compensation for all contemporary individuals:
   a. $LC_i = f(ChanceLC_i, \alpha \epsilon_{iY})$
2. Given this function, for each time period, t, barring restricted periods (e.g., whether time periods before birth, before age 16, etc.), calculate each individual's Autonomous Effort Coefficient (AEC):
   a. $AEC_{it} = \frac{LC_i}{ChanceLC_i} = \frac{\$220{,}000_S}{\$250{,}000_S} = 0.880_S$
3. For each time period, t, calculate a Unit Measure (UM; the value of one share):
   a. $UM_t = \frac{\sum_{i \in N} Compensation_{it}}{\sum_{i \in N} AEC_{it}} = UM_{2008} = \frac{\$90{,}000}{2.005} = \$44{,}888$

4. Calculate each individual's Pre-*Just Deserts* allocation (PJD):
   a. $PJD_i = \sum_{\min(t)}^{\max(t)} [AEC_{it} * UM_{it}]$
   b. $PJD_S = \sum_{2008}^{2016} [0.880_S * UM_{it}] = [0.880_S * \$44,887.78_S] + [0.880_S * \$32,612.31_S] + [0.880_S * \$57,237.94_S] = \$39,501.25_S + \$28,698.84_S + \$50,369.38_S = \$118,569.47_S$
5. Calculate the Quarter-Century Annualized Growth Rate of Mean Compensation (QCAGRMC):
   a. $QCAGRMC = \left[\frac{AnnualCompensation_{\mu,t}}{AnnualCompensation_{\mu,t-25}}\right]^{1/25} - 1$
6. Calculate each individual's Lifetime Expectancy Coefficient (LEC):
   a. $LEC_i = (1 + QCAGRMC)^{\text{Lifetime Expectancy}_i - \text{Lifetime Expectancy}_\mu} = 1.1_S$
7. Calculate each individual's Longevity-Adjusted Pre-*Just Deserts* (LAPJD):
   a. $LAPJD_i = \frac{PJD_i}{LEC_i} = \frac{\$118,569_S}{1.1_S} = \$107,790_S$
8. Finally, calculate each individual's *Just Deserts*, making a proportional adjustment for accounting purposes:
   a. $JD_i = \frac{\sum_{i \in N} LC_i}{\sum_{i \in N} LAPJD_i} * LAPJD_i$
   b. $JD_S = \frac{\$360,000}{\$107,790_S + \$89,850_J + \$168,423_I} * \$107,790_S = \$106,005_S$

11.6.3 *Model #3:* Just Deserts *Lump-Sum Endowment {0,0}*

Here is the general formula for our third model:

1. First, at the end of time period, t, calculate the present value of Chance Lifetime Compensation for each individual according to the "best" model with respect to the sum of lifetime compensation for all contemporary individuals:
   a. $LC_i = f(ChanceLC_i, \alpha\epsilon_{iY})$
2. Given this function, calculate each individual's lump-sum tax (T) according to bivariate specification {0,0}:
   a. $T_i = [ChanceLC_\mu + \epsilon_A \sigma(\alpha\epsilon_{Endowment_A})] - [ChanceLC_i + \epsilon_i \sigma(\alpha\epsilon_{Endowment_i})]$ such that, $\{\epsilon_A, \epsilon_i\} = \{0, 0\}$
   b. $T_S = [\$126,667 + \$0] - [\$250,000_S + \$0] = -\$123,333_S$

- where $[ChanceLC_{\mu} + \epsilon_A \sigma(\alpha\epsilon_{Endowment_A})]$ is equal to the lifetime compensation of an individual in the population with mean Chance Lifetime Compensation who has exhibited ϵ_A standard deviations of autonomous effort;
- where $[ChanceLC_i + \epsilon_i \sigma(\alpha\epsilon_{Endowment_i})]$ is equal to the lifetime compensation of an individual in the population with identical Chance Lifetime Compensation to individual, i, who has exhibited ϵ_i standard deviations of autonomous effort;

3. Calculate each individual's Pre-*Just Deserts* allocation (PJD):
   a. $PJD_i = LC_i + T_i = \$220{,}000_S - \$123{,}333_S = \$96{,}667_S$
4. Calculate the Quarter-Century Annualized Growth Rate of Mean Compensation (QCAGRMC):
   a. $QCAGRMC = \left[\frac{AnnualCompensation_{\mu,t}}{AnnualCompensation_{\mu,t-25}}\right]^{1/25} - 1$
5. Calculate each individual's Lifetime Expectancy Coefficient (LEC):
   a. $LEC_i = (1+QCAGRMC)^{LifetimeExpectancy_i - LifetimeExpectancy_{\mu}} = 1.1_S$
6. Calculate each individual's Longevity-Adjusted Pre-*Just Deserts* (LAPJD):
   a. $LAPJD_i = \frac{PJD_i}{LEC_i} = \frac{\$96{,}667_S}{1.1_S} = \$87{,}879_S$
7. Finally, calculate each individual's *Just Deserts*, making a proportional adjustment for accounting purposes:
   a. $JD_i = \frac{\sum_{i \in N} LC_i}{\sum_{i \in N} PJD_i} * PJD_i$
   b. $JD_S = \frac{\$360{,}000}{\$87{,}879_S + \$126{,}667_J + \$136{,}667_I} * \$87{,}879_S = \$90{,}078_S$

11.6.4 *Model #4:* Just Deserts *Lump-Sum Endowment Minimum Reward, Balanced Vector* $\{\epsilon_A, \epsilon_i\}$

Here is the general formula for our fourth model:

1. Follow the *Just Deserts* Lump-Sum Endowment {0,0} Compensation model except change step (2) to the following:

2. IF the minimum *Just Deserts* allocation for the entire population is < \$0 under Lump-Sum {0,0},[25] calculate each individual's lump-sum tax (T) according to bivariate specification $\{\epsilon_A, \epsilon_i\}$ such that $\epsilon_A = \epsilon_i$, where both variables take an identical value such that the minimum *Just Deserts* allocation for the entire population is the minimum amount possible greater than \$0:
   a. $T_i = [ChanceLC_\mu + \epsilon_A \sigma(\alpha\epsilon_{Endowment_A})] - [ChanceLC_i + \epsilon_i \sigma(\alpha\epsilon_{Endowment_i})]$ such that, $\epsilon_A = \epsilon_i \wedge \epsilon_i = \max(\epsilon_i)$ such that $\min(JD_i) > \$0$

      - where $[ChanceLC_\mu + \epsilon_A \sigma(\alpha\epsilon_{Endowment_A})]$ is equal to the lifetime compensation of an individual in the population with mean Chance Lifetime Compensation who has exhibited ϵ_A standard deviations of autonomous effort;
      - where $[ChanceLC_i + \epsilon_i \sigma(\alpha\epsilon_{Endowment_i})]$ is equal to the lifetime compensation of an individual in the population with identical Chance Lifetime Compensation to individual, i, who has exhibited ϵ_i standard deviations of autonomous effort.

[25] Although this does not occur in our three-person population, it does in our Panel Study of Income Dynamics sample.

CHAPTER 12

Just Deserts Outcomes and Aggregate Analysis

What do these proposals mean in practice? Across all four models, this agnostic, data-driven proposal is both mathematically simpler than standard equal opportunity policies and more flexible, adapting to macroeconomic changes (and other systemwide, unobserved influences) because we use *ex post* measurements to make *ex post* adjustments. We are ignorant of all *ex ante* intervention policies, we are ignorant of whether a weak or robust equality of opportunity policy even exists *ex ante*. We accomplish, nonetheless, the theoretically maximum observable economic mobility in models JD.LE, JD.LS, and JD.LS.MR.BV[1]—that is, allocations simultaneously exhibit empirical independence from individual birth-endowment and sensitivity to autonomous effort.

By focusing on autonomous effort and a principle of desert linked to our fundamental moral intuition—the control principle as the core of agent responsibility—all models could potentially win the support and respect of individuals across the political spectrum as the most just principle on which to distribute economic resources. Although no individual will have to pay to implement distributive justice under conditions of homogeneous goods (nor under heterogeneous goods given the currently distortionary system of taxation), this more ethically appealing foundation upon desert implies that, even if it were necessary, individuals would be willing to pay

[1] The age-restriction of Model #2, on the other hand, ensures that economic mobility itself is restricted by one factor: age.

J. T. Dwyer, *Chance, Merit, and Economic Inequality*,
https://doi.org/10.1007/978-3-030-21126-4_12

more to see *Just Deserts* distributions, (Eq. (3.4)), than they would pay to reduce inequality on account of a principle of equality. Nonetheless, it is an empirical question as to how much the aggregate output of the currently distortionary economy would increase or decrease under the *Just Deserts* proposal. There is some cutting-edge research, however, that suggests that the current economy does in fact inhibit productivity by failing to implement *Just Deserts.*[2]

Furthermore, once we have committed ourselves to an actual model of the function of the observed outcome of interest and luck-egalitarian reward, we are then in a position to answer some of the more nuanced questions about desert raised in Shelly Kagan's work.[3] First, each individual does in fact deserve a precise amount of reward, and it is always worse if the individual receives either less or more than that precise amount. Second, no individual deserves a reward of less than $0. Unfortunately, I do not believe that *Just Deserts* can tell us how to proceed if someone must receive excessive (or insufficient reward). For example, four individuals deserve precisely $300,000 but currently hold $50,000, $150,000, $400,000, and $600,000, and we are constrained to only redistribute $100,000. Neither can *Just Deserts* answer the more relevant question to a public policy, how to prioritize collecting inputs from the latter two individuals and allocating outputs to the former two? It may be that we ought to use the principle of efficiency for collection and the principle of priority for allocation, but *Just Deserts* is not the source of this answer.

With respect to the individual models themselves, our *Just Deserts* Luck-Egalitarian model guarantees that individuals who exert identical autonomous effort toward the market-expressed demands of others control identical economic resources as the appropriate reward. By rewarding individuals for their autonomous effort according to desert rather than rewarding them for circumstances of chance—factors beyond their control and for which they are in no way agent responsible—we reward individuals for merit and overthrow the last despot to rule over a free people, chance, one of the most powerful causes of inequality and poverty in all hitherto societies, and the one and only cause of economic immobility and a lack of equality of opportunity.

[2] Marrero and Rodríguez (2013).
[3] Kagan (2012).

Our *Just Deserts* Age-Restricted Luck-Egalitarian model guarantees the above only for those contemporaries who share the same age restrictions. This allows laborers at the end of their compensation careers to control greater lifetime-allocations than laborers at the beginning of their compensation careers, despite the fact that they may have exhibited identical lifetime autonomous effort.

Our *Just Deserts* Lump-Sum Endowment {0,0} model guarantees the above only for those contemporaries who share the same birth-endowment. Furthermore, this model always perfectly satisfies the principle of efficiency. However, under conditions of heterogeneous goods, this model utilizes a second-best principle of desert in order to guarantee a Pareto-optimal economy.

Our *Just Deserts* Lump-Sum Endowment Minimum Reward, Balanced Vector $\{\epsilon_A, \epsilon_i\}$ model is identical to the {0,0} model except for the fact that no individual may be liable for a "liberty-infringing" lump-sum tax amount as we adjust our variables, $\{\epsilon_A, \epsilon_i\}$, to the value such that the minimum *Just Deserts* allocation is at or above sufficiency. Given our sample, $\epsilon_A = \epsilon_i = -0.389$ and the minimum allocation is $0.

12.1 Inequality

To begin the analysis proper, I will follow standard procedure such as that utilized by the United States Congressional Budget Office in that I estimate the results of fiscal policy without reflecting behavioral changes that would affect total output in the economy.[4]

From our dataset, for the sake of comparison and analysis we now construct distributions of the Original empirical lifetime labor income data that was dependent upon both circumstances of chance and autonomous effort as well as the distribution of such compensation according to our four different *Just Deserts* models (see Fig. 12.1).

The mean empirical present value in 2016 dollars of lifetime labor income at the end of calendar year 2016 of the 8932 unweighted participating individuals in our Panel Study of Income Dynamics sample[5]

[4] Their reason is that such estimates are "highly uncertain." CBO—Congressional Budget Office (2015).

[5] The Panel Study of Income Dynamics conducted annual surveys from 1968. From 1999 to the present, surveys have been biannual. Thus, as a simple imputation, I use the mean of

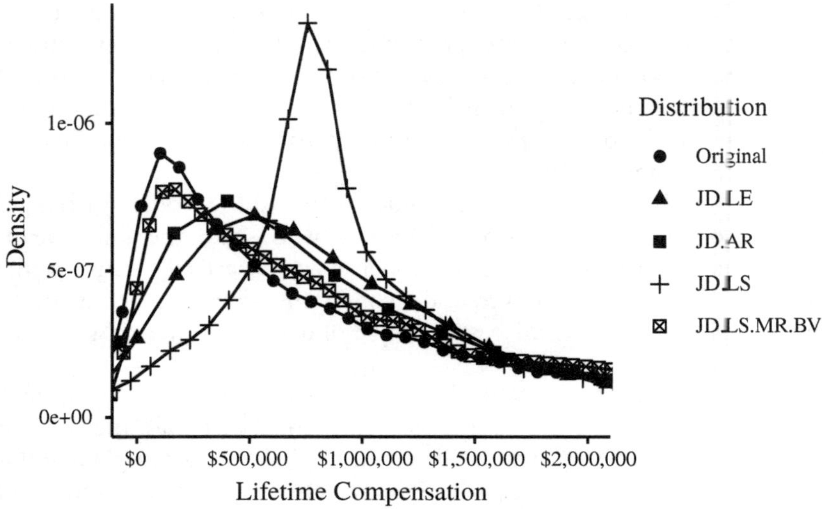

Fig. 12.1 Original and *Just Deserts* distributions, 2016

was $1,099,292. There are two reasons this dollar amount may appear too low. First, our dataset initially filtered out all individuals for whom we lack natural lottery information and thus the oldest individuals in our dataset were born in 1968 while their parents gave us natural lottery information for 1967. The age range of our simulated administrative dataset, however, is 18–100 (mean: 51, median: 52), requiring imputation to individuals born before 1967. While this weakness is unavoidable without administrative data that in fact contains natural lottery data for the entire

the two neighbor surveys as data for the missing even years, 1998–2016. Furthermore, since 1968, the Panel Study of Income Dynamics (PSID) has consistently measured the prior year's labor income of both the "family head" and the "family wife," if any. Thus 2017 survey data refer to 2016 labor income. The possibility that some included, and excluded, individuals have unmeasured labor income from years prior to family headship, or due to itinerant or temporary family headship, is a limitation of the dataset I cannot overcome. Noting once again the agnostic nature of the *Just Deserts* proposal, I use this specific model and its parameter estimates for illustrative purposes of how much unmerited inequality may be observed even when using an extremely conservative restriction on information inclusion. All data stem from values using the PSID 2017 longitudinal weights for individuals ages 16 and older to present a nationally representative analysis of individual labor income between 1967–2016.

Table 12.1 Distribution of lifetime compensation, 2016

	Original	JD.LE	JD.AR	JD.LS	JD.LS.MR.BV
Mean	$1,099,292	$1,099,292	$1,099,292	$1,099,292	$1,099,292
Median	$649,724	$787,389	$713,552	$830,274	$757,425
25th centile	$226,423	$430,832	$344,865	$617,616	$309,283
75th centile	$1,484,426	$1,353,468	$1,375,421	$1,288,614	$1,534,182
Std. dev.	$1,583,050	$1,202,882	$1,423,584	$1,382,362	$1,249,214
Minimum	$0	$1	$1	$−2,361,081	$0
Maximum	$42,307,831	$88,050,776	$120,886,446	$41,992,772	$28,647,763
90/10 ratio	40.6	11.0	15.4	8.4	22.2

population, this nonetheless constitutes, to my knowledge, the greatest age range yet utilized in a long-term or lifetime compensation model.[6] Second, unlike many studies interested in intergenerational earnings persistence and as mentioned in Chap. 9, our dataset does not remove either women or individuals with zero labor income. We are precisely interested in understanding the full distribution of lifetime compensation rather than the elasticity coefficient between full-time, full-year formal market working fathers' earnings and their correspondingly categorized sons.

While our models possess the same mean as the original distribution, they greatly differ otherwise. Most notably, the *Just Deserts* models show a right-shifted peak (mode of probability) that indicates that the elimination of unmerited inequality increases the rewards to labor of individuals with low lifetime labor income in the Original distribution (see Fig. 12.1).

Turning to specific statistics of the distributions, the elimination of unmerited inequality reduces the distance between the mean and median lifetime labor income values by roughly one third (see Table 12.1). These *Just Deserts* models have also reduced the standard deviation of lifetime labor income. This amounts to a change of −21.5% in the standard deviation of lifetime *log* labor income.[7] To put this in perspective, the

[6] Note, however, that by utilizing the *Just Deserts* theory, Sweden and Norway have longitudinal administrative datasets easily available to researchers that would far surpass what I have done for the United States using a survey. Cf. Aaberge et al. (2011); Björklund et al. (2011).

[7] Standard deviations are valid for normal distributions rather than the lognormal distributions seen in the chart. The standard deviations of the normal distribution of lifetime log labor income are ln(Original): 2.13 and ln(JD): 1.68 on two different means (ln(Original):

Table 12.2 Distribution of circumstances of chance and autonomous effort, 2016

	Circumstances of chance	Autonomous effort coefficient
Mean	$753,892	1.778
Median	$562,179	1.273
25th centile	$221,527	0.697
75th centile	$1,063,429	2.189
Std. dev.	$677,901	1.945
Minimum	$715	0
Maximum	$4,394,796	142.387
90/10 ratio	21.5	11.0

largest shift in the standard deviation of annual log income inequality in the past 50 years amounts to 20%: from 1967–1980 ($\sigma \ln(y) = 0.50$) to 1985–2000 ($\sigma \ln(y) = 0.60$).[8] Finally, we have also reduced the range of labor income between the minimum and maximum values—as well as the 90th and 10th centiles (the most frequently used interdecile ratio)[9]—of lifetime labor income.

These statistics differ for exactly one reason—*Just Deserts*' equalization of each individual's free lunch in order to reward everyone according to the same measure, the quantity of autonomous effort exhibited toward lifetime compensation. Table 12.2 shares the statistics of autonomous effort as well as circumstances of chance (dynamic endowment) with respect to lifetime labor income among the population. The small standard deviation of autonomous effort among the population tells us that the hardest working 2.5% of the population exhibit roughly three times more autonomous effort than the mean.

Table 12.3 shares the effective tax rates of our models. The fact that the median effective tax rate for all four *Just Deserts* models are negative means that distribution according to a principle of desert increases the economic resource allocations of more individuals than vice versa.

12.98, ln(JD): 13.34) (recall that exponentiated lognormal distributions with shared medians share a mean when log transformed while our exponentiated distributions share a mean, not a median).

[8] Card and DiNardo (2002).

[9] "The ratio between the ninetieth percentile of the income distribution and the tenth percentile." Piketty (2014), 267.

Table 12.3 Distribution of *Just Deserts* transfer rates, 2016

	Original	JD.LE	JD.AR	JD.LS	JD.LS.MR.BV
Mean	0%	−431.2%	−175.6%	−802,500.0%	−125,400.0%
Median	NA%	−10.3%	−12.8%	−22.3%	−4.8%
25th centile	NA%	−181.5%	−109.2%	−185.4%	−36.5%
75th centile	NA%	41.9%	34.9%	22.6%	11.3%
Std. dev.	0%	2703.6%	2507.4%	7,119,790.4%	1,569,150.3%
Minimum	NA%	−140,980.8%	−164,567.5%	-75,317,369.4%	-41,539,559.1%
Maximum	NA%	85.9%	80.7%	9,582,072.3%	33.3%
90/10 ratio	NA	−0.1	−0.2	−0.1	−0.2

Table 12.4 Distribution of *Just Deserts* transfer rates relative to actual transfers, by quintile, unweighted, 2016

	Original (%)	JD.LE (%)	JD.AR (%)	JD.LS (%)	JD.LS.MR.BV (%)
Quintile 1	−9.2	−3209.5	−1855.6	−7,382,419.8	−302,153.5
Quintile 2	−2.3	−342.2	−222.9	−169.2	−21.1
Quintile 3	1.6	−110.3	−98.9	−37.0	−7.0
Quintile 4	5.0	−30.7	−42.7	3.1	1.7
Quintile 5	13.8	21.6	3.7	17.6	10.5
All quintiles	7.7	−431.2	−175.6	−802,494.2	−125,420.2
81st–90th centiles	8.1	14.2	−4.4	18.4	6.7
91st–95th centiles	10.7	21.6	3.3	17.2	12.4
96th–99th centiles	15.1	40.1	24.4	17.9	16.0
Top 1	20.1	38.2	21.4	7.5	25.4

Table 12.4 shares the average tax rates of our models alongside an illustrative comparison to 2010 average *personal* income tax rates.[10]

While these numbers already suggest a significant amount of unmerited inequality could be addressed, note that we lack important compensation

[10] These numbers, "Original," are not strictly comparable to the *Just Deserts* models due to different tax units (personal income tax rates from household quintiles vs. individual quintiles) and definition of income (before-tax income vs. labor income) but are for illustrative purposes only. CBO—Congressional Budget Office (2013), 9. "Before-tax income is the sum of market income and government transfers. Market income is composed of labor income, business income, capital gains, capital income (excluding capital gains), income received in retirement for past services, and other sources of income. Government transfers are cash payments and in-kind benefits from social insurance and other government assistance programs."

data on which to specify model parameters, including pre-birth data for some individuals near the end of their careers. This analysis begs the question: is the *Just Deserts* proposal likely to show stronger or weaker anti-inequality effects once data from older individuals becomes observable (rather than imputed) and we account for compensation dynamics across entire lifetimes?

For at least two as yet unmentioned reasons, we should see that the original distribution exhibits greater unmerited inequality when a full picture of lifetime compensation is taken into account. First, the age range of our observed data overweights the period when (some) contemporary women's compensation are most similar to men's, that is, prior to age 30. As later years are appended, we are likely to see stronger evidence of the gender wage gap and thus a greater difference between a *Just Deserts* proposal and the current distribution. Second, this age range overweights the period when differentially educated earners still show similar lifetime compensation. If one individual's first year of family headship labor income occurred after high school graduation at age 18 and by age 30, our dataset contains 13 years of labor income at $30,000 (sum: $390,000) while a second individual's first year of family headship labor income occurred after college graduation at age 23, allowing 8 years of labor income by age 30, even at $50,000 per year (66% greater than $30,000) their empirical lifetime labor income is $400,000, only 2.5% greater. Our model is, accordingly, likely to see young individuals' natural lottery endowments as more similar than they will appear to be after capturing more years of labor income data when the divergent slopes of lifetime labor income trajectories move away from their point of intersection. Of course, I stress again that the proposal is agnostic and only the *ex post* data can tell. As the economy changes, so does the annual model, avoiding any unnecessary or entangling commitments, theoretical or otherwise.

If we turn to those individuals in our sample who either received or gave the largest *Just Deserts* transfer, we see that the Luck-Egalitarian models make the largest transfers to those individuals who exhibited the largest autonomous effort toward formal market labor income while the Lump-Sum models' largest transfers are considerably smaller and go to individuals with $0 lifetime labor income (see Tables 12.5 and 12.6).

Table 12.5 Details of maximum *Just Deserts* transfers, 2016

	Original	JD.LE	JD.AR.LE	JD.LS	JD.LS.MR.BV
Transfer	NA	$87,675,776	$120,511,446	$753,174	$1,657,556
Circumstances of chance	NA	$2634	$2634	$715	$3,983,568
Autonomous effort coefficient	NA	142.387	142.387	0.000	0.218
Original allocation	NA	$375,000	$375,000	$0	$868,634
Just Deserts allocation	NA	$88,050,776	$120,886,446	$753,174	$2,526,190

Table 12.6 Details of minimum *Just Deserts* transfers, 2016

	Original	JD.LE	JD.AR.LE	JD.LS	JD.LS.MR.BV
Transfer	NA	$−27,228,712	$−22,373,286	$−3,640,940	$−13,660,068
Circumstances of chance	NA	$1,994,066	$1,994,066	$4,394,796	$1,069,422
Autonomous effort coefficient	NA	19.793	19.793	0.373	39.561
Original allocation	NA	$39,468,495	$39,468,495	$1,639,187	$42,307,831
Just Deserts allocation	NA	$12,239,783	$17,095,210	$−2,001,752	$28,647,763

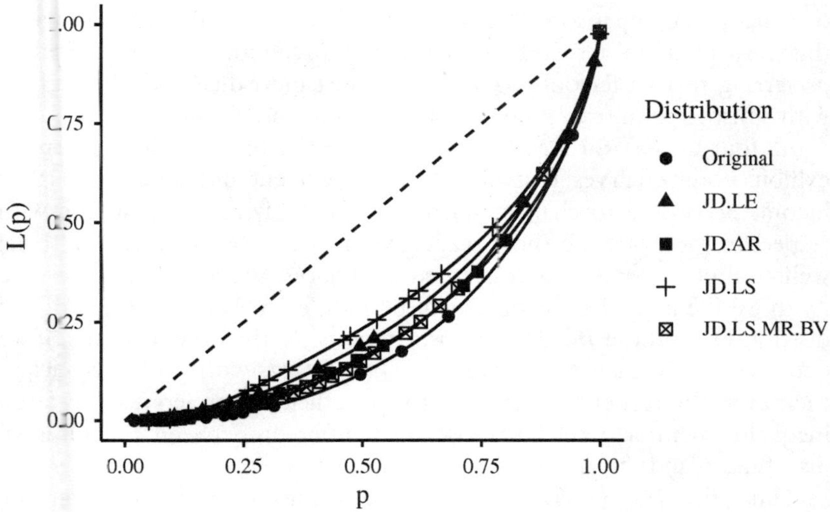

Fig. 12.2 Lorenz curves of original and *Just Deserts* distributions, 2016

12.1.1 Lorenz Curves and Gini Coefficients

Another way that economists view inequality is through Lorenz curves. Lorenz curves represent a portion of the population (ordered from poorest to richest) on the horizontal axis, from 0–1, and the corresponding portion of aggregate income belonging to that portion on the vertical axis, 0–1. If each member of the population had an equal allocation of resources, the Lorenz curve would look like a straight line from bottom-left (0,0) to top-right (1,1) while inequality is always represented by downward departures from that line, always conforming to a monotonically increasing function (see Fig. 12.2). Using the Atkinson theorem,[11] we may assert normative weight to distributions if certain conditions are met. Principally, as long as the observer's imposed utility-of-income function is strictly increasing and concave, they should always prefer a distribution that may be represented by a dominant Lorenz curve, that is, one which is greater than

[11] Although previously published in less elegant form by Kolm and later developed by Kakwani and Shorrocks.

or equal to a comparison Lorenz curve at all points.[12] Roughly speaking, this means that an observer with egalitarian preferences—even as small as preferring to transfer only $1 to the poorest individual—will be happier with a distribution represented by a dominant Lorenz curve.[13]

All four of our *Just Deserts* models, except Lump-Sum Endowment,[14] exhibit Lorenz curves that dominate the current distribution of labor income according to chance and merit. To clarify, in the first case with respect to the worst off, those readers with a pure Rawlsian leximin social welfare function and thus concerned only about the worst-off individual (with $0 lifetime labor income) will be indifferent between the Original distribution and the *Just Deserts* distributions. At the other extreme, if we could costlessly transfer according to *Just Deserts* with no leaky bucket, then even the reader with the most strict efficiency preference, perfectly inequality neutral, would likewise be indifferent between the Original distribution and the *Just Deserts* distributions.

Thus, the *Just Deserts* proposal is unanimously preferred over the Original distribution by observers with any consequentialist egalitarian preferences at all (including strict egalitarians), while it is considered identically just in comparison with the Original distribution by both individuals with perfect preferences for priority (concerned only with the worst off) and, with respect to the Lump-Sum policy variations, efficiency (concerned only with aggregate output). For those with perfect preferences for robust equality of opportunity, only the Luck-Egalitarian model will be maximally satisfactory under conditions of heterogeneous goods, while all *Just Deserts* models will be maximally satisfactory to those who require only weak equality of opportunity—a dubious possibility through current *ex ante* public policies.

[12] Lambert (2001), 2.31. Also note that our mean labor incomes are the same under all distributions and so the Lorenz curve and Shorrock's generalized Lorenz curve are equivalent. Lambert (2001), chap. 3.

[13] We do not expect the ethical observer, a socially concerned and personally disinterested individual, to have a convex utility-of-income function, that is, prefer more inequality to less for the sake of inequality alone, although this is, strictly speaking, a logical possibility that the *Just Deserts* proposal would also fail to satisfy.

[14] With negative distributions, these individuals did not receive sufficient lifetime labor income to pay their current *Just Deserts* liabilities. While these individuals may not pay with compensation they did not earn, assets may be used for payment.

Other measures also show that we have reduced inequality. The Gini coefficient for our Original distribution based on chance and merit is 0.566 and has been reduced to 0.467, 0.516, 0.446, and 0.507 (JD.LE, JD.AR, JD.LS.E, and JD.LS.E.MR.BV, respectively).[15] For Atkinson, a reduction in the Gini coefficient of 0.03 is a "salient reduction"[16] and the *Just Deserts* models show reductions of 0.099, 0.050, 0.119, and 0.059.[17] Furthermore, other scholars of just distributions have found similar percentage reductions in the Gini coefficient of around 25% on *single-year analyses* while also suggesting that the simple linear model used here may exhibit biased *underestimation* of this percent reduction when compared with other semi-parametric methods and nonlinear models.[18]

Lastly, following Piketty I present the "social tables" of each distribution.[19] In these tables, I present the share of total labor income received by the bottom 50% of laborers, the next 40% of laborers, the top 10% of laborers, the top 5% of laborers, and the top 1% of laborers for each *Just Deserts* distribution, including the Original. While the top 5% of laborers within the specified distribution (these are not necessarily the same individuals across different policies) received 25% of all labor income under the Original distribution, they receive between 21% and 25% of labor income under the four new *Just Deserts* policies (see Table 12.7). Another way to view the same information is to understand the percent difference of labor income shares relative to the Original distribution. Here we see that the total share of income going to the bottom 50% of laborers changes by anywhere from 29% to 87% under the four new *Just Deserts* policies (see Table 12.8). Thus, it is clear across a number of measures that implementation of a distributive principle of desert reduces inequality.

[15] The Ricci-Schutz coefficient (or Pietra's measure) is less popular but easier to interpret than the Gini coefficient, as it is equivalent to the percent of population compensation that would need to be transferred from above the mean to below the mean in order to reach perfect equality. The original Ricci-Schutz coefficient for the unweighted sample is 0.479 and has been reduced, respectively, to 0.370, 0.425, 0.229, and 0.442 (JD.LE, JD.AR, JD.LS.E, and JD.LS.E.MR.BV, respectively). Proper weights will change this, but not much, so it is only suggestive at this point.

[16] Atkinson (2015).

[17] Peragine defines the difference in pre- and post-implementation Gini coefficients as the "opportunity redistribution" statistic. Peragine (1998).

[18] Pistolesi (2007).

[19] Piketty (2014), 246–270.

Table 12.7 Details of *Just Deserts* income shares, 2016

	Original (%)	JD.LE (%)	JD.AR (%)	JD.LS (%)	JD.LS.MR.BV (%)
Top 1%	10	8	9	9	7
Top 5%	25	23	25	22	21
Top 10%	39	34	38	33	34
Middle 40%	50	47	47	45	51
Bottom 50%	12	19	16	22	15

Table 12.8 Details of difference in *Just Deserts* income shares, 2016

	Original (%)	JD.LE (%)	JD.AR (%)	JD.LS (%)	JD.LS.MR.BV (%)
Top 1%	NA	−20	−4	−6	−26
Top 5%	NA	−12	−1	−13	−18
Top 10%	NA	−12	−3	−15	−13
Middle 40%	NA	−5	−6	−9	4
Bottom 50%	NA	62	36	87	29

12.2 Desert

The above analysis focuses on the social welfare preferences for a principle of equality that we have satisfied through a distributive justice principle of desert. Yet, might we construct social welfare preferences for desert itself?[20] I construct an original Desert curve[21] by ordering the population in the typical manner, from those with the least compensation to the greatest. The Desert curve, however, represents the cumulative sum of autonomous effort along the horizontal axis and the cumulative sum of rewards allocated to individuals on the vertical axis.[22] For example, 40% of aggregate autonomous effort (with the population ordered by lifetime

[20] The following discussion may be seen as a step toward answering Ferreira and Peragine's call for robust measures. Ferreira and Peragine (2015), 31.

[21] For alternative constructions of Lorenz curves for "equal opportunity" or "fairness," cf. Peragine (1998); Almås et al. (2011); For alternative constructions of Lorenz curves for "equal opportunity" and "fairness," cf. Lefranc et al. (2009).

[22] Note that this looks like a formalization of a measure of the satisfaction of Kagan's "bell motion" as well as Arneson's argument for "a form of consequentialism that is prioritarian both in the domain of desert and in the domain of well-being and gives extra priority to achieving well-being gains for those who are comparatively more deserving." Arneson (2007), 264; Kagan (2012).

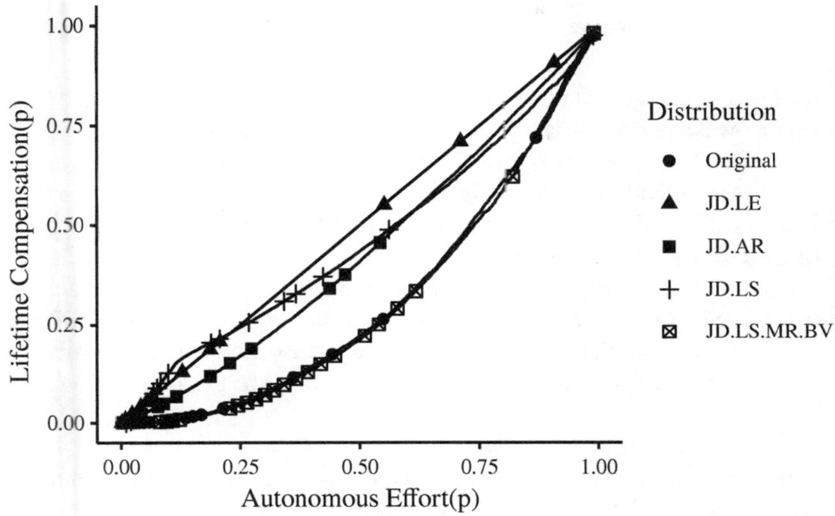

Fig. 12.3 Merit curves of original and *Just Deserts* distributions, 2016

labor income) yields ~10% of reward under the Original distribution (see Fig. 12.3). Given the above, the area between a Desert curve and the 45° line between (0,0) and (1,1) should be understood as a lower-bound estimate of the distance between that distribution and true *Just Deserts*.[23]

One difference between Desert curves and Lorenz curves is that individuals may actually receive too much of the reward, thus crossing above the 45 line between (0,0) and (1,1) while Lorenz curves may never do so. Note that in our case, the Lump-Sum Endowment curve does exactly this. Similar to typical Lorenz curves, each Desert Curve may be further simplified to a Gini coefficient. The Gini coefficients for the Original distribution is 0.376 and our Desert Curves are 0.000, 0.159, 0.151, and 0.294 (JD.LE, JD.AR, JD.LS, and JD.LS.MR.BV, respectively).

[23] Ramos and Van de Gaer (2012); Ferreira and Gignoux (2011).

12.3 Economic Mobility

I made a few bold claims in the introduction, one claim being that *Just Deserts* would maximally increase observable economic mobility and overthrow chance as the last tyrant of a free people. I argue that I have done so with the *Just Deserts* proposal as individual rewards are statistically independent of individual dynamic birth-endowment while perfectly sensitive to autonomous effort. Some scholars have suggested, to the contrary, that not only is it likely impossible to reduce the intergenerational correlation between parental compensation and those of their adult children to zero (a small piece of *Just Deserts*), but that we *ought not* reduce that correlation to zero. That is to say, that there exist purported reasons why the transmission of economic, and perhaps social, advantages ought to be reduced, but not absolutely.[24]

The typical arguments in favor of decreasing this intergenerational correlation rely upon principles of economic efficiency, economic inequality, and social justice. Yet, not one of these principles requires a full reduction to zero correlation. On the other hand, these scholars suggest that principles including privacy and parental partiality through both self-interest and altruism positively argue against zero correlation.[25] The argument says: it is possible that optimal efficiency, inequality, and social justice may recommend a correlation greater than 0.0 and, furthermore, much of this correlation would be due to genes, preferences, and norms with which social policy has no right to interfere given their place within the private bounds of the family or the individual.[26] In addition, all of these are simply reinforced by assortative mating practices—practices that again forbid interference.[27]

These arguments fail to hit the target, however, when confronted by the *Just Deserts* proposal—one that is an *ex post* intervention upon rewards rather than an *ex ante* intervention upon circumstances of chance such as

[24] Bowles et al. (2005a), 21–22; Harding et al. (2005), 131–140; Swift (2005).

[25] More technically, they reject the desire to distribute resources such that our estimate of the correlation to be exhibited by the true underlying data generating processes would be statistically indistinguishable from 0.

[26] Swift (2005); This is also a classic conservative objection to egalitarianism according to Anderson, cf. Anderson (1999), 288.

[27] Assortations show wealth correlations of 0.4 that contribute to greater household wealth inequality as well. Charles et al. (2013).

genes and other family gifts. Using an extremely conservative amount of information, our models have already demonstrated that we may decrease this correlation to 0 in ways that very few contemporary privacy arguments would begrudge. The only piece of information in our models to which the federal government may not already have explicitly authorized access might be "parental educational attainment prior to the individual's birth."

As an *ex post* intervention, the *Just Deserts* proposal has thus not recommended interventions upon genes, norms, preferences, or even (under some conditions) relative prices![28] Similarly, the *Just Deserts* proposal has completely avoided a Plato's *Republic* interference in mating decisions, parental self-interest, or parental altruism. There is no compulsion for high-, low-, or middle-endowment individuals to adjust their mating decisions, to restrict their investments or expenditures on their children, nor even to assist others' children in any way whatsoever. In other words, parents may justly "read bedtime stories to their children."[29] Granted, the richest individuals—now those individuals who exhibit the most hard work—may still seek the most exclusive, elite forms of education (human capital and behavioral formation opportunities) for their children. Nonetheless, rewards will continue to be independent of the natural lottery and dependent solely upon autonomous effort as long as the *Just Deserts* proposal is empowered to accurately measure compensation and immutable circumstances prior to, and at the time of, the natural lottery.

12.4 Poverty

There is a strong case in both the philosophical and economic literatures on distribution, as well as a human rights framework, to turn our attention to sufficiency or priority for the worst off rather than utilizing a distributive principle of equality, *per se*.[30] Equality simply suggests that, *ceteris paribus*, eliminating absolute or relative differences between individuals is better. The challenge from proponents of these other two principles is the suggestion that we are less tolerant of equality when it increases poverty and more tolerant of inequality when it has no impact on poverty.

[28] Recall that lump-sum taxes allow one to change the economy without "distorting" the economy.

[29] Segall (2013); Mason (2006).

[30] Parfit (2000); Feldstein (2005), 12.

Thus, Rawls' leximin suggests placing priority on the worst-off member of society[31] and allowing any and all inequality until it is bad for the worst off. Adherents of a principle of sufficiency suggest that the worst off receives a minimum allocation such that no individual is below the sufficiency threshold. Neither, however, specifies a unique, determinate mapping that describes from which other individuals in the population these transfers originate—the richest individual, the wealthiest, a uniform tax rate on all above the threshold, and so on.

To answer these concerns, although we might empirically examine poverty under the Original distribution and the *Just Deserts* distributions for more detailed analysis, we will defer for reasons of time and space. Nonetheless, I should note that we can first make a theoretically powerful statement, continuing to use Lorenz curves (as well as TIP curves for the incidence, intensity, and inequality of poverty). Using two poverty theorems which state that rank and generalized Lorenz dominance guarantee reduced poverty headcount ratio and reduced poverty deficit, we may choose any conceivable ***individual-based*** poverty line and based upon the above Lorenz curve dominance, guarantee that, in comparison to the Original distribution, our *Just Deserts* distributions reduce poverty as well.[32]

12.5 Imperfect Models and Just Outcomes

Amartya Sen has asked that we step away from attempts to identify transcendental justice—the absolute perfect system of justice—and toward comparative justice, simply identifying when one non-ideal system or outcome is more just than another.[33] Imagine for a moment that our particular first-order approximation model is imperfect but we nevertheless

[31] Tungodden and Vallentyne (2007).

[32] Lambert (2001), 77. We technically need to exclude zero incomes for this to hold, however, given that the generalized Lorenz curve of our multiple *Just Deserts*' distributions never falls below that of our original chance plus merit distribution, we can say more strictly that poverty is reduced for all poverty lines above the lowest non-zero income in the population. Thus, all conceivable poverty lines for the United States show less poverty under *Just Deserts* than we see today. Of course, it must be noted that this poverty measure follows the methodological individualism of the *Just Deserts* proposal and completely forgoes any analysis of households and excludes all those who are not moral agents.

[33] Sen (2009).

decide to implement the *Just Deserts* proposal in accordance with the calculations of this imperfect model. What consequences might we expect and must we reject the good on behalf of perfect justice, forced to wait until we have found that year's ***absolutely perfect*** model of the way formal labor market lifetime compensation depend upon circumstances of chance before implementation might be considered just? As we shall see, there are good reasons to implement an imperfect model as I have described.[34]

First, to fix ideas, imagine that our current *Just Deserts* Luck-Egalitarian model, JD.LEv1.1 is properly executed by April 15, 2017 for lifetime compensation up to December 31, 2016. Unfortunately, we discover five months later that there is a model, JDv2.1, that becomes the new "best current model," indicating different allocations of rewards are necessary to realize *Just Deserts.* Has the implementation of the *Just Deserts* proposal generated an (objectionable) injustice?

First, due to responsible bookkeeping, we have tracked the present value of *Just Deserts* Adjustments Due and Adjustments Rendered each year and may thus easily take account of any necessary changes. For example, if Sherlock had previously received compensation of $500,000 in the formal labor market and exhibited a transfer of −$200,000 in accord with *Just Deserts* principles in 2017 but our new model suggests that a transfer of −$150,000 would more precisely reward his autonomous effort, it is a simple matter to make each individual whole. Sherlock now holds the same present value as he would have held had the new model been previously implemented in April 2017 and his only loss is temporal rather than financial. Perhaps he bought a smaller house, or consumed fewer luxury pipes, but this deferred consumption of a larger house and fine pipes and his control of capital has been rectified. While not every individual will possess a future discount rate identical with the inflation rate used to calculate present value, it is hard for Sherlock to complain of injustice when, consuming only $300,000 instead of $350,000, he has been paid back with interest for his lost opportunity with respect to the extra $50,000.

More forcefully to my mind, let us turn to the case of Irene who had previously earned $200,000 and exhibited a credit transfer of +$100,000 in

[34] At the very least, I think I can meet Wolff's criteria: "All that is required is a policy that will approximately achieve the goal. If some errors creep in, that may be inevitable, but as long as the broad shape of resulting distributions reflects the underlying principle or value, that may well be enough." Wolff (2003), 227.

2017, for a total allocation of \$300,000, while the new model suggests that a transfer of +\$150,000 to her account would be more appropriate. What can we say to Irene who has died unexpectedly? We cannot pay her back for the lost opportunity to consume this \$50,000. Has the implementation of the *Just Deserts* proposal generated an (objectionable) injustice? This is a tougher case, but let me continue before I resolve it.

To complete our story, let us imagine that Sherlock's brother, Mycroft, is a civil servant who dislikes the *Just Deserts* proposal as he is certain that, unmerited though they may be, he would consume and control more economic resources without it. Without an argument against the theory of desert, he suggests that it is because of cases like those of himself and his brother, as well as tragic cases such as that of Irene, that we should abolish the *Just Deserts* proposal, that is, because the proposal is imperfect, giving some individuals more or less than their *ideal Just Deserts.*

In response to Mycroft, the existence of imperfections is a weak argument with respect to the *Just Deserts* proposal. As shown above, the *currently governing* economic system of rewards absent the *Just Deserts* proposal is in fact a *Just Deserts* proposal itself, JD.LEv0.1, with an extremely deficient model that assumes that lifetime compensation among the population is already exclusively sensitive to autonomous effort in 2016:

A Priori Model #1: Joe's LC depends solely upon Joe's Autonomous Effort

$$LC_{Joe} = f(0, AutonomousEffort_{Joe}) \tag{12.1}$$

Thus, Mycroft would find himself in the uncomfortable position of rejecting one *Just Deserts* model in favor of another that is demonstrably more unjust with respect to rewarding agent responsibility—model JD.LEv1.1 empirically compels the belief that luck varies among the population and that lifetime compensation depends upon that luck while model JD.LEv0.1 simply makes an assumption. To be utterly clear, to prefer our current system of distribution over *Just Deserts* is to prefer a reward system that will always reward a *greater number of individuals* with an allocation that is a *greater distance from ideal Just Deserts* than any reward system predicated upon a "best current" *Just Deserts* model as described in Chap. 10. That is, there will be more cases equivalent to those of Sherlock and Irene, and in greater amounts, if we follow Mycroft's recommendation.

Finally, what if *Just Deserts*, rather than adjusting Sherlock's allocation closer to true *Just Deserts* (although too small), adjusts his allocation further from *Just Deserts* than it was under the Original distribution? That is to say, model JDv0.1—the current economy—rewarded Sherlock with $500,000, v1.1 now rewarded Sherlock with $300,000, but we will imagine that if we were omniscient, the ideal *Just Deserts* model would have rewarded Sherlock with $600,000.

Although not everyone is a consequentialist, I imagine that one must be at the extreme end of the deontological end of the spectrum to prefer "*allowing*" more of this kind of harm under JDv0.1 to "*committing*" less of this kind of harm under JDv1.1.[35] Again, the current distribution contains more cases of injustice exactly such as Mycroft objects to and in greater amounts than the *Just Deserts* proposal—or, stated inversely, *Just Deserts* comes "closest to giving everyone what he or she deserved despite at the same time giving rise to some undeserved inequalities."[36] It is unfortunate that all systems and practices of human justice have flaws, but to ask the entire population to bear a greater amount of the identical injustice by "allowing" harm so as to avoid "committing" an identical harm of making any individual (1) worse off than they deserve or (2) further from *Just Deserts* strikes me as mistaken.[37] Furthermore, I think it is highly questionable to assert that leaving in place the *status quo* public policy is to "allow," but not "commit," harm—the current economic distribution does not arise in the state of nature and requires active support and implementation for its existence.[38] As such, I think the argument is rather strongly in favor of imperfect implementation of the *Just Deserts* proposal as a species of comparative justice rather than choosing the *status quo* while we hope transcendental justice will somehow become feasible.

[35] For a brief review of consequentialism in relation to distributive justice, cf. Adler (2011), 22ff.

[36] Young (1999), 252; Also, cf. Sher (1987), 33; Goldman (1987).

[37] This argument ought to account, in domains beyond *Just Deserts*, for self-ownership rights that may trump public policy intervention.

[38] This argument does not apply to those such as Nagel arguing in favor of no redistribution.

CHAPTER 13

The *Just Deserts* Economy

As all good theories of distributive justice must win allies, I hope to tie up some loose ends in this chapter and forge some alliances by describing what the US economy might look like after implementation of the *Just Deserts* proposal. Here, I only briefly sketch some interesting results we might expect to see in the *Just Deserts* economy for philanthropy, feminists, and disability rights.

13.1 Economic Markets and Philanthropy

Some readers may question my choice of present value of lifetime compensation as the measure of the "basal grounds" of desert for economic rewards. The argument might look something like this: if society chooses to reward formal labor market compensation in part because it instrumentally makes everyone better off, why not narrow the measure to only that compensation that actually contributes to the social good? Perhaps tax evasion lawyers, financial speculators, coal plant employees, agricultural tobacco laborers,[1] and even minimum wage food service workers all participate in producing something with negative externalities, monopolies, information asymmetries, and so on whose costs are borne by the rest of society? Refinements of the ideal, and more importantly, non-ideal desert-relation are of course encouraged and easy to absorb into the *Just Deserts* proposal.

[1] Cf. Arneson (2007), 270–210.

J. T. Dwyer, *Chance, Merit, and Economic Inequality*,
https://doi.org/10.1007/978-3-030-21126-4_13

Alternatively, some may feel that I wish to define the measure of a person's worth through the value of their formal market production or that *Just Deserts* expresses "contemptuous pity" for poorly endowed individuals.[2] Recall that luck-egalitarian desert divides the universe into mutually exclusive, exhaustive, and independent classes, that is, circumstances of chance and autonomous effort. The moral agent only has genuine control over autonomous effort. The principle of desert begins with the control principle, that "people cannot be morally assessed for what is not their fault, or for what is due to factors beyond their control."[3] As such, if it were to find motivation in contempt, which I do not believe to be the case, that contempt would be for low-value autonomous effort rather than low-value circumstances of chance.

Lastly, perhaps it seems unfair that non-profit and government workers receive fewer rewards because they serve those without the means to pay or because they serve the public good—which many want, but no one wants to pay for? Would we not expect everyone to take high-paying jobs in financial services rather than non-profits? While the economy will surely change, as previously stated, each individual will continue to compare the "whole of the advantages and disadvantages of the different employments" to find the occupation with the highest net advantages. The market filter on the desert-basis, from an ideal standpoint, must be deficient—certainly individuals sometimes contribute value outside of market exchanges. Nonetheless, it would be hard to find a better policy mechanism. Lastly, it is likely that individuals who stand to gain from the *Just Deserts* proposal might seek to monetize their contributions, over time weakening the force of this concern.

Among many interesting consequences of the *Just Deserts* economy, I should point out that there will likely be greatly reduced need for philanthropists, charities, and non-profit organizations to serve the needs of those unlucky in the natural lottery with respect to lifetime compensation. Not only does the *Just Deserts* proposal reduce inequality by at least 17.5% and significantly reduce poverty—plausibly reducing the need for some current philanthropic expenses—but the *Just Deserts* proposal has maximally increased economic mobility, reducing the need for charity and non-profits that focus on ***unlucky*** populations who carry one or more of

[2] Anderson (1999), 289; Sugin (2011).
[3] Nagel (1979), 24.

the tags in our administrative dataset. As it was philanthropists, non-profits, and government agencies that helped make the *Just Deserts* proposal possible to defend in theory (as *Just Deserts* formalizes the concepts "privilege" and "structural inequality," or at least a shared core thereof), I therefore hope that they will support its implementation as the *Just Deserts* proposal realizes core outputs of their mission statements.

In addition, as a great deal of chance is removed from this economy, there will be need instead for response to a smaller number of disadvantaged individuals, including those who exhibit less than average autonomous effort as well as those who carry natural lottery disadvantages for which we have no administrative data. It is here that I hope philanthropists focus most of their *Just Deserts* energy, in addition to making the case for better, universal data collection in order to more nearly approximate ideal allocations of *Just Deserts* via a more sophisticated endowment tax. Further, a changing economy offers significant scope for philanthropists, non-profits, and government agencies to adapt to serve a new set of human needs, perhaps considering consumer welfare and financial regulation as a second important focus during the transition to a mature *Just Deserts* economy where those unaccustomed to income and wealth now control a great deal more thereof.

13.2 Women and Men[4]

One of the original motivations for this book was the economic gap between the sexes, yet a number of previous commentators on endowment taxes have argued that such taxes would further hurt women given their different relationship to formal market labor and compensation.[5] To the contrary, individuals whose natural lottery circumstances of chance include "female" show some of the largest gains under this particular *Just Deserts* model. While scholars such as Mimi Abramovitz have compellingly documented the ways in which social welfare policy has often regulated, rather than empowered, women,[6] I would argue that the simple *ex post* implementation of the luck-egalitarian endowment tax—one that breaks

[4] Of course, *Just Deserts* can accommodate any sex or gender classification beyond individual control that humans can measure.

[5] Anderson (1999).

[6] Abramovitz (1996).

the unnecessary link between outcomes and rewards—eschews any such regulation (see Chap. 4). That is to say, luck-egalitarian endowment taxes are ignorant of causal mechanisms of economic injustice and completely avoid intrusive *ex ante* interventions yet nonetheless realize robust equality of opportunity and, as such, are the simplest, most accurate, and most effective way to end the gender pay and wealth gaps.

Currently, the full-time, full-year gender pay gap is 22%—meaning that among these workers, women's pay is 22% less than men's in our economy. Weichselbaumer and Winter-Ebmer have suggested that at present rates, it will take six decades to cut this pay gap in half![7] Note, however, that the *Just Deserts* proposal will actually reverse the sign of this statistic in year one of implementation—the mean female will now control greater lifetime economic resources than the mean male. To be clear, this is no reversal of hierarchy nor is it affirmative action, it is simply the result of ensuring that relative rewards track relative autonomous effort—it is the elimination of the average male's free lunch.

Mean formal market lifetime labor income among the male population under the pre-*Just Deserts* distribution is estimated to be 118.0% greater than that of the mean female, \$1,547,029 over \$709,737 (see Table 13.1). Females' mean formal market lifetime labor income increases by 72.2% over females' pre-*Just Deserts* distribution (\$1,222,517 vs. \$709,737) and surpasses males' post-intervention mean by 27.7% (\$1,222,517 vs. \$957,662). While this reversal of the gender pay gap also holds true for median post-luck-egalitarian endowment tax holdings, this fails to be true for the 25th centile. Despite the fact that females at the 25th centile are poorer than males at the 25th centile after the luck-egalitarian endowment tax, the post-intervention 25th centile females' allocation is still 155.5% greater than the pre-*Just Deserts* allocation of 25th centile females, now \$425,980 rather than \$166,738.

In sum, *Just Deserts* already realizes robust equality of opportunity for economic rewards with respect to biological sex at birth. As such, the *Just Deserts* proposal clearly advances women's economic power and position while possessing the flexibility to address intersectional economic injustice via the same method. It is my hope that feminist economists will be among those most enthusiastic to take up the *Just Deserts* proposal as a new tool in the rich feminist literature to combat gender inequity.

[7] Weichselbaumer and Winter-Ebmer (2005).

Table 13.1 Distribution of lifetime compensation, by sex, 2016

	Original	*Original (M)*	*Original (F)*	*JD.LE*	*JD.LE (M)*	*JD.LE (F)*
Mean	$1,099,292	$1,547,029	$709,737	$1,099,292	$957,662	$1,222,517
Median	$649,724	$1,041,704	$460,875	$787,389	$709,712	$910,848
25th centile	$226,423	$357,076	$166,738	$430,832	$433,342	$425,980
75th centile	$1,484,426	$2,085,768	$990,896	$1,353,468	$1,146,609	$1,549,275
Std. dev.	$1,583,050	$2,061,408	$814,296	$1,202,882	$1,025,776	$1,325,789
Minimum	$0	$0	$0	$1	$1	$1
Maximum	$42,307,831	$42,307,831	$15,170,178	$88,050,776	$29,857,593	$88,050,776
90/10 ratio	40.6	36.1	35.7	11	7.5	15.6

13.3 Disability

Once implemented, the most difficult piece of the *Just Deserts* proposal will be to adjudicate grievances at the bar of justice under non-ideal circumstances. While I argue that we possess a clear and concise method for such adjudication, it will not reduce the initial friction of a transition from a society that rewards observed outcomes of interest—the combination of circumstances of chance and autonomous effort—to one whose rewards are exclusively sensitive to autonomous effort. Many hyper-endowment individuals will correctly complain that they are worse off in comparison to our current system of unmerited economic rewards. As we are confident, however, that *Just Deserts* rewards them with no more and no less than they deserve, we shall not worry. The more difficult problem will be the hypo- and hyper-endowed individuals who, according to our best scientific estimations, have put forth less than average autonomous effort toward lifetime compensation but who claim at the bar of justice that this estimation is not the result of a lack of autonomous effort but is due instead to a latent disability—a negatively valued circumstance of chance that is not captured in our administrative dataset. I say this with the hope that disability rights theorists and activists will support and strengthen the implementation of the *Just Deserts* proposal.

Under *Just Deserts*, I believe that disability theory might even move to the center of mainstream political debate. As I see it, the *Just Deserts* proposal shifts the framework of disability away from a debate between biological and social models of "root causes" and toward a framework of *diverse abilities* that we can precisely measure as the functional value of one's circumstances of chance with respect to any observed outcome of interest. Yet what of latent disabilities within the *Just Deserts* system that nonetheless seem to be clear disabilities to society, that is, disabilities with a post-natural lottery etiology.

> Imagine that Very Unlucky is struck by a meteorite on her forty-fifth birthday, an outcome completely beyond her control that constitutes a negatively valued circumstance of chance with respect to her lifetime compensation over the next 5 years. Must the *Just Deserts* proposal tell her that justice demands that she reduce her standard of living and transfer undeserved resources to those who deserve them because we do not collect post-birth data on circumstances of chance?

First, the percent of individuals with a post-natural lottery disability is a small minority. The nationally representative 2010 Survey of Income and Program Participation, using a rather expansive questionnaire-based definition of non-severe and severe disability, found that less than 17% of individuals aged 21–64 had a disability. While only 2.3% of children under the age of 3 are classified as with a disability, this number rises rapidly to 12.2% among those ages 6–14. This suggests that there is ample room for early, valid gathering of non-manipulable, individual-level information in order to improve the accuracy of the *Just Deserts* proposal as currently envisioned in order to ensure that individuals of all tastes and talents receive no more and no less than what they deserve. In addition, the labor force participation among the disabled was 50% of the participation rate of the non-disabled and average labor income, among those disabled who did participate, were 72% of non-disabled individuals' labor income.[8] Together, these two facts suggest that there is a large disability pay and wealth gap plausibly dependent upon circumstances of chance one might, with adequate measurement, observe at birth. It is my hope that the disability rights community will support implementation of the *Just Deserts* proposal as the simplest, most accurate, and most effective way to end the disability pay and wealth gaps.

Second, note that Very Unlucky had plenty of economic reward during her lifetime, far surpassing her reward had she labored in the old economy, and was quite capable of purchasing insurance policies in a well-functioning insurance market against latent circumstances of chance (those unobserved by the *Just Deserts* model) such as post-natural lottery disabilities. It is this insurance system, not the *Just Deserts* proposal, that (until skeptics no longer have political force) will continue to oversee the verification, management, and auditing of these cases. There are, however, two broad classes of individuals this insurance system will likely not cover.

First, while the insurance system in which Very Unlucky purchased a policy may be able to observe some, but not all, changes in an individual's talent for formal market compensation (given non-manipulable measurements of gross damage to the body and/or its systems), I would imagine that it would currently be prohibitively expensive to purchase an insurance policy against observable changes in an individual's taste.

[8] Brault (2012), 10–12, also cf. Table 1. Note, by individuals I refer to civilian, non-institutionalized persons.

> Imagine that Very Unlucky's twin sister, Falsely, wishes to take early retirement on her forty-fifth birthday and invents claims to have suffered a change in taste upon observing her sister's injury, an outcome completely beyond her control. While Falsely's average autonomous effort previously received $30,000 in compensation, she now claims that every hour that she is not watching a bullfight in Spain is pure misery and so the identical autonomous effort now only receives $5,000 in compensation while she vacations in Spain. How would an insurance system verify her claims?

Given current technology, I see little possibility for an insurance system to directly and cheaply measure circumstances of chance with respect to taste, although it may be true that *Just Deserts* captures correlates of taste via other circumstances of chance. Note, however, that we do not reject Falsely's claims because she identifies with her (new) taste Against the views of Dworkin, Arneson,[9] Scanlon,[10] Lake,[11] and Fleurbaey,[12] we are uninterested in individuals' subjective representations of their relationship to outcomes. That is, as the book has argued from the beginning, the principle of desert decisively sides with "control" (Cohen) rather than "preference" (Dworkin) as dispositive for responsibility given that preferences (one's taste),[13] in identical fashion as one's talent, may be exogenously dependent upon circumstances of chance.[14] Thus, neither the non-ideal policy implementation of *Just Deserts* nor current insurance markets will realize distributive justice for those individuals whose tastes, with respect to formal labor market compensation, change due to chance.

The second class of uncovered individuals will be children and others without the economic reward or legal standing sufficient to purchase an insurance policy. They will have little recourse against injuries and illnesses that impact their (future) ability to contribute value to others and thereby

[9] Arneson (2007).

[10] Scanlon (1986), 116–117.

[11] Lake (2001), 57.

[12] Dworkin argues that individuals should be responsible for preferences with which they identify. Dworkin (1981a); Fleurbaey is also very interested in the subjective elements of responsibility. Fleurbaey (2008), chap. 6.

[13] Preferences should here be understood to mean first-order or second-order desires or volitions as long as such may be exogenously dependent upon circumstances of chance. Frankfurt (1971), 7–14.

[14] Cohen (1989); Roemer (2012), 166.

receive market compensation. As a solution,[15] the *Just Deserts* proposal might require all individuals to contribute to a public insurance fund for all those persons outside the *Just Deserts* population. One may wonder why we shouldn't allow parents to choose to insure or not insure their children. The answer is, to my mind, that it would be patently unjust to say to an individual that their lifetime economic reward is catastrophically decreased based upon any circumstances of chance, whether or not those circumstances of chance happen to be their parents' genuine choices to adequately provide for their basic needs as children. Although we might have an insurance system for all persons outside the *Just Deserts* population, this appendix to the proposal is limited to the injuries and illnesses we can currently measure and identify, not all bad luck. That is, we are not accidentally employing an *ex ante* policy, we simply prevent children from suffering catastrophic illness and death with a basic health insurance system using reasonable resources (e.g., Medicaid).

Finally, although the biggest gap missed by the *Just Deserts* proposal and a well-functioning insurance market is changes in taste due to chance, there is also the possibility that neither Very Unlucky nor her sister Falsely purchased insurance (due to genuine choice or a lack of an insurance market). Ought we require a universal insurance system against a chance post-natural lottery change in taste or talent with respect to formal labor market compensation? In the absence of perfect information, a system of universal insurance makes those with safe tastes worse off (and those with risky tastes better off) through no fault or choice of their own. Likewise, a system of private insurance makes those without insurance struck by meteorites worse off (and those not so struck better off) through no fault or choice of their own. On the assumption, however, that the latter types of "worse off" are much more severe than the former, I would lean toward an initial creation of a universal insurance system as the best approximation to eliminating the power of luck over our lifetimes. I should take care to note that this dilemma is not a weakness of the principle of desert but of its non-ideal implementation. Under ideal circumstances, if we could measure the full vector of non-responsibility characteristics (luck) with respect to a given observed outcome of interest and knew the function of that same

[15] Admittedly, I would like to give more thought to the question of what we owe, if anything, to children under a *Just Deserts* proposal. Here I proceed tentatively and assume that the skeptic has not persuaded us that post-birth humans are moral agents.

outcome, it would be trivial to make the corresponding reward exclusively sensitive to the vector of responsibility characteristics with respect to that same outcome, and there would be zero need for an insurance market as individuals would have absolute and unreserved choice over their reward. Given the centrality of different abilities in the real-world implementation of the *Just Deserts* proposal, however, it is my hope that disability rights proponents will be avid supporters of its implementation.

CHAPTER 14

Conclusion

We now possess the power to implement this ancient idea of justice, a distributive principle of desert. Simultaneously, we have the capacity to robustly understand the consequences of such implementation at both a macroeconomic and microeconomic level, and the results look highly promising. As I have argued, the luck-egalitarian principle of desert is based upon the shared, fundamental moral intuition of the *control principle*. This intuition leads us to a normative ideal of *agent responsibility* and *luck-egalitarian desert*. When translated into principled public policy, the luck-egalitarian principle of desert actually maximizes *equality of opportunity*, maximizes *efficiency* under broad conditions that are always accessible to our public policy, and maximizes *liberty* with respect to one's place in the distribution by encompassing the Lockean and Nozickean provisos. Furthermore, its implementation significantly reduces the moral wrong that motivated this book by eliminating meaningful quantities of *unmerited* inequality and poverty while it simultaneously realizes the maximum feasible *economic mobility*. In sum, *Just Deserts* is far superior to our current economy on a host of fundamental distributive principles.

Moreover, this book has not only addressed these moral wrongs, but it has supplied a unique, determinate answer to the demanding question, "How ought we justly allocate economic resources among individuals?" By offering a rigorous formalization of luck-egalitarian desert, a formalization that is identical to economists' *endowment* as well as concepts such as *privilege* and *systemic inequality*, we may strip away all the chance differ-

J. T. Dwyer, *Chance, Merit, and Economic Inequality*,
https://doi.org/10.1007/978-3-030-21126-4_14

ences among various individuals and allocate rewards based upon the only factor genuinely and completely within individual control, *autonomous effort*. This allows us, under conditions of *homogeneous* and *heterogeneous goods*, under a balanced or imbalanced economy, to allocate to each individual precisely what they deserve while always satisfying Fleurbaey's "compensation principle."

Cohen wrote that the responsibility-sensitive literature from which I have heavily drawn "[…] has performed for egalitarianism the considerable service of incorporating within it the most powerful idea in the arsenal of the anti-egalitarian right: the idea of choice and responsibility."[1] This book has argued that a responsibility-sensitive distribution accords at least as well with a principle of desert, an extremely underutilized principle of distributive justice with the power to gather far greater, effective philosophical and political support for a just distribution of economic reward than currently dominant principles of equality, priority, sufficiency, or efficiency.

Desert is a powerful normative ideal. In this book I have traversed multiple disciplines in order to argue that not only ought we to implement this principle of distributive justice, but that it is already feasible to do so. Thus, I take great joy in the possibility that, if I am truly lucky, I have helped us take one step closer to the day when each individual's economic reward will be no more and no less than precisely their *Just Deserts*.

[1] Cohen (1989), 933.

References

26 U.S. Code § 63 - Taxable Income Defined. 2000.

Aaberge, Rolf, Magne Mogstad, and Vitorocco Peragine. 2011. Measuring Long-Term Inequality of Opportunity. *Journal of Public Economics* 95 (3): 193–204.

Abramovitz, Mimi. 1996. *Regulating the Lives of Women: Social Welfare Policy from Colonial Times to the Present*. Boston, MA: South End Press.

Adler, Matthew. 2011. *Well-Being and Fair Distribution: Beyond Cost-Benefit Analysis*. Oxford: Oxford University Press.

Allaire, J.J., et al. 2018. *rmarkdown: Dynamic Documents for R*. R package version 1.11.

Almås, Ingvild, et al. 2011. Measuring Unfair (in)Equality. *Journal of Public Economics* 95 (7–8): 488–499.

Alperovitz, Gar, and Lew Daly. 2008. *Unjust Deserts: How the Rich Are Taking Our Common Inheritance and Why We Should Take It Back*. New York, NY: The New Press.

Alstott, Anne, and Bruce A. Ackerman. 1999. *The Stakeholder Society*. New Haven, CT: Yale University Press.

Anderson, Elizabeth. 1999. What Is the Point of Equality? *Ethics* 109 (2): 287–337.

—. 2015. The Fundamental Disagreement Between Luck Egalitarians and Relational Egalitarians. In *Distributive Justice and Access to Advantage: G. A. Cohen's Egalitarianism*, ed. Alexander Kaufman, 21–39. Cambridge: Cambridge University Press.

Aristotle. 1999. *Nicomachean Ethics*. 2nd ed. Trans. Terence Irwin. Indianapolis, IN: Hackett Publishing Company, Inc.

J. T. Dwyer, *Chance, Merit, and Economic Inequality*,
https://doi.org/10.1007/978-3-030-21126-4

Arneson, Richard J. 1989. Equality and Equal Opportunity for Welfare. *Philosophical Studies* 56 (1): 77–93.

—. 1990. Liberalism, Distributive Subjectivism, and Equal Opportunity for Welfare. *Philosophy & Public Affairs* 19 (2): 158–194.

—. 2003. The Smart Theory of Moral Responsibility. In *Desert and Justice*, ed. Serena Olsaretti, 233–258. Oxford: Oxford University Press.

—. 2004. Luck Egalitarianism Interpreted and Defended. *Philosophical Topics* 32 (1/2): 1–20.

—. 2007. Desert and Equality. In *Egalitarianism: New Essays on the Nature and Value of Equality*, ed. Nils Holtug and Kasper Lippert-Rasmussen, 262–293. Oxford: Oxford University Press.

Atkinson, Anthony Barnes. 2015. *Inequality*. Cambridge, MA: Harvard University Press.

Atkinson, Anthony Barnes, and Joseph E. Stiglitz. 1980. *Lectures on Public Economics*. Maidenhead: McGraw-Hill.

Baker, Michael, and Gary Solon. 1999. *Earnings Dynamics and Inequality Among Canadian Men, 1976–1992: Evidence from Longitudinal Income Tax Records*. Working Paper 7370. NBER - National Bureau of Economic Research.

Barrett, Malcolm. 2018. *ggdag: Analyze and Create Elegant Directed Acyclic Graphs*. R package version 0.1.0.

Barry, Brian. 1965. *Political Argument*. New York, NY: Humanities Press.

—. 1991. *Liberty and Justice: Essays in Political Theory*. Vol. 2. Oxford: Oxford University Press.

BEA - Bureau of Economic Analysis. 2015. *Table 6.6D. Wages and Salaries Per Full-Time Equivalent Employee by Industry*. http://bea.gov/iTable/iTable.cfm?reqid=9&step=1#reqid=9&step=3&isuri=1&904=2005&903=201&906=q&905=2014&910=x&911=0.

Becker, Gary S. 1988. Family Economics and Macro Behavior. *American Economic Review* 78: 1–13.

Beckert, Jens. 2008. *Inherited Wealth*. Princeton, NJ: Princeton University Press.

Bedau, Hugo. 1967. Radical Egalitarianism. In *Nomos IX*, ed. R. Pennock and J. Chapman, 3–27. Palo Alto, CA: Atherton Press

Behrman, Jere R., and Paul Tarbman. 1985. Intergenerational Earnings Mobility in the United States: Some Estimates and a Test of Becker's Intergenerational Endowments Model. *The Review of Economics and Statistics* 67 (1): 144–151.

Benshalom, Ilan, and Kendra Stead. 2010. Values and (Market) Valuations: A Critique of the Endowment Tax Consensus. *Northwestern University Law Review* 104 (4): 1511–1558.

Benus, Jacob, and James N. Morgan. 1975. Time Period, Unit of Analysis, and Income Concept in the Analysis of Income Distribution. In *The Personal Distribution of Income and Wealth*. National Bureau of Economic Research

Studies in Income and Wealth, ed. James D. Smith, vol. 39. New York, NY: Columbia University Press.

Björklund, Anders, Markus Jäntti, and John E. Roemer. 2011. *Equality of Opportunity and the Distribution of Long-Run Income in Sweden*. Discussion Paper 5466. Bonn: Forschungsinstitut zur Zukunft der Arbeit (IZA).

BLS - Bureau of Labor Statistics. 2014. *Employer Costs for Employee Compensation*. http://www.bls.gov/news.release/ecec.nr0.htm.

—. 2015. National Compensation Measures. In *Handbook of Methods*. Washington, DC: BLS - Bureau of Labor Statistics.

Boeninger, Brian Pocock. 2011. *Partial Freedom and Degrees of Moral Responsibility: The Metaphysics of Influence and Libertarianism*. Ph.D., University of Notre Dame.

Bok, Hilary. 1998. *Freedom and Responsibility*. Princeton, NJ: Princeton University Press.

Bourguignon, Francois, Francisco H. G. Ferreira, and Michael Walton. 2007. Equity, Efficiency and Inequality Traps: A Research Agenda. *Journal of Economic Inequality* 5: 235–256.

Bowles, Samuel, Herbert Gintis, and Melissa Osborne. 2001. The Determinants of Earnings: A Behavioral Approach. *Journal of Economic Literature* 39: 1137–1176.

Bowles, Samuel, Herbert Gintis, and Melissa Osborne Groves. 2005a. Introduction. In *Unequal Chances: Family Background and Economic Success*, ed. Samuel Bowles, Herbert Gintis, and Melissa Osborne Groves, 1–22. Princeton, NJ: Princeton University Press.

—, eds. 2005b. *Unequal Chances: Family Background and Economic Success*. Princeton, NJ: Princeton University Press.

Bradford, David F. 1984. *Blueprints for Basic Tax Reform*. 2nd ed. Arlington, VA: Tax Analysts.

Brandolini, Andrea. 1992. *Nonlinear Dynamics, Entitlement Rules and the Cyclical Behaviour of the Personal Income Distribution*. Discussion Paper 84. Centre for Economic Performance, London School of Economics and Political Science.

Brault, Matthew W. 2012. *Americans with Disabilites: 2010*. Report P70-131. Washington, DC: US Census Bureau.

Bredgaard, Thomas, and Arthur Daemmrich. 2012. The Welfare State as a Growth Strategy: Denmark, Flexicurity, and the Politics of Globalization. http://ilera2012.wharton.upenn.edu/RefereedPapers/BredgaardThomas%20ArthurDaemmrich.pdf.

Brody, Baruch. 2000. Redistribution without Egalitarianism. In *Left-Libertarianism and Its Critics: The Contemporary Debate*, ed. Peter Vallentyne and Hillel Steiner, 31–47. New York, NY: Palgrave.

Campbell, C. A. 2003. Has the Self Free Will? In *Freedom, Determinism, and Responsibility: Readings in Metaphysics*, ed. Neil Campbell, 49–63. Upper Saddle River, NJ: Prentice-Hall.

Cappelen, Alexander W., Erik Ø. Sørensen, and Bertil Tungodden. 2010. Responsibility for What? Fairness and Individual Responsibility. *European Economic Review* 54 (3): 429–441.

Card, David, and John E. DiNardo. 2002. Technology and US Wage Inequality: A Brief Look. *Federal Reserve Bank of Atlanta Economic Review* 87 (3): 45–62.

Carens, Joseph H. 2015. The Egalitarian Ethos as a Social Mechanism. In *Distributive Justice and Access to Advantage: G. A. Cohen's Egalitarianism*, ed. Alexander Kaufman, 50–78. Cambridge: Cambridge University Press.

CBO - Congressional Budget Office. 2013. *The Distribution of Household Income and Federal Taxes, 2010.* Report. Washington, DC: CBO - Congressional Budget Office.

—. 2015. *Processes.* https://www.cbo.gov/about/processes.

Charles, Kerwin Kofi, Erik Hurst, and Alexander Killewald. 2013. Marital Sorting and Parental Wealth. *Demography* 50 (1): 51–70.

Chetty, Raj, et al. 2014. Where Is the Land of Opportunity?: The Geography of Intergenerational Mobility in the United States. *Quarterly Journal of Economics* 129 (4): 1553–1623.

Christiano, Thomas. 2007. A Foundation for Egalitarianism. In *Egalitarianism: New Essays on the Nature and Value of Equality*, ed. Nils Holtug and Kasper Lippert-Rasmussen, 83–97. Oxford: Oxford University Press.

Cohen, G. A. 1989. On the Currency of Egalitarian Justice. *Ethics* 99 (4): 906–944.

—. 1993. Equality of What? On Welfare, Goods and Capabilities. In *The Quality of Life*, ed. Martha C. Nussbaum and Amartya Sen. Oxford: Oxford University Press.

—. 1995. *Self-ownership, Freedom, and Equality.* Cambridge: Cambridge University Press.

—. 2011a. Expensive Taste Rides Again. In *On the Currency of Egalitarian Justice, and Other Essays in Political Philosophy*, ed. Michael Otsuka, 81–115. Princeton, NJ: Princeton University Press.

—. 2011b. Fairness and Legitimacy in Justice, and: Does Option Luck Ever Preserve Justice? In *On the Currency of Egalitarian Justice, and Other Essays in Political Philosophy*, ed. Michael Otsuka, 124–143. Princeton, NJ: Princeton University Press.

—. 2011c. How to Do Political Philosophy? In *On the Currency of Egalitarian Justice, and Other Essays in Political Philosophy*, ed. Michael Otsuka, 225–235. Princeton, NJ: Princeton University Press.

—. 2011d. On the Currency of Egalitarian Justice. In *On the Currency of Egalitarian Justice, and Other Essays in Political Philosophy*, ed. Michael Otsuka, 3–43. Princeton, NJ: Princeton University Press.

Coronado, Julia Lynn, Don Fullerton, and Thomas Glass. 2000. *The Progressivity of Social Security*. Working Paper 7520. NBER - National Bureau of Economic Research.

Cupit, Geoffrey. 1996a. Desert and Responsibility. *Canadian Journal of Philosophy* 26 (1): 83–99.

—. 1996b. *Justice as Fittingness*. Oxford: Oxford University Press.

Damico, Anthony Joseph. 2019. *Lodown: Locally Download and Prepare Publicly-Available Microdata*. R package version 0.1.0.

Daniels, Norman. 1996. *Justice and Justification: Reflective Equilibrium in Theory and Practice*. Cambridge: Cambridge University Press.

Danziger, Sheldon, Robert Haveman, and Eugene Smolensky. 1976. *The Measurement and Trend of Inequality: A Basic Revision - Comment*. Discussion Paper 335-76. University of Wisconsin - Madison: Institute for Research on Poverty.

Darrick Hamilton, and William Darity Jr. 2010. Can 'Baby Bonds' Eliminate the Racial Wealth Gap in Putative Post-Racial America? *Review of Black Political Economy* 37: 207–216.

Davis, Alyssa, and Lawrence Mishel. 2014. *CEO Pay Continues to Rise as Typical Workers Are Paid Less*. Issue Brief 380. EPI - Economic Policy Institute.

Delignette-Muller, Marie-Laure, Christophe Dutang, and Aurelie Siberchicot. 2018. *fitdistrplus: Help to Fit of a Parametric Distribution to Non-censored or Censored Data*. R package version 1.0-11.

Diamond, Peter A. 1982. Wage Determination and Efficiency in Search Equilibrium. *The Review of Economic Studies* 49 (2): 217–227.

Dick, James C. 1975. How to Justify a Distribution of Earnings. *Philosophy & Public Affairs* 4 (3): 248–272.

Dowle, Matt, and Arun Srinivasan. 2018. *data.table: Extension of 'data.frame'*. R package version 1.11.8.

Duncan, Greg, et al. 2005. The Apple Does Not Fall Far from the Tree. In *Unequal Chances: Family Background and Economic Success*, ed. Samuel Bowles, Herbert Gintis, and Melissa Osborne Groves, 23–79. Princeton, NJ: Princeton University Press.

Dworkin, Ronald. 1981a. What Is Equality? Part 1: Equality of Welfare. *Philosophy & Public Affairs* 10 (3): 185–246.

—. 1981b. What Is Equality? Part 2: Equality of Resources. *Philosophy & Public Affairs* 10 (4): 283–345.

Eastwood, Clint. 1992. *Unforgiven*. Film (Distributor: Warner Bros, Alberta, Canada).

Ewin, R. E. 1981. *Co-operation and Human Values: A Study of Moral Reasoning*. New York, NY: St. Martin's Press.

Feinberg, Joel. 1963. Justice and Personal Desert. In *Nomos VI: Justice*, ed. C. J. Friedrich and John W. Chapman. New York, NY: Atherton Press.

—. 1970a. Action and Responsibility. In *Doing & Deserving: Essays in the Theory of Responsibility*, ed. Joel Feinberg, 119–151. Princeton, NJ: Princeton University Press.

—. 1970b. Causing Voluntary Actions. In *Doing & Deserving: Essays in the Theory of Responsibility*, ed. Joel Feinberg, 152–186. Princeton, NJ: Princeton University Press.

—. 1970c. *Doing & Deserving: Essays in the Theory of Responsibility*. Princeton, NJ: Princeton University Press.

—. 1970d. Justice and Personal Desert. In *Doing & Deserving: Essays in the Theory of Responsibility*, ed. Joel Feinberg, 55–94. Princeton, NJ: Princeton University Press.

—. 1970e. Problematic Responsibility in Law and Morals. In *Doing & Deserving: Essays in the Theory of Responsibility*, ed. Joel Feinberg, 25–37. Princeton, NJ: Princeton University Press.

—. 1970f. Sua Culpa. In *Doing & Deserving: Essays in the Theory of Responsibility*, ed. Joel Feinberg, 187–221. Princeton, NJ: Princeton University Press.

—. 1970g. What Is So Special About Mental Illness? In *Doing & Deserving: Essays in the Theory of Responsibility*, ed. Joel Feinberg, 272–292. Princeton, NJ: Princeton University Press.

—. 1999. Justice and Personal Desert. In *What Do We Deserve?: A Reader on Justice and Desert*, ed. Louis P. Pojman and Owen McLeod, 70–83. Oxford: Oxford University Press.

Feldman, Fred. 1995a. Adjusting Utility for Justice: A Consequentialist Reply to the Objection from Justice. *Philosophy and Phenomenological Research* 55 (3): 567–585.

—. 1995b. Desert: Reconsideration of Some Received Wisdom. *Mind* 104 (413): 63–77.

—. 1996. Responsibility as a Condition for Desert. *Mind* 105 (417): 165–168.

Feldman, Fred, and Brad Skow. 2015. Desert. In *The Stanford Encyclopedia of Philosophy*, ed. Edward N. Zalta.

Feldstein, Martin. 2005. Rethinking Social Insurance. *American Economic Review* 95 (1): 1–24.

Fernholz, Ricardo, and Robert Fernholz. 2014. Instability and Concentration in the Distribution of Wealth. *Journal of Economic Dynamics and Control* 44: 251–269.

Ferreira, Francisco H. G., and Jérémie Gignoux. 2011. The Measurement of Inequality of Opportunity: Theory and an Application to Latin America. *Review of Income and Wealth* 57 (4): 622–657.

Ferreira, Francisco H. G., and Vitorocco Peragine. 2015. *Equality of Opportunity: Theory and Evidence*. Working Paper 7217. World Bank.

Fields, Gary S. 2003. Accounting for Income Inequality and Its Change: A New Method, with Application to the Distribution of Earnings in the United States. *Research in Labor Economics* 22 (3): 1–38.

Fischer, John Martin, and Mark Ravizza. 1998. *Responsibility and Control: A Theory of Moral Responsibility*. Cambridge: Cambridge University Press.

Fishkin, Joseph. 2014. *Bottlenecks: A New Theory of Equal Opportunity*. Oxford: Oxford University Press.

Fleurbaey, Marc. 1995a. Equal Opportunity or Equal Social Outcome? *Economics and Philosophy* 11 (1): 25–55.

—. 1995b. Equality and Responsibility. *European Economic Review* 39: 683–689.

—. 2008. *Fairness, Responsibility, and Welfare*. Oxford: Oxford University Press.

Fleurbaey, Marc, and Vitorocco Peragine. 2013. Ex Ante Versus Ex Post Equality of Opportunity. *Economica* 80 (317): 118–130.

Fox, John, Sanford Weisberg, and Brad Price. 2018. *car: Companion to Applied Regression*. R package version 3.0-2.

Frankfurt, Harry G. 1969. Alternate Possibilities and Moral Responsibility. *The Journal of Philosophy* 66 (23): 829–839.

—. 1971. Freedom of the Will and the Concept of a Person. *The Journal of Philosophy* 68 (1): 5–20.

Freeman, Richard Barry. 1997. Solving the New Inequality. *Boston Review*. http://new.bostonreview.net/BR21.6/freeman.html.

Freeman, Richard Barry, and Robert B. Reich. 1999. In *The New Inequality: Creating Solutions for Poor America*, ed. Joshua Cohen and Joel Rogers. Boston, MA: Beacon Press.

Freiman, Christopher, and Shaun Nichols. 2011. Is Desert in the Details. *Philosophy and Phenomenological Research* 82 (1): 121–133.

Gibbard, Allan. 1976. Natural Property Rights. *Noûs* 10 (1): 77–86.

—. 2000. Natural Property Rights. In *Left-Libertarianism and Its Critics: The Contemporary Debate*, ed. by Peter Vallentyne and Hillel Steiner, 23–30. New York, NY: Palgrave.

Goldman, Alan H. 1987. Real People (Natural Differences and the Scope of Justice). *Canadian Journal of Philosophy* 17 (2): 377–393.

Goodin, Robert E. 1985. Negating Positive Desert Claims. *Political Theory* 13 (4): 575–598.

—. 1999. Negating Positive Desert Claims. In *What Do We Deserve?: A Reader on Justice and Desert*, ed. by Louis P. Pojman and Owen McLeod, 234–244. Oxford: Oxford University Press.

Gosepath, Stefan. 2011. Equality. In *The Stanford Encyclopedia of Philosophy*, ed. Edward N. Zalta.

Graaff, Johannes de Villiers. 1957. *Theoretical Welfare Economics*. London: Cambridge University Press.

Groves, Melissa Osborne. 2005. Personality and the Intergenerational Transmission of Economic Status. In *Unequal Chances: Family Background and Economic Success*, ed. by Samuel Bowles, Herbert Gintis, and Melissa Osborne Groves, 208–231. Princeton, NJ: Princeton University Press.

Grunebaum, James O. 1987. *Private Ownership*. London/New York: Routledge/Kegan Paul.

Guyon, Isabelle, et al. 2010. Model Selection: Beyond the Bayesian/Frequentist Divide. *The Journal of Machine Learning Research* 11: 61–87.

Hahn, Frank H. 1973. On Optimum Taxation. *Journal of Economic Theory* 6 (1): 96–106.

Handcock, Mark S. 2016. *reldist: Relative Distribution Methods*. R package version 1.6-6.

Harding, David J., et al. 2005. The Changing Effect of Family Background on the Incomes of American Adults. In *Unequal Chances: Family Background and Economic Success*, ed. by Samuel Bowles, Herbert Gintis, and Melissa Osborne Groves, 100–144. Princeton, NJ: Princeton University Press.

Hardoon, Deborah. 2015. *Wealth: Having It All and Wanting More*. Report. Oxford: Oxfam.

Harrell, Frank E Jr. 2018. *Hmisc: Harrell Miscellaneous*. R package version 4.1-1.

Hart, H. L. A. 1968. *Punishment and Responsibility*. Oxford: Clarendon Press.

Hart, H. L. A., and Tony Honoré. 1959. *Causation in the Law*. Oxford: Clarendon Press.

Hayek, Friedrich A. von. 1978. *New Studies in Philosophy, Politics, Economics, and the History of Ideas*. London: Routledge & Kegan Paul.

Heathcote, Jonathan, Kjetil Storesletten, and Giovanni L. Violante. 2008. Insurance and Opportunities: A Welfare Analysis of Labor Market Risk. *Journal of Monetary Economics* 55 (3): 501–525.

Heckman, James J. 2014. *"Going Forward Wisely": Speech for the White House Early Childhood Education Summit*. Chicago: University of Chicago.

Heckman, James J., Robert J. Lalonde, and Jeffrey A. Smith. 1999. The Economics and Econometrics of Active Labor Market Programs. In *Handbook of Labor Economics*, ed. Orley C. Ashenfelter and David Card, vol. 3, 1st ed., chap. 31, 1865–2097. Amsterdam: Elsevier.

Hill, Martha S. 1992. *The Panel Study of Income Dynamics: A User's Guide*. Newbury Park, CA: Sage Publications.

Hirose, Iwao. 2014. *Egalitarianism*. New York, NY: Routledge.

Hobbes, Thomas. 1991 (1651). *Leviathan*. Cambridge Texts in the History of Political Thought. Cambridge: Cambridge University Press.

Holtug, Nils, and Kasper Lippert-Rasmussen. 2007. An Introduction to Contemporary Egalitarianism. In *Egalitarianism: New Essays on the Nature and Value of Equality*, ed. Nils Holtug and Kasper Lippert-Rasmussen, 1–37. Oxford: Oxford University Press.

Hunt, David P. 2000. Moral Responsibility and Unavoidable Action. *Philosophical Studies* 97: 195–227.

Hurka, Thomas. 2003. Desert: Individualistic and Holistic. In *Desert and Justice*, ed. Serena Olsaretti, 45–68. Oxford: Oxford University Press.

Hurley, S. L. 2003. *Justice, Luck, and Knowledge*. Cambridge, MA: Harvard University Press.

Hurley, Susan. 2011. The Public Ecology of Responsibility. In *Responsibility and Distributive Justice*, ed. Zofia Stemplowska and Carl Knight. Oxford: Oxford University Press.

Hyslop, Dean R. 2001. Rising U.S. Earnings Inequality and Family Labor Supply: The Covariance Structure of Intrafamily Earnings. *American Economic Review* 91 (4): 755–777.

Jed Wing, Max Kuhn. Contributions from, et al. 2018. *caret: Classification and Regression Training*. R package version 6.0-81.

Kagan, Shelly. 1999. Equality and Desert. In *What Do We Deserve?: A Reader on Justice and Desert*, ed. Louis P. Pojman and Owen McLeod, 298–314. Oxford: Oxford University Press.

—. 2003. Comparative Desert. In *Desert and Justice*, ed. Serena Olsaretti, 93–122. Oxford: Oxford University Press.

—. 2012. *The Geometry of Desert*. Oxford: Oxford University Press.

Kane, Bob, and Bill Finger. 1942. Two-Face (Harvey Dent). *Batman*.

Kant, Immanuel. 1993 (1784). *Grounding for the Metaphysics of Morals*. 3rd ed. Trans. James W. Ellington. Indianapolis, IN: Hackett Publishing Company, Inc.

Katz, Lawrence F., and David H. Autor. 1999. Changes in the Wage Structure and Earnings Inequality. In *Handbook of Labor Economics*, ed. Orley C. Ashenfelter and David Card, vol. 3A. Amsterdam: North-Holland Publishing.

Kaufman, Bruce E., and Julie L. Hotchkiss. 2000. *The Economics of Labor Markets*. 5th ed. Fort Worth, TX: Harcourt College Publishers.

King, Desmond. 1999. *In The Name of Liberalism: Illiberal Social Policy in the United States and Britain*. Oxford: Oxford University Press.

Kleiber, Christian, and Achim Zeileis. 2017. *AER: Applied Econometrics with R*. R package version 1.2-5.

Kleinig, John. 1973. *Punishment and Desert*. The Hague: Martinus Nijhoff.

—. 1999. The Concept of Desert. In *What Do We Deserve?: A Reader on Justice and Desert*, ed. Louis P. Pojman and Owen McLeod, 84–92. Oxford: Oxford University Press.

Knight, Frank Hyneman. 1935. *The Ethics of Competition*. New York: Harper & Brothers.

Knight, Carl. 2009. *Luck Egalitarianism: Equality, Responsibility, and Justice*. Edinburgh: Edinburgh University Press.

—. 2011. Responsibility, Desert, and Justice. In *Responsibility and Distributive Justice*, ed. Zofia Stemplowska and Carl Knight. Oxford: Oxford University Press.

Knight, Carl, and Zofia Stemplowska. 2011. Responsibility and Distributive Justice: An Introduction. In *Responsibility and Distributive Justice*, ed. Carl Knight and Zofia Stemplowska, 1–23. Oxford: Oxford University Press.

Kohn, Melvin L., and Carmi Schooler. 1982. Job Conditions and Personality: A Longitudinal Assessment of Their Reciprocal Effects. *American Journal of Sociology* 87 (6): 1257–1286.

—. 1983. *Work and Personality: An Inquiry into the Impact of Social Stratification.* Norwood, NJ: Ablex.

Lake, Christopher. 2001. *Equality and Responsibility*. Oxford: Oxford University Press.

Lambert, Peter. 2001. *The Distribution and Redistribution of Income*. 3rd ed. Manchester: Manchester University Press.

Lamont, Julian. 1994. The Concept of Desert in Distributive Justice. *Philosophical Quarterly* 44 (174): 45–64.

—. 1995. Problems for Effort-Based Distribution Principles. *Journal of Applied Philosophy* 12 (3): 215–229.

—. 1997. Incentive Income, Deserved Income and Economic Rents. *Journal of Political Philosophy* 5 (1): 26–46.

Lamont, Julian, and Christi Favor. 2014. Distributive Justice. In *The Stanford Encyclopedia of Philosophy*, ed. Edward N. Zalta.

Latus, Andrew. 2000. Moral and Epistemic Luck. *Journal of Philosophical Research* 25: 149–172.

Lefranc, Arnaud, Nicolas Pistolesi, and Alain Trannoy. 2009. Equality of Opportunity and Luck: Definitions and Testable Conditions, with an Application to Income in France. *Journal of Public Economics* 93 (11): 1189–1207.

Lerner, Melvin. 1980. *The Belief in a Just World: A Fundamental Delusion*. New York, NY: Springer.

Lewis, Charlton T., and Charles Short. 1879. In *Compos*, ed. Charlton T. Lewis and Charles Short. Oxford: Clarendon Press.

Lippert-Rasmussen, Kasper. 2011. Luck Egalitarianism and Group Responsibility. In *Responsibility and Distributive Justice*, ed. Zofia Stemplowska and Carl Knight. Oxford: Oxford University Press.

—. 2014. Justice and Bad Luck. In *The Stanford Encyclopedia of Philosophy*, ed. Edward N. Zalta.

Locke, John. 1690. *An Essay Concerning Human Understanding*. New York, NY: Dover Publications.

—. 1997 (1689). Second Treatise of Government. In *Classics of Modern Political Theory: Machiavelli to Mill*, ed. Steven M. Cahn, 213–292. New York: Oxford University Press.

Logue, Kyle, and Joel Slemrod. 2008. Genes as Tags: The Tax Implications of Widely Available Genetic Information. *National Tax Journal* LXI (4.2): 843–863.

Mahto, Ananda. 2018. *splitstackshape: Stack and Reshape Datasets After Splitting Concatenated Values*. R package version 1.4.6.

Markovits, Daniel. 2008. Luck Egalitarianism and Political Solidarity. *Theoretical Inquiries in Law* 9 (1): 271–308.

Marrero, Gustavo A., and Juan G. Rodríguez. 2013. Inequality of Opportunity and Growth. *Journal of Development Economics* 104: 107–122.

Marshall, Gordon, et al. 1999. What Is and What Ought to Be: Popular Beliefs about Distributive Justice in Thirteen Countries. *European Sociological Review* 15 (4): 349–367.

Mason, Andrew. 2006. *Levelling the Playing Field: The Idea of Equal Opportunity and Its Place in Egalitarian Thought*. Oxford: Oxford University Press.

Matravers, Matt. 2011. Mad, Bad, or Faulty? Desert in Distributive and Retributive Justice. In *Responsibility and Distributive Justice*, ed. Zofia Stemplowska and Carl Knight. Oxford: Oxford University Press.

Mazumder, Bhashkar. 2001a. *Earnings Mobility in the US: A New Look at Intergenerational Inequality*. Working Paper 2001-18. Federal Reserve Bank of Chicago.

—. 2001b. *The Mis-Measurement of Permanent Earnings: New Evidence from Social Security Earnings Data*. Working Paper 2001-24. Federal Reserve Bank of Chicago.

—. 2003. *Revised Estimates of Intergenerational Income Mobility in the United States*. Working Paper 2003-16. Federal Reserve Bank of Chicago.

—. 2005. The Apple Falls Even Closer to the Tree than We Thought: New and Revised Estimates of the Intergenerational Inheritance of Earnings. In *Unequal Chances: Family Background and Economic Success*, ed. Samuel Bowles, Herbert Gintis, and Melissa Osborne Groves, 80–99. Princeton, NJ: Princeton University Press.

McCall, Leslie, and Lane Kenworthy. 2009. Americans' Social Policy Preferences in the Era of Rising Inequality. *Perspectives on Politics* 7 (03): 459–484.

McKerlie, Dennis. 2007. Egalitarianism and the Difference Between Interpersonal and Intrapersonal Judgments. In *Egalitarianism: New Essays on the Nature and Value of Equality*, ed. Nils Holtug and Kasper Lippert-Rasmussen, 157–173. Oxford: Oxford University Press.

McLeay, Michael, Amar Radia, and Ryland Thomas. 2014. Money Creation in the Modern Economy. *Bank of England Quarterly Bulletin* 2014 (Q1): 1–14.

McLeod, Owen. 1996. Desert and Wages. *Utilitas* 8 (2): 205–221.

—. 1999a. Desert and Institutions. In *What Do We Deserve?: A Reader on Justice and Desert*, ed. Louis P. Pojman and Owen McLeod, 186–196. Oxford: Oxford University Press.

—. 1999b. Desert and Wages. In *What Do We Deserve?: A Reader on Justice and Desert*, ed. Louis P. Pojman and Owen McLeod, 271–282. Oxford: Oxford University Press.

—. 2003. On the Comparative Element of Justice. In *Desert and Justice*, ed. Serena Olsaretti, 123–144. Oxford: Oxford University Press.

Mill, John Stuart. 1991. Utilitarianism. In *On Liberty and Other Essays*, ed J. Dunn. Oxford: Oxford University Press.

Miller, David. 1976. *Social Justice*. Oxford: Oxford University Press.

—. 1989. *Market, State, and Community*. Oxford: Oxford University Press.

—. 1999a. Desert and Determinism. In *What Do We Deserve?: A Reader on Justice and Desert*, ed. Louis P. Pojman and Owen McLeod, 135–139. Oxford: Oxford University Press.

—. 1999b. Deserts. In *What Do We Deserve?: A Reader on Justice and Desert*, ed. Louis P. Pojman and Owen McLeod, 93–100. Oxford: Oxford University Press.

—. 1999c. *Principles of Social Justice*. Cambridge, MA: Harvard University Press.

—. 2003. Comparative and Noncomparative Desert. In *Desert and Justice*, ed. Serena Olsaretti, 25–44. Oxford: Oxford University Press.

Milne, Heather. 1986. Desert, Effort and Equality. *Journal of Applied Philosophy* 3 (2): 235–243.

Mirrlees, J. A. 1971. An Exploration in the Theory of Optimum Income Taxation. *The Review of Economic Studies* 38 (2): 175.

Mitnik, Pablo A., et al. 2015. New Estimates of Intergenerational Mobility Using Administrative Data. Statistics of Income Division, Internal Revenue Service.

Molander, Per. 2016. *The Anatomy of Inequality: Its Social and Economic Origins–and Solutions*. Brooklyn, NY: Melville House Publishing.

Mulligan, Thomas. 2018. *Justice and the Meritocratic State*. Abingdon: Routledge.

Murphy, Liam, and Thomas Nagel. 2004. *The Myth of Ownership: Taxes and Justice*. Oxford: Oxford University Press.

Nagel, Thomas. 1979. Moral Luck. In *Mortal Questions*, ed. Thomas Nagel, 24–38. Cambridge: Cambridge University Press.

—. 1991. *Equality and Partiality*. Oxford: Oxford University Press.

—. 2000. Equality. In *The Ideal of Equality*, ed. Matthew Clayton and Andrew Williams, 60–80. New York, NY: St. Martin's Press.

Nash, John. 1950. *Noncooperative Games*. Ph.D., Princeton University.

Nelkin, Dana K. 2013. Moral Luck. In *The Stanford Encyclopedia of Philosophy*, ed. Edward N. Zalta.

Noorman, Merel. 2012. Computing and Moral Responsibility. In *The Stanford Encyclopedia of Philosophy*, ed. Edward N. Zalta. Stanford, CA: Metaphysics Research Lab, Stanford University.

Norton, Michael I., and Dan Ariely. 2011. Building a Better America-One Wealth Quintile at a Time. *Perspectives on Psychological Science* 6 (1): 9–12.

Nozick, Robert. 2013. *Anarchy, State, and Utopia*. New York, NY: Basic Books

Nussbaum, Martha C. 2001. *Women and Human Development: The Capabilities Approach*. Cambridge: Cambridge University Press.

—. 2013. *Creating Capabilities: The Human Development Approach*. Cambridge, MA: Belknap Press.

Okun, Arthur M. 1975. *Equality and Efficiency: The Big Tradeoff*. Washington, DC: Brookings Institution Press.

Olsaretti, Serena. 2003a. Compensatory Desert. In *Desert and Justice*, ed. Serena Olsaretti, 187–204. Oxford: Oxford University Press.

—. 2003b. Introduction: Debating Desert and Justice. In *Desert and Justice*, ed. Serena Olsaretti, 1–24. Oxford: Oxford University Press.

—. 2004. *Liberty, Desert and the Market: A Philosophical Study*. Cambridge: Cambridge University Press.

—. 2015. Rescuing Justice and Equality from Libertarianism. In *Distributive Justice and Access to Advantage: G. A. Cohen's Egalitarianism*, ed. Alexander Kaufman, 249–270. Cambridge: Cambridge University Press.

Olsen, Henry. 2017. How the Right Gets Reagan Wrong: And What Will Happen If They Don't Start Getting Him Right. *Politico Magazine*.

Ostry, Jonathan D., Andrew Berg, and Charalambos G. Tsangarides. 2014. *Redistribution, Inequality, and Growth*. Staff Discussion Note SDN/14/02. International Monetary Fund.

Ostry, Jonathan D., Prakash Loungani, and Davide Furceri. 2016. Neoliberalism: Oversold? *IMF Finance and Development* 53 (2): 38–41.

Oswald, Florian. 2018. PsidR: Build Panel Data Sets from PSID Raw Data. https://cran.r-project.org/package=psidR.

Otsuka, Michael. 2003. *Libertarianism Without Inequality*. Oxford: Oxford University Press.

Paglin, Morton. 1975. The Measurement and Trend of Inequality: A Basic Revision. *The American Economic Review* 65 (4): 598–609.

Parfit, Derek. 1971. Personal Identity. *The Philosophical Review* 80 (1): 3–27.

—. 2000. Equality or Priority? In *The Ideal of Equality*, ed. Matthew Clayton and Andrew Williams, 81–125. New York: St. Martin's Press.

Parthemore, Joel, and Blay Whitby. 2013. What Makes Any Agent a Moral Agent? Reflections on Machine Consciousness and Moral Agency. *International Journal of Machine Consciousness* 5 (2): 105–129.

Pearl, Judea. 2016. *Causal Inference in Statistics: A Primer*. West Sussex: John Wiley & Sons.

Peragine, Vitorocco. 1998. *Measuring and Implementing Equality of Opportunity for Income*. Discussion Paper 11. University of York.

Pereboom, Derk. 2003. *Living Without Free Will*. Cambridge: Cambridge University Press.

Persson, Ingmar. 2007. A Defence of Extreme Egalitarianism. In *Egalitarianism: New Essays on the Nature and Value of Equality*, ed. Nils Holtug and Kasper Lippert-Rasmussen, 41–82. Oxford: Oxford University Press.
Pickett, Kate, and Richard Wilkinson. 2011. *The Spirit Level: Why Greater Equality Makes Societies Stronger*. New York, NY: Bloomsbury Press.
Piketty, Thomas. 2014. *Capital in the Twenty-First Century*. First English language edition edition. Trans. Arthur Goldhammer. Cambridge, MA: Belknap Press.
Pistolesi, Nicolas. 2007. Inequality of Opportunity in the Land of Opportunities, 1985–2001.
Plat, Didier. 2012. *IC2: Inequality and Concentration Indices and Curves*. R package version 1.0-1.
Pojman, Louis. 1997. Equality and Desert. *Philosophy* 72 (282): 549–570.
Pojman, Louis P. 1999. Does Equality Trump Desert? In *What Do We Deserve?: A Reader on Justice and Desert*, ed. Louis P. Pojman and Owen McLeod, 283–297. Oxford: Oxford University Press.
Pojman, Louis P., and Owen McLeod. 1999. *What Do We Deserve?: A Reader on Justice and Desert*. Oxford: Oxford University Press.
Pollin, Robert, and Jeannette Wicks-Lim. 2013a. *Technical Appendix and References for $10.50 Minimum Wage Petition*, PERI (Political Economy Research Institute). http://www.peri.umass.edu/fileadmin/pdf/resources/minwage_notesjune19.pdf.
—. 2013b. *The Costs to Fast-Food Restaurants of a Minimum Wage Increase to $10.50 per Hour*, PERI (Political Economy Research Institute). http://www.peri.umass.edu/fileadmin/pdf/research_brief/PERI_fast_food_wages.pdf.
Puma, Michael, et al. 2010. *Head Start Impact Study: Final Report*. Report. Washington, DC: U.S. Department of Health and Human Services, Administration for Children and Families.
R Core Team. 2019. *R: A Language and Environment for Statistical Computing*. Vienna: R Foundation for Statistical Computing.
Rachels, James. 1978. What People Deserve. In *Justice and Economic Distribution*, ed. John Arthur and William H. Shaw. Englewood Cliffs, NJ: Prentice-Hall.
Ramos, Xavier, and Dirk Van de Gaer. 2012. *Empirical Approaches to Inequality of Opportunity: Principles, Measures, and Evidence*. Working Paper 6672. Bonn: Forschungsinstitut zur Zukunft der Arbeit (IZA).
Rawls, John. 1985. Justice as Fairness: Political Not Metaphysical. *Philosophy and Public Affairs* 14 (3): 223–251.
—. 1999 (1971). *A Theory of Justice*. Cambridge, MA: The Belknap Press of Harvard University.
Revelle, William. 2018. *psych: Procedures for Psychological, Psychometric, and Personality Research*. R package version 1.8.10.

Riley, Jonathan. 1989. Justice Under Capitalism. In *Markets and Justice: Nomos XXXI*, ed. John W. Chapman and J. Roland Pennoct, 122–162. New York, NY: NYU Press.

Ripley, Brian. 2018. *MASS: Support Functions and Datasets for Venables and Ripley's MASS*. R package version 7.3-51.1.

Robeyns, Ingrid. 2005. The Capability Approach: A Theoretical Survey. *Journal of Human Development* 6 (1): 93–117.

Roemer, John E. 1986. Equality of Resources Implies Equality of Welfare. *The Quarterly Journal of Economics* 101 (4): 751–784.

—. 1996. *Theories of Distributive Justice*. Cambridge, MA: Harvard University Press.

—. 1998. *Equality of Opportunity*. Boston, MA: Harvard University Press.

—. 2002. Going Beyond Intergenerational Income Transition Matrices. http://time.dufe.edu.cn/wencong/johnroemer/EOpCorak.pdf.

—. 2012. On Several Approaches to Equality of Opportunity. *Economics and Philosophy* 28 (02): 165–200.

—. 2013. *Economic Development As Opportunity Equalization*. Policy Research Working Paper 6530. World Bank.

Rowe, William L. 1987. Two Concepts of Freedom. *Proceedings and Addresses of the American Philosophical Association* 61 (September): 43–64.

Ruse, Michael. 2003. Darwinism and Determinism. In *Freedom, Determinism, and Responsibility: Readings in Metaphysics*, ed. Neil Campbell, 26–44. Upper Saddle River, NJ: Prentice-Hall.

Ryan, The Honorable Paul. 2011. *Saving the American Idea: Rejecting Fear, Envy, and the Politics of Division* [**inlang**en]. Tech. rep. The Heritage Foundation.

Ryle, Gilbert. 1949. *The Concept of Mind*. London: Hutchinson's University Library.

Sadurski, Wojciech. 1985. *Giving Desert Its Due: Social Justice and Legal Theory*. Dordrecht: D. Reidel Publishing Company.

Saez, Emmanuel, and Thomas Piketty. 2003. Income Inequality in the United States, 1913–1998 (Tables and Figures Updated to 2012, September 2013). *Quarterly Journal of Economics* 118 (1): 1–39.

Saez, Emmanuel, and Gabriel Zucman. 2014. *Wealth Inequality in the United States since 1913: Evidence from Capitalized Income Tax Data*. Working Paper 20625. Cambridge, MA: NBER - National Bureau of Economic Research.

Sandel, Michael J. 1982. *Liberalism and the Limits of Justice*. Cambridge: Cambridge University Press.

Sandel, Michael. 1999. Liberalism and the Limits of Justice. In *What Do We Deserve?: A Reader on Justice and Desert*, ed. Louis P. Pojman and Owen McLeod, 177–185. Oxford: Oxford University Press.

Scanlon, T. M. 1986. Equality of Resources and Equality of Welfare: A Forced Marriage? *Ethics* 97 (1): 111–118.

—. 2000. *What We Owe to Each Other*. Cambridge, MA: Belknap Press.
Scheffler, Samuel. 1992. Responsibility, Reactive Attitudes, and Liberalism in Philosophy and Politics. *Philosophy and Public Affairs* 21 (4): 299–323.
—. 1999. Responsibility, Reactive Attitudes, and Liberalism in Philosophy and Politics. In *What Do We Deserve?: A Reader on Justice and Desert*, ed. Louis P. Pojman and Owen McLeod, 196–209. Oxford: Oxford University Press.
—. 2003. Distributive Justice and Economic Desert. In *Desert and Justice*, ed. Serena Olsaretti, 69–91. Oxford: Oxford University Press.
Schor, Juliet. 1991. *The Overworked American: The Unexpected Decline of Leisure*. New York: Basic Books.
Schor, Juliet, and Laura Leete-Guy. 1994. Assessing the Time Squeeze Hypothesis: Estimates of Market and Non-market Hours in the United States, 1969–1989. *Industrial Relations* 33 (1): 25–43.
Schwartz, Christine R. 2010. Earnings Inequality and the Changing Association between Spouses' Earnings. *American Journal of Sociology* 115 (5): 1524–1557.
Segall, Shlomi. 2009. *Health, Luck, and Justice*. Princeton, NJ: Princeton University Press.
—. 2013. *Equality and Opportunity*. Oxford: Oxford University Press.
Sen, Amartya. 1970. *Collective Choice and Social Welfare*. San Francisco: Holden Day.
—. 1976. Poverty: An Ordinal Approach to Measurement. *Econometrica* 44 (2): 219–31.
—. 1985. *Commodities and Capabilities*. Amsterdam: North-Holland Publishing.
—. 1987. *The Standard of Living*. Cambridge: Cambridge University Press.
—. 2009. *The Idea of Justice*. Cambridge, MA: Belknap Press.
Sewell, William H., and Robert M. Hauser. 1975. *Education, Occupation and Earnings: Achievements in the Early Career*. New York, NY: Academic.
Sharkey, Patrick. 2009. *Neighborhoods and the Black-White Mobility Gap*. Report. Pew Research Center.
Shaviro, Daniel. 2002. Endowment and Inequality. In *Tax Justice: The Ongoing Debate*, ed. Joseph J. Thorndike and Dennis J. Ventry Jr. Washington, DC: Urban Institute.
Sher, George. 1987. *Desert*. Princeton, NJ: Princeton University Press.
—. 2003. Effort and Imagination. In *Desert and Justice*, ed. Serena Olsaretti, 205–217. Oxford: Oxford University Press.
—. 2014. *Equality for Inegalitarians*. Cambridge: Cambridge University Press.
Sidgwick, Henry. 1999. Justice as Desert. In *What Do We Deserve?: A Reader on Justice and Desert*, ed. Louis P. Pojman and Owen McLeod, 47–55. Oxford: Oxford University Press.
Simon, William E. 1977. *Blueprints for Basic Tax Reform*. Report. U.S. Department of the Treasury.

Singer, Peter. 1972. Famine, Affluence, and Morality. *Philosophy & Public Affairs* 1 (3): 229–243.

Sjoquist, David L., ed. 2000. *The Atlanta Paradox*. New York, NY: Russell Sage Foundation.

Slote, Michael A. 1973. Desert, Consent, and Justice. *Philosophy and Public Affairs* 2 (4): 323–347.

—. 1999. Desert, Consent and Justice. In *What Do We Deserve?: A Reader on Justice and Desert*, ed. Louis P. Pojman and Owen McLeod, 210–223. Oxford: Oxford University Press.

Slottje, Daniel Jonathan, Stephen A. Woodbury, and Rod W. Anderson. 2000. Employee Benefits and the Distribution of Income and Wealth. In *Employee Benefits and Labor Markets in Canada and the United States*, ed. William T. Alpert and Stephen A. Woodbury. Kalamazoo, MI: W.E. Upjohn Institute for Employment Research.

Smart, J. J. C. 1973. An Outline of a System of Utilitarian Ethics. In *Utilitarianism: For and Against*, ed. J. J. C. Smart and Bernard Williams, 3–74. Cambridge: Cambridge University Press.

Smilansky, Saul. 1996. Responsibility and Desert: Defending the Connection. *Mind* 105 (417): 157–163.

—. 2000. *Free Will and Illusion*. Oxford: Oxford University Press.

Smith, Adam. 1976 (1776). *The Wealth of Nations*. Chicago, IL: University of Chicago Press.

Solon, Gary. 1992. Intergenerational Income Mobility in the United States. *American Economic Review* 82 (3): 393–408.

Solow, Robert M. 1990. *The Labor Market As a Social Institution*. Cambridge, MA: Blackwell.

Spiegelberg, Herbert. 1944. A Defense of Human Equality. *Philosophical Review* 53 (2): 101–124.

—. 1999. An Argument for Equality from Compensatory Desert. In *What Do We Deserve?: A Reader on Justice and Desert*, ed. Louis P. Pojman and Owen McLeod, 149–155. Oxford: Oxford University Press.

Stark, Kirk J. 2005. Enslaving the Beachcomber: Some Thoughts on the Liberty Objections to Endowment Taxation. *Canadian Journal of Law and Jurisprudence* 18: 47.

Steinberg, Laurence. 2013. Should the Science of Adolescent Brain Development Inform Public Policy? *Magazine* 28 (3).

Steiner, Hillel. 2009. Left Libertarianism and the Ownership of Natural Resources. *Public Reason* 1 (1): 1–8.

Stern, Nicholas. 1982. Optimum Taxation with Errors in Administration. *Journal of Public Economics* 17: 181–211.

Stiglitz, Joseph E. 2013. *The Price of Inequality: How Today's Divided Society Endangers Our Future*. New York: W. W. Norton & Company.

Strawson, Peter Frederick. 1962. Freedom and Resentment. *Proceedings of the British Academy* 48: 1–25.

Strawson, Galen. 1994. The Impossibility of Moral Responsibility. *Philosophical Studies* 75 (1): 5–24.

Sugin, Linda. 2011. A Philosophical Objection to the Optimal Tax Model. *Tax Law Review* 64: 229–281.

Survey Research Center, Institute for Social Research, University of Michigan. 2019. Panel Study of Income Dynamics, Public Use Dataset. Ann Arbor, MI.

Swift, Adam. 2005. Justice, Luck, and the Family: The Intergenerational Transmission of Economic Advantage from a Normative Perspective. In *Unequal Chances: Family Background and Economic Success*, ed. Samuel Bowles, Herbert Gintis, and Melissa Osborne Groves, 256–276. Princeton, NJ: Princeton University Press.

Tan, Kok-Chor. 2012. *Justice, Institutions, and Luck: The Site, Ground, and Scope of Equality*. Oxford: Oxford University Press.

Taylor, Richard. 2003. Fate. In *Freedom, Determinism, and Responsibility: Readings in Metaphysics*, ed. Neil Campbell, 15–26. Upper Saddle River, NJ: Prentice-Hall.

Temkin, Larry S. 1993. *Inequality*. New York, NY: Oxford University Press

—. 2000. Equality, Priority, and the Levelling Down Objection. In *The Ideal of Equality*, ed. Matthew Clayton and Andrew Williams, 126–161. New York, NY: St. Martin's Press.

—. 2011. Justice, Equality, Fairness, Desert, Rights, Free Will, Responsibility, and Luck. In *Responsibility and Distributive Justice*, ed. Zofia Stemplowska and Carl Knight. Oxford: Oxford University Press.

Thurow, Lester C. 1975. *Generating Inequality: Mechanisms of Distribution in the U.S. Economy*. New York, NY: Basic Books.

Trapletti, Adrian, and Kurt Hornik. 2018. *tseries: Time Series Analysis and Computational Finance*. R package version 0.10-46.

Tungodden, Bertil, and Peter Vallentyne. 2007. Who Are the Least Advantaged? In *Egalitarianism: New Essays on the Nature and Value of Equality*, ed. Nils Holtug and Kasper Lippert-Rasmussen, 174–195. Oxford: Oxford University Press.

Ushey, Kevin, et al. 2018. *packrat: A Dependency Management System for Projects and their R Package Dependencies*. R package version 0.4.9-3.

Vallentyne, Peter. 2000. Introduction: Left-Libertarianism - A Primer. In *Left-Libertarianism and Its Critics: The Contemporary Debate*, ed. Peter Vallentyne and Hillel Steiner, 1–20. New York, NY: Palgrave.

—. 2002. Brute Luck, Option Luck, and Equality of Initial Opportunities. *Ethics* 112: 529–557.

—. 2003. Brute Luck Equality and Desert. In *Desert and Justice*, ed. Serena Olsaretti, 169–185. Oxford: Oxford University Press.

—. 2008. Brute Luck and Responsibility. *Politics, Philosophy & Economics* 7 (1): 57–80.

—. 2015. Justice, Interpersonal Morality, and Luck Egalitarianism. In *Distributive Justice and Access to Advantage: G. A. Cohen's Egalitarianism*, ed. Alexander Kaufman, 40–49. Cambridge: Cambridge University Press.

van Buuren, Stef, and Karin Groothuis-Oudshoorn. 2018. *mice: Multivariate Imputation by Chained Equations*. R package version 3.3.0.

van Inwagen, Peter. 1986. Ability and Responsibility. In *Moral Responsibility*, ed. John Martin Fischer, 153–173. Ithaca, NY: Cornell University Press.

Van Parijs, Philippe. 1995. *Real Freedom for All: What (If Anything) Can Justify Capitalism?* Oxford: Clarendon Press.

Walker, Francis A. 1888. The Bases of Taxation. *Political Science Quarterly* 3: 1–16.

Wallace, R. Jay. 1998. *Responsibility and the Moral Sentiments*. Cambridge, MA: Harvard University Press.

Wang, Haidong, et al. 2013. Left Behind: Widening Disparities for Males and Females in US County Life Expectancy, 1985–2010. *Population Health Metrics* 11 (1): 8.

Weichselbaumer, Doris, and Rudolf Winter-Ebmer. 2005. A Meta-analysis of the International Gender Wage Gap. *Journal of Economic Surveys* 19 (3): 479–511.

Wetzel, Linda. 2014. Types and Tokens. In *The Stanford Encyclopedia of Philosophy*. Spring 2014, ed. Edward N. Zalta. Stanford, CA: Metaphysics Research Lab, Stanford University.

White, John Myles. 2018. *ProjectTemplate: Automates the Creation of New Statistical Analysis Projects*. R package version 0.8.2.

Wickham, Hadley. 2016. *plyr: Tools for Splitting, Applying and Combining Data*. R package version 1.8.4.

Wickham, Hadley, Jim Hester, and Winston Chang. 2018. *devtools: Tools to Make Developing R Packages Easier*. R package version 2.0.1.

Wicks-Lim, Jeannette. 2008. Mandated Wage Floors and the Wage Structure: New Estimates of the Ripple Effects of Minimum Wage Laws. In *A Measure of Fairness: The Economics of Living Wages and Minimum Wages in the United States*, ed. Robert Pollin et al. Ithaca, NY: Cornell University Press.

Williams, Bernard. 1981. *Moral Luck: Philosophical Papers 1973–1980*. Cambridge: Cambridge University Press.

Wolff, Jonathan. 2003. The Dilemma of Desert. In *Desert and Justice*, ed. Serena Olsaretti, 219–232. Oxford: Oxford University Press.

Wollner, Gabriel. 2015. Basic Equality and the Currency of Egalitarian Justice. In *Distributive Justice and Access to Advantage: G. A. Cohen's Egalitarianism*, ed. Alexander Kaufman, 180–203. Cambridge: Cambridge University Press.

Wood, Simon. 2018. *mgcv: Mixed GAM Computation Vehicle with Automatic Smoothness Estimation*. R package version 1.8-26.

Xie, Yihui. 2018a. *bookdown: Authoring Books and Technical Documents with R Markdown*. R package version 0.9.

—. 2018b. *knitr: A General-Purpose Package for Dynamic Report Generation in R*. R package version 1.21.

Young, Robert. 1999. Egalitarianism and the Modest Significance of Desert. In *What Do We Deserve?: A Reader on Justice and Desert*, ed. Louis P. Pojman and Owen McLeod, 245–258. Oxford: Oxford University Press.

Young, Garry. 2016. The Principle of Alternate Possibilities as Sufficient but Not Necessary for Moral Responsibility: A Way to Avoid the Frankfurt Counter-Example. *Philosophia* 44: 961–969.

Zaitchik, Alan. 1977. On Deserving to Deserve. *Philosophy and Public Affairs* 6 (4): 370–388.

Zeileis, Achim. 2014. *ineq: Measuring Inequality, Concentration, and Poverty*. R package version 0.2-13.

Zelenak, Lawrence. 2006. Taxing Endowment. *Duke Law Journal* 55: 1145–1181.

Zill, Nicholas, Gary Resnick, and Ruth Hubbell McKey. 1999. What Children Know and Can Do at the End of Head Start and What It Tells Us About the Program's Performance. In *Biennial Meeting of the Society for Research in Child Development*, ed. Society for Research in Child Development.

INDEX

Note: Page numbers followed by 'n' refer to notes.

J. T. Dwyer, *Chance, Merit, and Economic Inequality*,
https://doi.org/10.1007/978-3-030-21126-4

FSC
www.fsc.org
MIX
Papier | Fördert
gute Waldnutzung
FSC® C083411

Kolibri 360 GmbH
Ferdinand-Jühlke-Straße 7
99095 Erfurt, Deutschland
produktsicherheit@kolibri360.de